Planning for Earthquakes

Wreckage in the wake of the great 1886 Charleston earthquake. Photograph by George Cook. Courtesy of the Charleston Museum, Charleston, South Carolina.

PLANNING FOR EARTHQUAKES

Risk, Politics, and Policy

Philip R. Berke and Timothy Beatley

THE JOHNS HOPKINS UNIVERSITY PRESS
Baltimore and London

The Johns Hopkins University Press
701 West 40th Street
Baltimore, Maryland 21211-2190
The Johns Hopkins Press Ltd., London

∞ The paper used in this book meets the
minimum requirements of American National
Standard for Information Sciences—Permanence
of Paper for Printed Library Materials,
ANSI Z39.48-1984.

Library of Congress Cataloging-in-Publication Data

Berke, Philip, 1951–
   Planning for earthquakes : risk, politics, and policy /
   Philip R. Berke and Timothy Beatley.
      p.   cm.
   Includes bibliographical references and index.
   ISBN 0-8018-4255-7
   1. Earthquakes—United States. 2. Regional planning—
   United States. 3. Local government—United States.
   I. Beatley, Timothy, 1957– . II. Title.
   QE535.2.U6B47   1992
   363.3'495'0973—dc20   91-20703

To Alison, Jane, and Roger

CONTENTS

LIST OF ILLUSTRATIONS

LIST OF TABLES

PREFACE AND
ACKNOWLEDGMENTS

This book originates from our previous studies of land use planning and development management responses to environmental hazards. While these studies examined a limited number of state and local government efforts to mitigate coastal storm hazards, they were not sufficient for development of a broad theory of collective response to environmental hazards. We wanted information from a variety of other hazard-prone settings to develop the empirical base necessary to improve our understanding of how local government planning programs respond to hazards.

Another motivation for this study comes from our concern about how to improve local government capacity to undertake earthquake hazard mitigation actions. Seismically active areas experiencing intense pressures for urbanization, and the need to safeguard people and property are a crucial policy arena. We contend that flexible approaches to guiding development can balance these competing demands and can be acceptable to public and private decision makers. We are encouraged by empirical evidence from this study that supports this contention.

This book does not focus directly on private development mitigation actions. While private actions are obviously an important form of mitigation, our primary focus is actions that can be taken to strengthen local government capacity to anticipate and avoid the potential catastrophic impact of earthquakes. Evidence reported here suggests that strengthened local programs can be a strong factor in stimulating change in private land use and building practices.

Chapter 1 discusses potential disaster losses, the nature of disaster policy making, issues surrounding domestic and international organizational roles in disaster mitigation, and data and methods used in this study. Chapter 2 presents a typology of planning mitigation measures

xiv · PREFACE AND ACKNOWLEDGMENTS

and a conceptual framework for analyzing local planning efforts directed toward earthquake mitigation. The conceptual foundations of the typology and framework are reviewed and the factors that the planning and natural hazards literatures suggest are important influences upon mitigation planning are specified. Chapters 3 through 5 consist of case studies. Each case contains a detailed discussion of the progression of a locality's earthquake mitigation planning, how traditional land use and development practices are used for mitigation, and factors that explain local mitigation activity.

Chapter 6 covers a range of traditional and innovative planning measures available to local governments at risk to earthquakes, as revealed by the telephone survey. A discussion of how these measures can be "packaged" to form viable mitigation strategies is also provided. Chapter 7 describes the current state of mitigation practice in high-risk localities, based on the nationwide survey. Chapter 8 presents an analysis of survey data that identifies factors associated with adoption of mitigation practices. Finally, chapter 9 presents conclusions of study findings in light of the typology and conceptual framework presented in chapter 2 and gives recommendations for improving local mitigation efforts.

Numerous people contributed directly to this study. Among our Texas A&M University faculty colleagues, Alex McIntosh helped in the design and analysis of the survey of seismically vulnerable communities, Benigno Aguirre provided insightful comments that helped in developing the theoretical approach of the study, and Jesus Hinojosa assisted in the collection of case study data. We are grateful for the help given by two excellent graduate student research assistants—Suzanne Wilhite and Kim Ludeke.

The National Science Foundation (grant ECE-8421106) supported this study. Opinions, findings, and conclusions or recommendations expressed in this book are those of the authors and do not necessarily reflect the views of the foundation. Beyond funding, however, we express special appreciation to William Anderson, NSF Program Director, for his advice, patience, and administrative and intellectual support.

We are deeply appreciative to Peter May of the University of Washington for his comments on portions of an early draft of the manuscript, and to David Godschalk of the University of North Carolina for sending us information that proved to be highly relevant to this study. We also thank the many people from government, universities, and business and others who responded to our requests for information throughout this study.

We have benefitted greatly from our association with the Texas A&M University Hazard Reduction and Recovery Center directed by Dennis Wenger. Special thanks go to Ruth Bostic of the center. Her magic word processor accomplished the herculean task of keeping track of our additions and second thoughts. Bettie Hall of the University of Virginia was also especially helpful in word processing.

George Thompson, our editor at the Johns Hopkins University Press, offered guidance and encouragement, and made many helpful suggestions that greatly improved the manuscript for both academic and practicing audiences. We are indebted to the Earthquake Engineering Research Institute for permitting us to use portions of our article previously published in *Earthquake Spectra* (6, no. 1 (1989): 57–81), and to the Research Committee on Disasters of the International Sociological Association for allowing us to use portions of our article published in the *International Journal of Mass Emergencies and Disasters* (7 (March 1989): 35–56). We are grateful to the Charleston Museum, Charleston, South Carolina, for allowing us to print photographic material on the 1886 Charleston earthquake.

Finally, Philip Berke has deep appreciation for Roger J. Berke, who has influenced this study in many ways. The debts owed to him cannot be fully acknowledged in a few words. Philip Berke also thanks Jane Sell for her constant support and encouragement as well as intellectual companionship.

Planning for Earthquakes

1 • EARTHQUAKES
A National Problem

Earthquakes can induce sudden, swift, and untold devastation. On 7 December 1988, a massive earthquake struck Armenia of the Soviet Union. Media reports depicted high-rise apartments, hospitals, schools, businesses, and government office buildings toppled like dominos. Rescue workers worked around the clock for weeks to dig survivors and the dead from under the piles of rubble. At the same time survivors were seeking family, friends, housing, food, and medical supplies. More than 25,000 deaths and hundreds of thousands of injuries were reported by official sources. Shortly thereafter another devastating seismic event struck San Francisco, on 18 October 1989. Fatalities were remarkably low, but physical damages have been estimated to exceed $10 billion, making the San Francisco quake the costliest one in the history of the United States. The catastrophic consequences of the Armenia and San Francisco disasters are a dramatic and painful reminder of the awesome power of earthquakes in seismically active areas (see fig. 1-1).

The sobering fact is that such events are not unexpected. As urban growth in hazardous environments continues, the devastating potential of natural hazards escalates. At the same time, advances in building design to withstand destructive forces, mapping of hazardous areas, and assessment of population vulnerability have created new opportunities for reducing losses.

Disaster specialists have increasingly emphasized the importance of a proactive public policy that can prevent or lessen loss rather than a crisis-reactive approach taken when disasters strike. This book focuses on earthquake mitigation activities of local planning programs throughout the United States. Of key concern are the major difficulties of undertaking

Figure 1.1
Search-and-rescue workers comb the mass of rubble for survivors after the great Mexico City earthquake of 1985. Photographer unknown. *Source:* National Research Council 1987, 5.

such activities and the factors that facilitate effective public response to earthquakes.

Local planning, as conceived here, can be broadly construed to include not just standard land use practices but also building and construction standards. The general idea behind this approach is to prevent development in hazardous areas in the first place or to assure that structures are designed to withstand hazards. This approach has been characterized as one of the most promising ways to mitigate the destructive effects of earthquakes (Ender et al. 1988) and natural hazards generally (White and Haas 1975; Petak and Atkisson 1982).

While local planning is potentially an effective long-term solution to future threats to life and property, most localities do little to discourage development in earthquake-prone areas; sometimes they unwittingly encourage it. If the catastrophic impact of disasters is to be reduced, localities, as well as federal and state organizations, must change their practices.

Initiating change through planning is central to our study. Our basic question is how can public officials, particularly those at the local level where planning is carried out, stimulate mitigation efforts? More specifically, using data from in-depth local case studies and mail and telephone surveys, we seek to answer the following three sets of questions. First, what planning measures (land use controls and development regulations) have communities adopted for earthquake mitigation? How have these measures influenced the location, density, type, and quality of development? Why were these measures chosen, while others were neglected? Second, what activities do local governments undertake to advance mitigation efforts (e.g., coalition building, playing an advocacy role, committing resources, and seeking information)? How do these different activities influence a local government's capacity to put earthquake issues on the public agenda? Third, what characteristics shape the locality's external environment in which planning occurs (e.g., support of elected officials, demands from powerful interest groups, past disaster experience, and federal and state programs and policies)? How important are these characteristics, relative to activities used to stimulate mitigation responses, in explaining the use of planning measures for mitigation? These and related questions constitute the substance of the research reported here.

DISASTER LOSSES

Earthquakes are not, as is sometimes thought, a problem limited to California. Communities throughout the nation face the possibility of loss from an earthquake. Figure 1-2 shows locations of known earthquakes that have caused damage in the United States. All or parts of thirty-nine states lie in regions classified as having major or moderate seismic risk. Within these states, more than seventy million people are exposed to earthquake hazards of ground shaking, surface faulting, ground failures, and tsunamis (Hays 1980).

Population and economic growth have been escalating in earthquake-prone areas. Concerns are growing that catastrophic earthquakes, which can potentially kill thousands of people, cause billions of dollars of property damage, and wreak havoc on financial systems, lie in the nation's not-so-distant future.[1] For instance, a simulated repeat of the San Francisco earthquake, which in 1906 caused almost $170 million (1978 money) in property damage and took 700 lives, caused $24 billion in damage and about 5,000 deaths and 70,000 injuries from ground shaking alone (Wiggins 1979). Similarly, a repeat of the most severe earthquake known to have occurred in the continental United States, which struck the sparsely populated, seven-state area surrounding New Madrid, Missouri, in 1811–

1. Widely publicized predictions have been made, for example, that the chance is better than 50 percent that a severe earthquake will occur in California within the next thirty years (Scholl 1986).

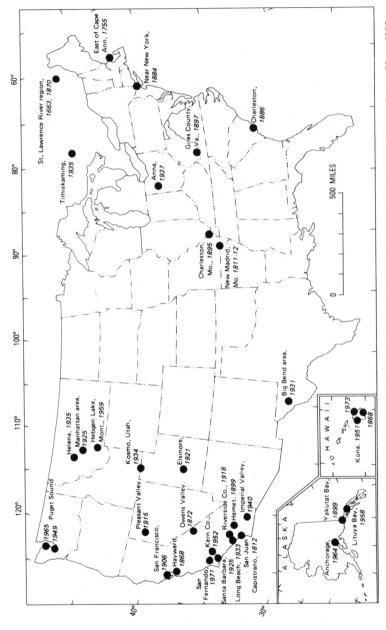

Figure 1.2 Locations of known historic earthquakes that caused notable damage in the United States. *Source:* Hays 1980, B5.

4

Figure 1.3 A massive landslide in Turnagain Heights subdivision was triggered by the great Alaskan earthquake of 1964. Parts of this suburban bluff moved up to 2,000 feet into a nearby bay. Photographer unknown. *Source:* National Research Council 1987, 6.

12, would result in unprecedented destruction. Property losses would be up to $51 billion, more than 4,900 people would die, and 460,000 would be rendered homeless (FEMA 1989).

Furthermore, the nation's insurance industry is not equipped to deal with a catastrophic earthquake event. While the existing private insurance system works well in spreading risk among U.S. and international underwriters and reinsurers, a catastrophic earthquake would severely cut into the industry's capital and result in numerous bankruptcies (Friedman 1984). Commenting on the ripple effect that such an event would cause throughout the economy, a respected insurance analyst concluded that, "suddenly desperate for cash, insurers would have to dump stocks and bonds onto the stock market . . . depressing the stock market . . . [which] would do more economic damage than a 500-point drop in the Dow" (*Washington Post*, 4 December 1988).

Thus a key concern for this book is the continuing urban growth in seismically active areas without corresponding growth in government capacity to reduce potential loss of life and property (see fig. 1-3). While some private developers recognize the risks (Reitherman 1983), govern-

ment action is needed to ensure a comprehensive and coordinated mitigation policy. Unless such a policy is adopted, individual decisions could
add up to a series of unprecedented disasters. Conversely, if the policy is
put in place, a gradual reduction in national vulnerability to disaster can
occur.

ACTIVE VERSUS APATHETIC DISASTER POLICIES: A POLICY DILEMMA

Disaster policy making has been characterized as either "active" politics
or "apathetic" politics (May and Williams 1986; Wright and Rossi 1981). In
active politics, researchers and practitioners have historically focused on
the immediate and highly visible stages of the disaster policy cycle: predisaster preparedness functions of advance planning and training necessary
for emergency operations; disaster response activities like evacuation,
search and rescue, and medical service delivery; and postdisaster recovery
actions designed to rebuild damaged property and put lives back together.
Here is where the disaster milieu attracts excitement, urgency, and media
attention. Planning programs centered on these salient activities tend to
be politically popular. The intention is to mobilize government and people
to respond to a disaster for a short but intense period in order to restore
a devastated area to normalcy.

In the apathetic world of disaster politics, mitigation activities are undertaken during a routine day, long before an uncertain event. Mitigation
typically has low political salience and, as a result, is relegated to the
backwaters of governmental agendas. Apathetic politics are marked by
disagreement among public officials about what risks are involved, their
costs, and what to do about them.

Evidence that individuals and governments assign low priority to disaster mitigation comes from several sources. Drabek et al. (1983) found
seismic safety to be of low political salience in their study of earthquake
mitigation in two states and attributed this finding to the tendency of
American political processes to be reactive rather than proactive and
anticipatory. This study concluded that public officials are reluctant to
invest in mitigation activities because disasters have low probability, even
though losses may be catastrophic when they occur.[2] Political and economic costs of mitigation are up front and highly visible, while mitigation
benefits are realized in the future, if at all. Wyner and Mann (1986) investigated thirteen community earthquake mitigation programs in California

2. During the past century, only four earthquakes have caused substantial destruction
in the United States. For a listing of major U.S. earthquakes—most of which produced
minimal damage—since 1811, see Hays (1980). Hays notes that four destructive events
have occurred during the past century. A fifth would obviously be the Loma Prieta
earthquake of October 1989 in San Francisco.

Figure 1.4 Buckled streets and slumped buildings dropped up to 13 feet in Anchorage during the great 1964 Alaskan earthquake. Much of the damaged area was rebuilt to prequake development densities. Photographer unknown. *Source:* National Research Council 1987, 49.

and found a similar lack of political urgency. Political salience, according to this study, is constrained by a variety of obstacles, including infrequent contact among relevant interest groups, insufficient advocates inside local government, lack of resources, and inadequate technical and administrative capacities for dealing with complex seismic problems.

Also relevant are the findings of Godschalk et al. (1989) of problems that arise during the postdisaster recovery stage, when public officials face strong pressures from disaster victims to rebuild damaged areas as quickly as possible (fig. 1-4). Opportunities to rebuild damaged structures to make them more hazard resistant or to prevent reconstruction in hazardous areas are often disregarded when mitigation is given low priority. There is not only a push to return to normalcy but also a substantial inflow of capital for reconstruction and both private and public restrictions against improving damaged structures beyond predisaster levels (Mader 1980). For example, financial institutions holding mortgages in damaged areas often give owners no alternative but to rebuild to predisaster standards of building construction and land use. Such practices recreate conditions for another disaster.

Herein lies the political dilemma characterized by May and Williams (1986). On the one hand, mitigation efforts that are believed most effective in reducing loss are of low political salience and therefore unlikely to receive attention in active disaster planning. On the other hand, the politically more popular, crisis-oriented approaches—preparedness, response, and recovery—that operate in active politics do little to control urban development in hazardous areas or to reduce damages.

Thus a challenge for planners, emergency managers, and other disaster specialists interested in predisaster planning is to stimulate effort to change apathetic predisaster planning. For this reason, political and institutional constraints on predisaster planning merit investigation. Study of the planning process regarding mitigation will not only explain the way such constraints can be overcome but also help to identify conditions that facilitate enactment of effective earthquake mitigation programs.

ISSUES SURROUNDING LOCAL, STATE, AND FEDERAL GOVERNMENT ROLES IN STIMULATING APATHETIC POLITICS OF PLANNING

The development of earthquake mitigation programs and policies is a product of the activities of a variety of participants in an intergovernmental setting. That is, governments at different jurisdictional levels (local, regional, state, and federal) have different responsibilities for mitigation and different ways to carry out their responsibilities. While the focus of this study is on local government, we also discuss the roles of federal and state governments in earthquake mitigation. In particular, the discussion centers on federal and state programs and policies that have strong potential influence on local capacity to advance mitigation.

Local Planning

Local governments play a crucial role in reducing earthquake risks. Generally they have authority for planning and regulating land use and for building design practices. The Constitution reserves these powers to the states, which, in turn, pass them on to local jurisdictions. Thus, local governments have great potential latitude in planning and regulating development.

The local planning and regulatory process has a general plan as its core. Sometimes called a master or comprehensive plan, the general plan is a long-range policy document that guides the location, design, density, and type of development within a community over a twenty- to thirty-year time frame. The plan is updated from time to time as local development trends and policy objectives change. Implementation of a general plan relies on a variety of traditional and innovative measures, including police power regulations, public spending, taxation, and land acquisition techniques. Because plan policies and implementation measures deal with widely recognized, day-to-day public needs, they tend to have broad political and administrative support (Godschalk et al. 1989).

A smaller number of local governments have adopted specific hazard mitigation policies. These policies seek to reduce human injuries and property losses from natural hazards by anticipatory urban growth guidance actions. Traditionally structured around a single type of hazard, such as floods, hurricanes, or earthquakes, such policies recently have started to become more generic in order to deal with multiple hazards (Mushkatel and Weschler 1985). Because they involve apathetic politics, however, such anticipatory hazard mitigation policies have not engendered broad political or administrative support (Rossi et al. 1982).

Both traditional planning and hazard mitigation policies typically use the same types of implementation measures to carry out their goals. Table 1-1 indicates six major categories of plans and associated implementation measures for guiding development. The table lists specific measures within each category as well as different planning approaches and briefly describes how each can be applied to earthquake mitigation. The approaches and implementation measures are discussed and assessed in greater detail in chapter 6.

Applying Local Planning to Hazard Mitigation

Traditional plan implementation measures can be applied to earthquake hazards in many innovative ways. One example is cluster development zoning. Through such zoning, development can be restricted to less hazardous areas, and high-hazard areas can be left as open space. In exchange for not developing high-hazard areas, developers are allowed to build at higher density than might otherwise be allowed in less hazardous areas. Another innovative example is transfer of development rights. Under this measure the rights to develop a parcel, presumably a parcel with some potentially hazardous feature, can be transferred to another parcel. In this manner, hazardous parcels remain undeveloped. In sum, these flexible approaches to guiding development can be tailored to mitigate seismic risks and still allow development.

Rather than applying only one type of traditional implementation measure to hazard mitigation, localities typically combine a variety of measures with different financing and administrative mechanisms into general hazard mitigation strategies (May and Bolton 1986). In choosing an appropriate combination of measures, localities might seek a strategy that balances expected loss, effectiveness in reducing risk, political acceptability, and cost.

Localities undertaking earthquake mitigation activities use strategies that incorporate various combinations of measures listed in table 1-1

Table 1.1 Planning Measures for Earthquake Hazard Mitigation

Plans and Implementation Measures	Application of Plans and Measures to Mitigation
Planning • Comprehensive or land use plan • Earthquake component of comprehensive plan • Recovery/construction plan	Identify hazardous areas and adopt mitigation policies that guide development and redevelopment in hazardous areas
Development regulations • Zoning ordinance • Subdivision ordinance • Fault setback ordinance	Control of type, location, and density of development in hazardous areas
Building standards • Building code • Special seismic resistance building standards • Retrofit standards for existing buildings	Strengthen existing development and require new development to withstand seismic forces
Land and property acquisition • Transfer of development potential from one site to another • Acquisition of undeveloped lands • Acquisition of development rights • Building relocation • Acquisition of damaged buildings	Remove existing development or prevent future development in hazardous areas
Critical and public facilities policies • Capital improvements programs • Location requirements for critical facilities (hospitals, schools) • Location of capital facilities (street, water) in less hazardous areas	Direct new development away from hazardous areas (or at least do not induce new development in hazardous areas)
Taxation and fiscal policies • Impact tax to cover additional public costs of building in hazardous areas • Reduced or below-market taxation for open space or nonintensive uses in hazardous areas	Maintain low density in hazardous areas
Information dissemination • Public information program • Hazard disclosure requirements	Inform the public and those involved in real estate transactions about hazards

(Olson et al. 1988; Beatley and Berke 1990; Wyner and Mann 1986; Selkregg et al. 1984). Palo Alto, California, for instance, combines development density bonuses specified in the city zoning ordinance with seismic retrofit standards to formulate a successful hazards abatement strategy. This strategy is elaborated in chapter 4.

In summary, this book explores two issues regarding local planning practices. The first issue addresses local experiences in the formulation of effective and politically acceptable earthquake mitigation strategies. Reactions of a variety of stakeholders (local planning staff, real estate interests, and elected officials) to various plan implementation measures or combinations of measures vary greatly. Consequently, the political support for particular measures also varies. Thus, examination of local efforts in "packaging" measures for mitigation illustrates the most effective measures under different community values, socioeconomic conditions, and hazard characteristics.

The second issue deals with the capacity of local governments to apply traditional planning concerns to earthquake mitigation. Local capacity is the level of activity that relevant local organizations devote to mitigation concerns. Among indicators of local capacity are strength of leadership, amount of funding, number of personnel, and degree of consensus concerning seismic activities. We focus on how local decision makers can enhance local government capacity to resolve the political dilemma in disaster policy making.

Federal and State Influence over Local Planning

In considering federal and state influence over land use and development practices, it is important to recognize that regulatory decisions regarding such practices are the responsibility of states, which, in turn, generally delegate authority to localities. In some cases there has been direct federal influence in local practices. Notable examples are the National Flood Insurance Program and the Coastal Zone Management Program, which use financial incentives for initiating local planning activities. There are also instances of direct state mandates governing local planning practices in seismic zones. California law mandates addition of a seismic safety element to the general plan of each local jurisdiction and requires localities to use seismic zone maps in making land use decisions near active faults. California, Utah, and Washington, among other states, require local governments to adopt special seismic building design standards. Yet, even under these federal and state programs, the enactment and enforcement of specific regulations governing land use and development is primarily the responsibility of local governments. While mandates (or incentives) are one form of influence, our primary focus is actions federal and state governments can take to strengthen local capacity to formulate and adopt effective mitigations programs.

Federal Influence. Given constitutional limitations on responsibility and authority, the role of the federal government in hazard mitigation is not to mandate direct changes in local planning but to provide information and resources to stimulate change. In 1977, Congress enacted the National Earthquake Hazards Reduction Act, which sets the scope and responsibilities of the federal government in earthquake mitigation. The act called for a comprehensive nationwide effort to reduce earthquake losses through research and research application. Goals are to support local efforts by improving seismic hazard information, developing better building design practices, and providing financial support (May 1991).

Three types of federal actions have attempted to achieve these goals. In the first, state and local officials have collaborated to establish regional mitigation and preparedness programs; the Federal Emergency Management Agency (FEMA) has been the lead actor. The first regional program—the Southern California Earthquake Preparedness Program (SCEPP)—was initiated by FEMA and California in 1980. A similar program—the San Francisco Bay Area Earthquake Preparedness Program (BAREPP)—was established in 1983. The main concern of the programs' staff is to translate technical information for the public and to assist local government efforts in earthquake loss reduction. Based on the success of the California programs, FEMA has recently initiated support for fifteen similar earthquake hazard reduction programs in high-risk areas throughout the nation.

The second type of action is to conduct detailed studies that assess seismic risk for selected urban areas; here, the U.S. Geological Survey (USGS) is the lead actor. The key component of this federal effort is translation of geological information into detailed hazards maps for use by local planning staffs. Such maps provide an information base that enables local officials to justify hazards mitigation measures. In some areas engineering geologists have been hired with state and federal funds as part of local planning staffs to provide assistance in using technical information.

To date, major seismic studies have been completed in three urban areas—Los Angeles, San Francisco, and the Wasatch Front (Provo, Salt Lake City, and Ogden) of Utah. A fourth study, of the Puget Sound area of Washington, has been initiated. Limited, but ongoing, development of data bases is underway in various urban areas of the central and eastern United States as well as Alaska and Hawaii.

The third type of federal action is to encourage private organizations to develop standards for construction, banking, and insurance practices;

FEMA, the National Science Foundation (NSF), and the National Bureau of Standards (NBS) are the lead actors. Activities center on reducing fragmentation in the development of building codes and of standards for new technologies. Fragmentation has contributed to continued use by communities of out-of-date codes, which can lead to additional building costs (Dillon 1985). A major federal effort completed in 1985 was a trial design study in nine cities—Charleston, Chicago, Fort Worth, Los Angeles, Memphis, New York, Phoenix, St. Louis, and Seattle—to standardize seismic safety provisions for various structural systems and regional hazard severities (FEMA 1989). To date, Charleston and Seattle have amended their building codes to incorporate seismic provisions recommended by the study.

In sum, the federal approach has been to stimulate local efforts to change land use and building practices in jurisdictions for which requisite information exists or can be developed. Given the necessity of such information for establishing local mitigation activities, the federal emphasis upon information collection and translation appears appropriate. Yet, whether these efforts have been effective in stimulating changes in local practices is unknown because they have not been evaluated. While our study is not an evaluation of federal programs, a key question we address is whether credible information resulting from federal efforts alone can stimulate local adoption of mitigation policies. As mentioned in the discussion of apathetic politics, many political and administrative obstacles can constrain local response to seismic risk.

State Influence. State governments are responsible for the safety of their citizens and thereby have legislative mandates to mitigate hazards. California has most directly required localities to apply land use and development practices to earthquake mitigation. The state mandates localities to adopt minimum seismic building standards for new development, to initiate a retrofit program for existing development, to review proposals for development near active faults under the Alquist-Priolo Special Studies Zones Act, and to enact seismic safety elements as part of general plans. Another major effort in California is to raise public awareness and to promote local innovative hazard mitigation programs through joint financial support with FEMA of SCEPP and BAREPP.

The impact of California's initiatives on local practices can vary widely. Wyner and Mann's study (1986), as cited earlier, found the impact of two initiatives to be strikingly different. In the case of the special study zones legislation, they found that aside from controversy in some locations where the fault traces were not well documented, few, if any, structures have been built astride known faults and that "this specific and limited effort at state intervention in local land use planning seems successful"

(25). In contrast, they found seismic safety elements to have little impact on local practices. The state mandate induced formulation and adoption of safety policies, but local enforcement has been weak.[3]

To date, earthquake mitigation policy in states other than California is generally in the beginning stages (see Drabek et al. 1983; Lambright 1984). Direct involvement in land use and development practices has been confined to establishment of statewide model building codes with seismic provisions. These codes, however, have had little impact on local jurisdictions. Arnold (1988), for example, found that seventeen local jurisdictions in Idaho, including two that sustained significant damage from the Borah Peak earthquake of 1983, had not adopted provisions of the state code.

The dominant activities for states other than California have been directing the attention of public and private officials to the need for mitigation, interpreting technical information, and facilitating application of such information. Organizing tabletop earthquake simulation exercises, publishing reports and brochures about earthquakes, and establishing state seismic safety task forces to stimulate and coordinate federal, state, and local efforts are examples of such activity. These efforts, however, have generally had limited success. Drabek et al. (1983), for instance, examined the efforts of two states, Missouri and Washington, to stimulate earthquake mitigation. The study found that most state-initiated mitigation activities were short-lived and that, aside from raising public consciousness, they had little influence on state and local land use and development practices.

On the positive side, a few state initiatives outside of California have advanced mitigation activities. Christensen's assessment (1987) found a technical assistance program in Utah to have strengthened local mitigation practices. Under this program, the state, upon local request, provides a geotechnical review of proposed developments in hazardous areas. In most instances mitigation measures recommended in the reviews were enforced by local governments. This study concluded that few, if any, of these developments would have incorporated mitigation measures if the state had not provided technical assistance. Other instances of successful state initiatives include: Washington's mandate that the state undertake geotechnical reviews for the siting of major energy facilities; Oregon's requirement that localities inventory hazards (including earthquakes) and avoid damage-prone development in such areas; and Colorado's develop-

3. A study by the California Seismic Safety Commission (1985) on the effectiveness of local seismic safety elements had a more positive view. The study concluded that local governments are giving more attention to seismic concerns than they would otherwise have done without the elements. Nevertheless, it maintained that localities have a long way to go in achieving the full potentials of the elements.

ment of model geological hazard control regulations, which have been adopted by several localities.[4]

Various studies of intergovernmental policy making regarding hazards identify conditions that affect local efforts to carry out state or federal programs (Drabek et al. 1983; Lambright 1984; Wyner and Mann 1986). These conditions can be summarized as follows: clarity of guidelines and explanations of what needs to be done; adequacy of local technical training; adequacy of knowledge about levels of risk, costs, and benefits of various mitigation measures; extent of information about political interests of affected groups and individuals; and degree of coordination among relevant public organizations. We focus upon the extent to which these and other conditions are met by state and federal programs in building the capacity of local jurisdictions to carry out hazard mitigation programs. The key decisions regarding formulation and enactment of state and federal policies are made at the local level.

THE INTERNATIONAL AND UNITED STATES DECADE OF NATURAL DISASTER REDUCTION: AN OPPORTUNITY FOR HAZARD MITIGATION?

Practitioners and researchers in natural hazards have been challenged by the proposal to make the 1990s an International and United States Decade for Natural Disaster Reduction—a period devoted to improved and vitalized efforts to reduce the impact of natural disasters on people and the built environment. The concept of an international decade was initiated by Frank Press, President of the U.S. National Academy of Sciences, in 1984 at the Eighth World Conference on Earthquake Engineering. He envisioned a decade that would take advantage of recent scientific and engineering advances to reduce the growing toll of natural disasters throughout the world.

The United Nations General Assembly in 1987 adopted a resolution endorsing the international decade. The U.N. resolution urges each member nation to establish a national program for a decade of hazard reduction within its boundaries and, unilaterally or multilaterally, across boundaries with other member nations. As stated in a National Academy of Sciences report (National Research Council 1987), the rationale for the international decade is twofold. First, the toll exacted by natural disasters is significant and rising, "yet heavy losses at the hands of nature are not inevitable" (1). Second, "experience demonstrates that we have enough knowledge

4. For reviews of state-initiated earthquake mitigation activities outside of California, see Christensen (1987) and Scholl (1986).

already, if properly applied, to reduce both human and property losses substantially" (1). While the report maintains that disaster research needs ongoing support, it emphasizes application of existing research and technology, particularly at the local level.

Soon after the U.N. endorsement, the U.S. Congress passed legislation in 1988 establishing a U.S. decade serving two purposes (Natural Hazard Research and Applications Center 1989). First, it provides a focal point for participants in natural hazard reduction activities within the United States to share information and become more aware of each other. Second, it provides a framework in which the United States can cooperate with other U.N. member nations to reduce the toll of natural disasters worldwide. U.S. participants can benefit from exposure to lessons learned from other hazard reduction programs.

The decade is gaining momentum, as exemplified by the establishment of a U.S. National Committee for it by the National Academy of Sciences in 1989. The committee consists of sixteen representatives of private industry, media, academia, and federal, state and local government. Its principal objectives are to assess the magnitude of the risk posed by natural hazards in the United States and to make recommendations for national policy for reducing the risk. Other activities reflecting interest in the decade include declarations of the 1990s as Natural Disaster Reduction Decade by the governors of Utah, California, and Tennessee. While these activities demonstrate greater involvement and support for hazard reduction in the United States, they are indicative of a program in the initial stages of development. A workable decade program and its impact on local mitigation policy will take time to emerge.

At a recent workshop organized by the Natural Hazards Research and Applications Center (NHRAC) of the University of Colorado, experts highlighted several constraints to the development of the U.S. decade, such as low commitment among federal agencies, funding limitations, and insufficient staff (NHRAC 1989, 12). Workshop participants, however, maintained that these constraints could be addressed by a strong mandate from the executive branch and the creation of a federal interagency coordinating task force (NHRAC 1989, 13). Participants suggested that such actions would require low levels of funding and could minimize duplication of effort, enhance sharing of staff expertise, and raise the saliency of the decade among federal agencies.

In sum, given its inevitable shortcomings, we believe that the decade holds considerable promise for advancing hazards mitigation. However, because it is only in the emergent stages, assessment of its impact on local government earthquake mitigation efforts is not within the scope of this study. Nevertheless, our study findings should be useful to those charged with designing and implementing decade programs.

DATA AND METHODS

Typically, planning and public policy studies take one of two forms: an in-depth case study of the outcomes of a program, or an overview of the activities of a class of programs. The case approach has the advantage of providing detailed information, but it does not permit generalizations about results. When only one program is examined, it is difficult to specify the specific causes of success or failure and to know if an unsuccessful program would be successful in a different environment. An overview approach can provide information on the importance of program activities and environment at a specific point in time, but it often lacks an in-depth examination of the dynamics of program operation.

Taking advantage of the strengths of both approaches, this study relies on a nationwide survey of mitigation efforts of local government planning programs and three case studies of such programs. The survey was designed to provide an overview of the characteristics that shape localities' external environment, program activities used to advance mitigation policy, and specific land use and development measures used for mitigation. The case studies were designed to provide an in-depth assessment of local mitigation activities.[5] Data collection under both approaches was guided by a conceptual framework that is presented in chapter 2.

Mail Questionnaire

The mail questionnaire was designed to obtain three categories of information. The first included questions on the physical, socioeconomic, legal, and political environment of communities that are prone to earthquakes. The second category contained questions on the activities planners and other decision makers use to advance mitigation policies in their communities. These activities included, for example, use of the media, pursuance of an advocacy role, modes of intergovernmental coordination, and application of resources, including funds, trained staff, and detailed hazards maps. The last category included questions on various community responses to earthquake hazards, including priority of mitigation on local government political agendas, adoption of specific mitigation measures, and effectiveness of such measures in reducing potential loss.

The questionnaire was sent to communities in twenty-two states that contain high seismic risk areas. These states fall within seismic zones 3 to 4 as illustrated in figure 1-5. A Modified Mercalli Intensity (MMI) of VIII or greater is likely to occur in both zones. An intensity of MMI VIII

---

5. Qualitative research methods, such as case studies, are generally accepted in hazards research (Yin 1984). Even Campbell, originally a staunch advocate of quantitative methods, has come to accept the legitimacy of case studies, which are primarily based on interviews and documentary information, as an evaluation method (Campbell 1975).

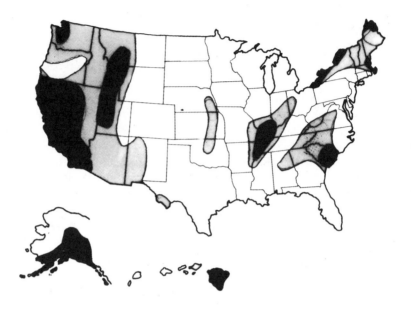

LEGEND

Zones 0 and 1: No damage and minor damage, respectively, corresponds to intensity VI and lower of the MMI scale.

Zone 2: Moderate damage, corresponds to intensity VII of the MMI scale.

Zones 3 and 4: Severe damage, corresponds to intensity VIII and higher of the MMI scale.

Figure 1.5 Map of the seismic zones of the U.S. Uniform Building Code. *Source:* Algermissen 1969.

causes major damage to the built environment. Seismic zones 3 and 4 are distinguished because zone 4 areas are determined to contain certain major fault systems. Zone 3 areas have no such fault systems. Communities in areas of lower risk (MMI VII and below) were not included in the survey. To be certain that communities were capable of establishing at least a minimal program, those with permanent populations of less than 10,000 (as determined by the 1980 U.S. Census) were excluded, since many of them lack the resources to initiate a minimal planning effort.

A random sample of communities in California was used. The sample size of 104 communities of the 256 communities in the state was deter-

Table 1.2 Survey Population and Respondents by Region and State

	Survey Communities	Survey Responses	Response (%)
Northeast			
Maine	1	1	100.0
New York	26	16	61.5
Pennsylvania	1	1	100.0
Massachusetts	24	17	70.8
New Hampshire	1	1	100.0
Southeast			
South Carolina	16	15	93.8
Midwest			
Arkansas	5	3	60.0
Illinois	5	5	100.0
Indiana	1	1	100.0
Kentucky	7	4	57.1
Mississippi	1	1	100.0
Missouri	3	2	66.7
Tennessee	8	5	62.5
Mountain-West			
Arizona	1	1	100.0
Idaho	4	4	100.0
Montana	3	3	100.0
Nevada	3	3	100.0
Utah	21	19	90.5
Pacific			
Alaska	1	1	100.0
California	103	85	82.5
Hawaii	1	1	100.0
Washington	23	18	78.3
Totals	259	207	79.9

mined according to a procedure developed by McNamara (1978). Because of the small number of communities in each of the remaining twenty-one states, all 156 communities were surveyed. Data from communities in the twenty-two states were obtained from a mail survey administered during the fall of 1986.

The survey was conducted with techniques developed by Dillman (1978). The response rate was 82.5 percent for California and 78.2 percent for other states. The response rate for the total sample was 79.9 percent. Table 1-2 indicates, by region, the number of communities in each state that received a questionnaire and the number of respondents.

To maximize the reliability of data returned by communities, all letters and questionnaires were sent to the jurisdictions' planning directors. Of those who answered the questionnaire in California, 83.5 percent were planning directors or planning staff members, 9.4 percent were city managers, and the remainder were building inspectors, city engineers, and emergency planners. In other states, 74.6 percent were planning directors or planning staff members, 12.9 percent were city managers, 8.2 percent were building inspectors, and the remainder were city engineers, emergency planners, and a community attorney.

The Case Studies

The case studies entailed detailed investigations of specific mitigation efforts of local governments. On the basis of four criteria, three localities were selected for the study. First, only jurisdictions in high earthquake hazard areas in the United States were selected. The high-hazard areas were within seismic zones 3 and 4 as indicated in figure 1-5. We also used localized information, if available, on geological hazards and land use to assure that concentrations of development within a jurisdiction were at risk.

Second, the jurisdictions selected represented a range of earthquake experiences from recent experience of an earthquake event (which includes being on the periphery of an earthquake) to no recent experience. The occurrence of an earthquake was presumed to provide strong impetus for mitigation activity, whereas the absence of such an event would make the adoption of effective mitigation measures less likely. It was also assumed that jurisdictions on the periphery of a large earthquake would gain insight into the effects of a significant event and therefore be inclined to initiate mitigation policy-making activities.

Third, the jurisdictions selected represented a range of political, cultural, and economic conditions. At one end of a continuum were communities like Salt Lake County, where the political culture was oriented toward individualism and private property and the economy performed poorly; at the other, communities like Palo Alto, where the culture was activist and public spirited and the economy strong. We assumed that a jurisdiction with a conservative political culture and a poorly performing economy was less likely to adopt earthquake mitigation measures than one with a progressive culture and strong economy. The intent was to determine the importance of factors that shape a jurisdiction's capacity to advance mitigation (e.g., the presence of advocates and interorganizational coordination), relative to the political and economic conditions, in explaining the level of mitigation effort. While these considerations were little more than speculative, they nevertheless guided the choices made in the selection process.

Finally, selection of jurisdictions depended on whether there was a minimal level of activity or interest in earthquake mitigation. Localities where concern was almost nonexistent were avoided.

With the general site selection criteria in mind, two information sources were developed. First, returned questionnaires were used to identify the level of mitigation activity and past disaster experience. Available agency reports, previous studies, and other pertinent documentary information were also relied upon.[6] On the basis of this information, twenty potential case jurisdictions were identified in California and sixteen in other earthquake-prone states.

Second, telephone interviews were conducted with planning staff of these jurisdictions. Subjective evaluations about earthquake hazards within each jurisdiction, previous earthquake experience, local reactions to previous experiences, and local mitigation practices were obtained. We also asked those interviewed to send general plans, relevant ordinances, minutes of public hearings, and technical reports such as those on geological hazards within the jurisdiction. (The plans and ordinances were also useful for developing a comprehensive review of planning measures that are in use or could be used for mitigating seismic hazards.) Using information from the two sources, we selected the following three localities: Charleston, South Carolina; Palo Alto, California; and Salt Lake County, Utah.

All on-site interviews were conducted during four- to five-day visits between September 1988 and April 1989. They were rich in information about substantive mitigation concerns and perspectives on earthquake hazards. The interviews usually lasted nearly an hour, rarely less than a half hour, sometimes up to three hours. Interviews were conducted with planning and building inspection departmental staff, elected officials, consultants, representatives of real estate interests, and state agency staff. A total of thirty-six interviews were conducted in the three case jurisdictions. During the interviews, informants were asked to suggest other relevant data sources. A wide variety of plans, ordinances, agency reports, research publications, newspaper accounts, and other documentary materials pertinent to this study were cited.

The interviews were loosely structured. That is, an interviewer would have a list of topics to be covered but not a fixed set of questions to be asked across interviews. Further, they were free to follow leads that did not necessarily reflect the specified topics. At the start of each interview it was made clear that all information given by the informant would be kept strictly confidential. Interviewers would then typically ask about general earthquake problems, specific earthquake mitigation practices in

6. From telephone interviewing and collecting documentary information, we found several counties as potential case jurisdictions that were not included in the mail survey. Because county governments in states like California and Utah have planning programs and regulatory powers similar to municipalities, we decided to include counties that met the site selection criteria. This reasoning explains why Salt Lake County was selected as a case study.

each jurisdiction, modes of interaction among various participants in the earthquake mitigation policy process, and the priority of seismic mitigation policy on the local government agenda.

To assure accuracy of essential facts and evidence of the case studies, draft reports of each case were reviewed by key informants. From a methodological viewpoint, the corrections made through this review process enhanced the accuracy and hence increased the validity of the studies. The likelihood of falsely reporting an event or the perspectives of different participants in mitigation policy making was thus reduced.

2 • A CONCEPTUAL FRAMEWORK
OF LOCAL PLANNING RESPONSE
TO NATURAL HAZARDS

This chapter outlines a typology of mitigation measures and a conceptual framework for analyzing local earthquake mitigation programs. They are based on the literature regarding planning and policy making for hazards. While this literature is limited by comparison with research on individual and organizational behavior immediately before and after a disaster (Drabek 1986), it has advanced enough to provide a conceptual foundation for understanding different mitigation responses to risk and the factors that might account for them.

Pioneering work on hazard mitigation was largely derived from the general school of thought promoted by Harlan Barrows (1923) as "human ecology" and its specific application by Gilbert White and others to water problems, river basin development, and the flood hazard.[1] One early study by White (1945) examined development and growth patterns in hazard-prone areas and introduced the concept of land use planning as an alternative to building and structural design measures. White et al. (1958) also investigated why flood-engineering mitigation measures were preferred over others and then, despite investments in them, why loss was increasing. For example, projects to dam and channel rivers had resulted in a reduction in the number of floods, but these fewer floods

---

1. The "human ecology" school of thought emphasizes relations of human aggregates with their natural environment. It considers human collectives as adaptive units that respond to the environment. Specifically, investigations in this field seek determinants of behavior in the natural environment (including hazards) and processes that facilitate human adjustment to the physical world through social organization. For a discussion of the fundamental principles of human ecology see Duncan (1964), and for reviews of its application to natural hazards see Mileti (1980) and Palm (1990, ch. 5).

resulted in even greater damages. Another study focused on the economic and political issues surrounding land use planning and the extent to which planning was used by localities (Murphy 1958). A key conclusion of these studies is that, of all possible mitigation measures, land use planning has the greatest potential to reduce loss from natural hazards.

Subsequent investigations attempted to understand better the process by which localities initiate, adopt, and implement mitigation plans and policies (Burton and Kates 1964; Burton et al. 1978; Haas and Mileti 1976; Kates 1978; Slovic et al. 1974; White 1974; White and Haas 1975). All these studies point to the complexities of planning and policy making. All maintain that planning is not strictly a technical exercise, but an intensely political one as well. Furthermore, all suggest that the process is altered by inaccurate appraisals of risk, inadequate time and resources devoted to complex problem solving by decision makers, and multiple and conflicting preferences of affected groups.

Much of the planning literature has focused on two general approaches to understanding planning. The process approach examines the process through which organizational plans are made and the factors that comprise organizational commitment and capacity to achieve goals (Ackoff 1970; 1981; Ansoff 1985; Nutt 1984). The content perspective focuses on the specification of planning strategies and how such strategies set the direction for the organization (Mintzberg and Waters 1985; Taylor 1984; Wind and Mahajan 1981). Regardless of orientation (process or content), theories of planning and strategic management generally have been concerned with private business organizations, not with public organizations.

Only recently has work in planning begun to explore the process and content of planning in public organizations (Bryson and Roering 1987). For example, studies have examined how public organizations increase their capacity to take intended, self-directed action in the fields of local health care delivery (Van de Ven 1980), metropolitan planning (Bryson 1983; Bryson and Boal 1983), and state environmental, public works, and utilities policy (Wechsler and Backoff 1987). This emerging literature holds that rather than being formed in response to the requirements of markets, plans that are formulated and carried out by public agencies are products of organizational capacity and various physical, political, and socioeconomic contexts.

In the planning and public policy literature oriented toward hazards, studies have tended to take either the process or the content approach, but not both. For example, Cochran (1975), May and Bolton (1986), and Olson and Nilson (1982) take the content approach by specifying the planning measures available for mitigation and examine how such measures can be packaged into politically acceptable and technically effective mitigation strategies.[2] Alesch and Petak (1986), Berke (1989), Lambright (1984), and Mittler (1988) use the process approach in examining how public organizational policies are made and how various factors (e.g., support of elected officials, demands of powerful interest groups, roles of advocates, and occurrences of disastrous events) influence outcomes of the process.

Further, several studies assess the influence of process activities and contexts on specific types of hazard reduction outcomes. In a study of community disaster preparedness planning, Kartez and Lindell (1987) examine the influence of context (past disaster experience) and process (updating emergency plans and standard operating procedures, and holding emergency exercises and joint critiques) on adoption of emergency planning practices or outcomes (establishing emergency equipment contracts, media centers, and telephone hotlines). This approach has also been used in explaining community adoption and implementation of earthquake (Berke et al. 1989), coastal storm (Godschalk et al. 1989), and flood (Burby and French 1981, 1985; Hansen and Hirsch 1983; Kaiser and Burby 1987) hazard mitigation measures (reconstruction plans, shoreline setback controls, and building strengthening regulations). The studies cited, however, do not examine the content of such outcomes.

As a result, the hazards planning and policy literature has two shortcomings. First, while the process literature focuses on factors that influence policy making, existing conceptual frameworks in this literature do not examine how specific planning measures can be combined into viable mitigation strategies. This poses a major problem for determining how various measures might be used, given variations in factors that comprise organizational capacity and different decision-making environments. Second, the content literature generally does not account for the temporal dimension of strategy building. A viable planning strategy should have different characteristics at different times, given changes in organizational capacity or environmental factors. For example, due to increased support from elected officials, a voluntary strategy is revised to include an incentive measure to further entice target group compliance.

In addition, a third shortcoming in the hazards planning and policy literature is that existing conceptual frameworks tend to underestimate the capacity of public agencies to influence the planning process. While most process studies discuss the importance of program resources, past experience with disasters, and characteristics of the spatial distribution of

2. May and Bolton (1986) introduce a typology of mitigation measures and make assessments of how different local commitment and capacity factors could constrain local efforts to implement each type of measure.

development in hazardous areas, among other influences, many neglect the ability of public agencies to provide strong support for advocates of mitigation, to develop cooperative relationships with other organizations, and to raise hazard issues on the public agenda. As mentioned, the content literature explores the characteristics of mitigation strategies but does not focus on how political, economic, and administrative factors influence strategy formulation.

The first two limitations discussed above are addressed in the conceptual framework presented in this chapter by combining the process and content approaches. On the one hand, knowledge of planning strategy characteristics enhances understanding of how to formulate appropriate strategies for different decision-making environments. On the other hand, knowledge of the dynamics of such environments improves understanding of how to adapt mitigation strategies to assure their viability over time. As compared to any single approach, combining both approaches gives a more complete understanding of public planning response to hazards. Finally, the conceptual framework addresses the third limitation by developing a set of factors that reflect the capacity of public agencies to influence the planning process.

The remainder of this chapter draws on hazards policy process and content literatures to develop a conceptual framework for understanding public agency response to risks posed by hazards. More specifically, the chapter examines the characteristics according to which planning measures might be classified, the process by which such measures are used to formulate, adopt, and implement mitigation strategies, and the factors that can facilitate or constrain this process.

A TYPOLOGY OF MITIGATION MEASURES

Localities can take a variety of actions to reduce loss of life, damage to the built environment, and social and economic disruption. These actions comprise the range of planning measures (see table 1-1) that can be used for mitigating risks posed by hazards. Some measures are widely practiced; others are used infrequently but hold considerable promise for application in mitigation (Godschalk and Brower 1985).

A locality's strategy for mitigation can be found in the actions it takes to influence the future design, density, timing, and location of development. The strategy can be determined by identifying the various combinations of planning measures used by the locality. An understanding of the appropriate combination of measures to take in response to variations in interest group demands, budgetary constraints, hazard characteristics, and technical and administrative capacity is crucial for successful mitigation efforts (Olson and Nilson 1982) and in carrying out public policies in general (Lowi 1964).

The range of planning measures that could be used in formulating a mitigation strategy can be classified into three broad categories: (1) regulatory measures, which are coercive in that they attempt to control the activity of specific interest groups; (2) incentives measures, which are noncoercive in that they aim to induce, rather than require, desired development; and (3) informational measures, which enable people who might deal with hazards to make informed decisions. This typology is similar to May and Bolton's classification (1986) of planning measures available for mitigation. The following are examples of measures representative of each response category:

Regulatory—building code provisions for new construction, hazardous building retrofit provisions for old construction, subdivision codes, zoning, critical facility permits, and lifeline location restrictions

Incentives—purchase of development rights, capital improvement programs, property acquisition, and taxation schemes

Informational—hazards area impact reviews, real estate disclosure requirements, comprehensive and reconstruction plans, and building construction workshops

Furthermore, this typology can be useful in understanding local response over time. Specifically because local mitigation programs typically operate in dynamic environments that impose numerous rapidly changing demands, mitigation strategies must be adapted over time to remain viable (May and Bolton 1986; Olson and Nilson 1982; Sorensen and White 1980). For example, a building retrofit strategy in Provo, Utah, had to be modified to reflect changes in the local economy (May and Bolton 1986). That is, what began as a regulatory strategy became ineffective because of the inability of building owners to cover retrofit costs as a result of a decline in local economic performance. Thus, to enhance building owner compliance, the local retrofit program incorporated incentive measures (e.g., low-interest loans and development density bonuses) in the overall strategy.

How does this typology relate to other work on plan and policy content? As noted earlier, the typology provides a basis for understanding a range of possible mitigation responses, whereas much of the previous research has not deciphered the characteristics of such responses. Thus, the typology can help determine which measures are likely to succeed or fail given variations in local political and economic conditions, as well as in organizational capacity. Also, the typology can be used to account for the dynamics of mitigation responses. As mentioned, previous research does not provide insight into how strategies can be adapted to maintain technical, political, and economic viability.

PLANNING PROCESS

Until the 1970s the traditional view of hazards mitigation planning and the policy process was premised on a theoretical model that approximated Simon's "rational man" (1957). Slovic et al. (1974) proposed, for example, that if participants involved in hazards policy decisions followed such a model they would: (1) clearly define goals; (2) set objectives that would specify measurable achievement of goals; (3) collect information on all possible policy alternatives and associated costs and benefits; and (4) select an alternative or mix of alternatives that provides maximal achievement of public goals at minimal public costs.

The rational mode of planning does not accurately depict reality. A number of studies characterize the process quite differently. Studies of community planning and risk management focused on the structure of power and influence as keys to understanding the planning and policy process (Faupel and Bailey 1989; Kunreuther and Linnerooth 1984). One of the most important conclusions of these studies was that different groups pursue their own goals rather than some simplified community-wide goals that attempt to optimize public welfare. These studies also strongly substantiate March and Simon's work (1958) on organizational behavior, which maintains that the ability of human beings to process information is more limited than the rational approach would claim. People are unable to canvass many alternatives, keep them simultaneously in their minds, and compare them systematically.

Other recent empirical studies of state (Drabek et al. 1983; Lambright 1984; Mittler 1988) and local (Ender et al. 1988; Kartez and Lindell 1987; Wyner and Mann 1986) hazards mitigation planning have criticized the rational approach. These studies point to the complexities of planning and the constraints on rationality. They characterize successful planning as both technically and politically motivated. Accordingly, key activities for success are process oriented or procedural (e.g., coalition building, interorganizational communication, and leadership).

Another line of criticism of the rational planning model stems from analysis of local seismic retrofit policy (Alesch and Petak 1986). Like the work of Cohen et al. (1972) and Kingdon (1984) in organizational decision making under uncertainty, Alesch and Petak's study criticizes the orderly, sequential nature of the rational model. These researchers' characterization of planning suggests that people do not first clearly recognize hazards problems and then seek solutions to them. The processes of problem definition and solution development do not occur in sequence. Problems and solutions exist independently. Some problems have no apparent solutions, and some solutions are suggested in the absence of a matching problem.

In sum, for most planning efforts concerning mitigation, the process by which plans and policies are adopted and implemented does not conform to the rational approach. Instead, the process tends to reflect the characteristics discussed above. A variety of factors can facilitate or constrain this process, as is discussed below.

LOCAL PLANNING RESPONSE TO HAZARDS

As illustrated in figure 2-1, the process of local response to hazards consists of four stages. The first stage is *environmental risk*. Risk is a threat to life, health, and property as a potential consequence of a hazardous event, such as an earthquake (Fischoff et al. 1981). In the case of earthquakes, it is produced by interaction between seismic hazards and the built environment. Environmental risk determines the character of the next three stages of the process.

The second stage is *policy initiation*. Initiation involves efforts to place the risk problem on the governmental agenda. Once on the agenda, the problem is likely to receive active consideration by authoritative decision makers (Kingdon 1984). Specifically, achieving agenda status means getting hazard issues on city council calendars, on a priority list for bill introduction by an elected official, or on the schedule of a public agency. However, achieving agenda status is not easy. High-consequence, infrequent events like earthquakes are typically given low priority by public officials and their constituents; immediate day-to-day problems (e.g., traffic congestion, crime, and jobs) are commonly viewed as more important.

The third stage involves *formation and adoption* of planning measures. These measures set the direction for local government efforts to guide development in seismic areas. In formulating the appropriate combination of measures, public officials seek strategies that balance expected risk, effectiveness in reducing risk, political acceptability to various interest groups, and cost. The decisions within this stage implicitly answer the question, What is an acceptable level of risk? If a mitigation proposal is considered technically feasible, accommodates the main concerns of influential interest groups, and poses acceptable loss levels, then the proposal is adopted. If a proposal is not viable, either a different combination of measures is reintroduced or no action is taken.

The final stage of the process involves *implementation* of adopted measures. Plans and policy measures remain largely statements of intention until they are translated into operational programs. Indeed, the impact of such measures depends upon how they are implemented. Thus, what

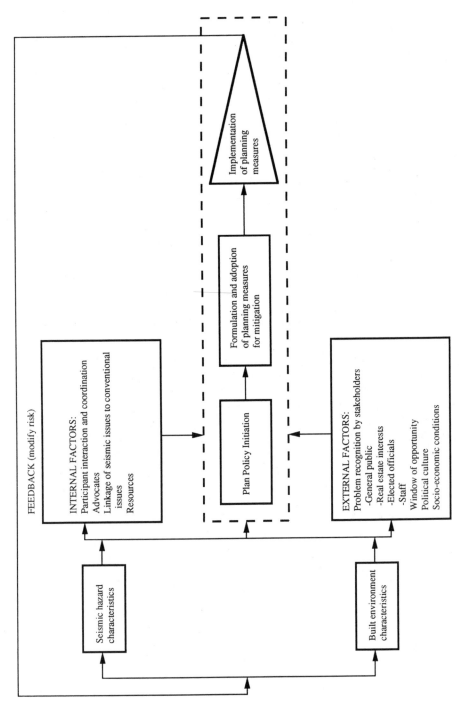

Figure 2.1 Conceptual framework of planning response to earthquake hazards. Conceived by the authors, 1990.

30

government is doing about risk problems relates to how the programs have been implemented (May and Williams 1986). The effectiveness of implementation dictates the degree of change in one or a combination of seismic hazard and built environment characteristics. Consequent changes in potential risk levels can require renewed or continued planning efforts to mitigate environmental risk.

As figure 2-1 indicates, two categories of factors influence stages 2 through 4 of the planning process (Weschler and Backoff 1987). First, internal factors are activities (interorganizational communication and co-ordination, advocacy, provision of resources, and linkage of hazards to conventional activities) that can be undertaken by public officials to advance mitigation. These activities constitute the capacity of public agencies to influence the planning process. As mentioned, previous research tends to neglect public agency capacity to advance mitigation programs. Second, external factors (e.g., problem recognition by stakeholders; past disaster experience; political, cultural, and socioeconomic conditions) make up the environment within which planning operates. Of key importance to this study is the balance of influence between these categories of factors. If a locality has a high capacity to advance mitigation, then its policies reflect the intentions of its participants. In contrast, if external factors predominate, then a locality's mitigation efforts are far less relevant and its policies arise from environmental circumstances instead of its own actions.

FACTORS THAT INFLUENCE PLANNING AND POLICY

In this section we develop both internal and external factors. These two categories serve well to integrate the findings of recent research in hazards planning and policy making.

Internal Factors

Participant Interaction. Participants are players in a given public planning arena. Some players are elected officials. Others are government specialists, such as emergency managers or city planners. Still others represent real estate or environmental interests.

Participant interaction varies tremendously from one public arena to another. Some arenas are tightly knit and have frequent and sustained interaction. The capacity to diffuse, adopt, and implement planning innovations is high. Other arenas are more diverse and fragmented. Participant interaction in planning activities tends to be infrequent and transitory. The potential for enactment of innovations in loosely knit arenas is low.

When high levels of interaction are maintained, participants share common information that generates common outlooks and ways of thinking (Berke 1989; Drabek et al. 1983; Mileti, 1980). They become more aware of the interests and activities of others. Issues of local concern, for instance, have a greater chance of being communicated to state and federal government agencies. Technical and financial support from high levels of government are more likely to fit the specific needs of localities. There is more opportunity for bargaining, compromise, and adoption and implementation of acceptable planning policies for a broad range of stakeholders.

The consequences of public planning without substantial interaction among stakeholders have been addressed by several hazards planning studies. Ender et al. (1988), for one, suggests that traditional comprehensive planning relies on expert knowledge and does not incorporate the values and spirit of the community. Reliance on experts does not induce commitment and participation because it eliminates the need for various participants to come together and work to solve problems in the cooperative spirit that forms community cohesion. In addition, Rohe and Gates' work (1985) on neighborhood planning maintains that because the business community has citywide interests and is usually organized, it often participates to a much greater extent than other stakeholder groups. Downtown merchants, for instance, are accustomed to monitoring local issues that may affect their interests. They become involved with a proposal at the early stages of discussion and understand its consequences on their interests early on. In contrast, members of the general public tend to become aware that something is afoot and then take some time to organize. Thus, traditional comprehensive planning has tended to favor commercial interests over those of residents.

In the area of natural hazards, Drabek et al. (1983) investigated seismic mitigation activities in Missouri and Washington, two states at risk from earthquakes. A key study finding was that numerous seismic activities were placed on the public agenda in Washington, whereas few were placed on the agenda in Missouri. These researchers contend that an important factor explaining this difference is the extent of interaction among key participants. Interaction in Washington was sustained and frequent. It was sporadic and infrequent in Missouri. They concluded that the energies, skills, and values each participant brings into the arena help to identify relevant issues and consequences of alternative solutions that would be neglected in a fragmented public arena.

Presence and Role of Advocates. Advocates are participants in the planning process who are willing to invest their resources—time, energy, and money—to assure that a particular problem is raised on governmental agendas and is given priority. Advocates can be a moving force in planning (Lambright 1984). They can be found in many locations in a given public arena, such as a local government planner or a seismologist from a private consulting firm.

The most critical characteristics contributing to the success of advocates, according to Kingdon (1984), are expertise in the subject area, political skill in forming coalitions around a given proposal, and, most important, persistence. Kingdon contends that persistence implies a willingness to invest substantial resources over a long period of time to create a political climate receptive to change.

In the natural hazards field, Alesch and Petak (1986) examined the influence of advocates in advancing earthquake mitigation in three California communities. A major conclusion was that strong advocates were a key factor in stimulating adoption of a seismic retrofit ordinance. Advocates played a strong role in formulating an acceptable ordinance that dealt with a variety of stakeholders, ranging from low-income tenants to building owners. Another conclusion was that "muddling through" tends to be the prevailing mode of planning, with periodic spurts of activity largely attributable to the persistent efforts of advocates.

Several hazards policy studies (e.g., Berke 1989; Lambright 1984; Olson and Nilson 1982) recommend that scientists, planners, and public officials in general should act as advocates for groups and issues that typically are underrepresented in public planning. These studies found that plans are often expressions of the values of a few powerful special interests and do not meet the needs of the general public. A key conclusion of these studies is that public officials should advocate alternative proposals for underrepresented clients and issues. The very act of advocacy was found to clarify assumptions and enhance communication, and thereby to promote accurate judgments about potential consequences. Thus, the advocacy role is educational: those that are underrepresented learn about their rights, opportunities, and resources in the context of the public debate.

Linkage to Well-established Precedents. When landmark legislation is passed or a public agency adopts a particular planning innovation, precedent is established. Once that occurs, planning and its attendant policies in that arena are never quite the same. Establishing a precedent does not necessarily imply that a policy or program actually has taken a dramatic new turn, at least not in the short run. The step might or might not be small. The importance of such events lies in their precedent-setting nature. Precedents are important because people become accustomed to the new way of doing things and build new practices into their standard operating procedures. Inertia sets in, and it becomes difficult to divert the system from its new direction.

Once a precedent is established in one arena, it can be used to open windows gradually and to promote similar change in another arena that is like the first in some way. For example, passage of structural flood control legislation in the 1930s resulted in legislation for mapping flood hazards and nonstructural floodplain management, dam inspection, coastal land use planning, earthquake prediction technology, and other diverse fields (Clary 1985).

Spillover is promoted when advocates are persistent in their efforts and use their expertise to develop linkages. For an issue to progress from one arena to another, it must be linked to an issue in the second arena. In other words, the two issues need to be placed in the same category of public concern. For example, people may easily move from one issue (e.g., adverse environmental impact of rapid urbanization) to the next (e.g., impact of new development on hurricane evacuation times) because they are linked to the common category of urban growth. Beatley and Godschalk (1985) and Godschalk et al. (1989) maintain that natural hazard mitigation efforts can be advanced by linking mitigation issues to traditional measures of local development management. Measures guiding development would then be applied to mitigation, and, in turn, hazard mitigation would become more feasible because it would be integrated with politically acceptable measures of development management. Thus, the two activities would cease to operate as separate administrative functions.

Availability of Resources. Planning proposals can wax or wane according to the availability of resources. Resources can be monetary or nonmonetary. Monetary resources can be translated into additional staff, studies of geology or structural engineering, and consultants. The principal nonmonetary resource for hazard mitigation activities is staff time.

When resources are available, problems can be evaluated and alternatives generated. The result can be improved understanding of risks and an increased likelihood of formulating a viable proposal. Moreover, resources available during the early stages of planning, when participants are most open to suggestions, can have a significant impact. That is, a significant knowledge base about both problems and their potential solutions available at the outset can forestall decisions that would constrain viable courses of action.

Resources for seismic mitigation, however, usually are not adequate. Drabek et al. (1983) and Wyner and Mann (1986) suggest that low accomplishment by communities is largely due to inadequate resources. These studies maintain that when resource constraints are severe, efforts to undertake seismic mitigation have been virtually paralyzed.

External Factors

Recognition of Problem. The perception of risk from natural hazards is crucial to setting the public agenda. There must be a perception that the current situation reflects a disparity between what is and what ought to be. The chances of a problem being given high priority in public planning forums are markedly enhanced if the problem is perceived to involve potentially catastrophic loss of people and property.

Participants in the public arena attend to a long list of problems. Local government officials in earthquake-prone communities, for example, investigate the costs of providing public infrastructure (e.g., roads, sewers, water systems), deficiencies in the job market, and safety issues related to earthquakes. While developers may be concerned for the safety of residents, they are likely to be more worried about the immediate economic implications of meeting new development or land use codes. Obviously, each participant gives attention to some problems and ignores others.

In the case of low probability–high consequence events like earthquakes, achieving high agenda status is not easy because people typically place a low value on them. It is difficult to convince key decision makers to devote time and attention to a low-probability problem when the public agenda is full of generally acknowledged problems that constituents view as more pressing and important (Alesch and Petak, 1986; Rossi et al. 1982). This situation is particularly true when low-probability problems generate immediate political and economic costs but yield only long-term benefits.

Kingdon (1984) indicates two key ways in which a problem captures attention. Sometimes a systematic indicator shows there is a problem. Indicators abound in public arenas because both governmental and nongovernmental agencies routinely monitor various activities and events. They may suggest problems ranging from a declining number of jobs to rising crime rates. In the case of earthquake hazards, indicators might include detailed maps illustrating seismic hazard zones and reports that indicate dam safety problems or structurally inadequate critical facilities such as schools and hospitals. Such information has been shown to raise awareness about the risk and draw attention to the need for action (Mushkatel and Nigg 1987a, b).

A second way is a focusing event. Problems associated with low probability–high consequence events are often not made evident by indicators. They need a push to get attention. The push in the case of natural hazards is provided by a disaster event that calls for immediate attention. Such an event moves key participants from general awareness to action-oriented decision making (Abney and Hill 1966; Godschalk et al. 1989; Mileti, 1980; others).

Window of Opportunity. Cohen et al. (1972) define windows as occasions during which a problem becomes pressing, creating an opportunity for advocates to push their proposals as solutions. In the natural hazards field, windows are opened by a disastrous event such as an earthquake.[3] If proposals are ready, the disaster provides an opportunity to argue for enactment.

Once the window opens, however, it does not stay open long. If solutions are not enacted quickly, the window closes. The disaster that prompted the window to open passes from the scene. A crisis event by its nature is of short duration. People can stay excited only for so long. Plan proposals must develop well in advance of the time when the window opens. Without earlier consideration, decision makers cannot take advantage of the open window.

Alesch and Petak's study (1986) of local efforts to enact seismic mitigation building codes found that when the 1971 San Fernando Valley earthquake occurred, local officials in Long Beach were prepared. They were aware of the problem, a solution was available in the form of recommendations made in a consulting report on retrofit, and key advocates were poised for an intensive effort (Alesch and Petak 1986). In Los Angeles, local officials were not prepared when the window opened. Fourteen years passed before another window opened—the 1985 Mexico City earthquake. This time, however, Los Angeles officials were ready. Immediately after the earthquake, while elected officials' and the politic's memory of television reports was still vivid, a stringent seismic building retrofit ordinance was adopted.

Social and Economic Conditions. There are two ways in which social and economic conditions can influence local support for new initiatives and, hence, the degree of success in formulating solutions for seismic hazards (Bryson 1983). First, social and economic conditions reflect overall community wealth and the availability of resources to carry out new initiatives (Alterman and Hill 1978; Burby and French 1985). A prosperous community with a growing fiscal capacity (high-income residents and a growing economy and tax base) makes possible governmental innovation that would be nearly impossible in times of economic stagnation and tax base erosion. Tight fiscal conditions lead public and private groups to be conservative, to protect what they have, and to avoid big changes. Many

---

3. Alesch and Petak (1986), Cohen et al. (1972), and Kingdon (1984), among others, suggest that windows of opportunity can open not only because of crises like earthquakes but also through other events. These events might include passage of a state mandate requiring localities to undertake a specific activity (e.g., preparation of a seismic element for local comprehensive plans) or the election of a politician with a new agenda.

proposals fail to obtain serious consideration because the future looks bleak.

A prosperous community, however, creates slack resources, which free up organizations. Governmental agencies may have more opportunities for experimentation and more resources to sink into the production of innovations. Real estate developers are likely to be more willing to absorb unproductive costs, such as seismic retrofit of buildings. Thus, proposals have a better chance of surviving because expected fiscal conditions make them obtainable.

Social and economic conditions may also reflect perceived needs for public action related to hazard mitigation (Kunreuther and Linnerooth 1984, ch. 8; Rowe 1977; Wyner and Mann 1986). Facts such as expected damages or loss of life from earthquakes may support a need for hazard mitigation, but the need is also subject to interpretation. In affluent communities, the costs of hazard mitigation may be viewed as acceptable in view of the benefits of loss reduction. In communities of low affluence, the costs of mitigation are of greater concern and are likely to be found unacceptable. There is thus no absolute level of acceptable loss; rather, there is likely to be a close relationship between the acceptability of loss and the social and economic setting in which loss might occur.

Political Culture. The political culture reflects prevailing local attitudes toward private property and government regulation of private development. Different cultural perspectives on property and regulations can result in different local responses to environmental risk. Particularly affected are those planning measures that involve regulation of private rights to the use of land (Petak and Atkisson 1982).

Conservative attitudes toward regulation of development rights are exacerbated by the timing and distribution of benefits, and the costs associated with, such regulatory approaches. As Baker and McPhee (1975) observe, land use planning measures are often not feasible because of the long time span before benefits can accrue. Often benefits cannot be "seen" by the public. Moreover, many types of measures, such as zoning and subdivision controls, involve short-term costs. It is difficult for public officials in a conservative political climate to endure short-term political costs if they are weighed against more indefinite and long-term community benefits.

Pioneering work by Banfield and Wilson (1963) suggests that the extent to which constituents hold "public-regarding" values strongly influences the degree of support they give to hazard mitigation. These researchers found that when such values exist, constituents are likely to support expenditures that do not benefit them directly. Elazar (1966) expanded the notion of political culture by identifying three forms, each with distinctive characteristics and implications for government and politics. They are individualistic, moralistic, and traditionalistic. The individualistic political culture emphasizes "the centrality of private concerns [and] places a premium on limiting community intervention—whether governmental or nongovernmental—into private activities to the minimum necessary to keep the marketplace in proper working order" (86, 87). The traditionalistic political culture supports some government intervention, but primarily maintains existing political and social relations.

In contrast to these two political cultures, and particularly to the utilitarian and reactive individualistic culture, is the moralistic culture. Here politics is considered an activity intended to promote the public interest and the good of society. Elazar suggests that this form of political culture "creates a greater commitment to active government intervention into the economic and social life of the community" (92). Public officials initiate new governmental activities to tackle problems that are often not perceived by the majority of the citizenry.

In sum, localities characterized as less public regarding, more individualistic, and more private property oriented tend to give less support to hazard mitigation. In such localities, mitigation program activities tend to be very limited.

CONCLUSIONS

This chapter presented a typology of mitigation measures and a conceptual framework for understanding the dynamics of planning for earthquake mitigation. The typology can help determine which measures are likely to succeed or fail, given variations in a range of technical, economic, and political factors, It can also provide insight into how mitigation strategies can be adapted when such factors change over time.

An essential premise of the conceptual framework is that planning in turbulent environments, like the public arena of earthquake mitigation, does not necessarily follow the simplified, orderly, sequential process of the rational approach. Decision makers discover preferences through action more than they act on clearly defined goals. Decisions require considerable judgment and are often made without full knowledge of the consequences of alternative proposals.

To explain the dynamics of public planning, the framework consists of a sequence of four stages: environmental risk; policy initiation; policy formulation and adoption; and policy implementation. Internal and external factors that shape the evolution of planning policies for mitigation are derived. Of particular interest are the internal factors that constitute the capacity of public agencies to achieve their intentions. These factors represent activities that can be undertaken by public agency staff to advance mitigation programs. The balance of influence exerted by internal and external factors determines the extent to which local public organizations influence their own plans and policies.

Finally, the typology and conceptual framework will be used to interpret the survey and case study data collected for this study. As mentioned in chapter 1, the mail survey covers communities in the twenty-two states that contain high-hazard earthquake zones. Forty follow-up telephone surveys of localities were selected from those included in the mail survey to review a range of mitigation measures. Three follow-up case localities were selected from those surveyed for more detailed analysis.

3 • SEISMIC HAZARD MITIGATION IN UTAH
The Salt Lake County Natural Hazards Ordinance

Salt Lake County, located southeast of the Great Salt Lake, lies along a region known as the Wasatch Front. This five-county region is the most heavily populated portion of Utah, containing 90 percent of the state's population of 1.6 million. The 1987 county population was approximately 700,000, or more than 40 percent of the state population (Utah Office of Planning and Budget 1988). Within its geographical boundaries lies Salt Lake City and twelve other incorporated municipalities.

Historically, the local economy has depended heavily upon resource activities such as mining and oil and gas production. Such dependence was evident when the economy took a sharp downturn in the early 1980s due to closings of several large mining operations in the region and the fall of world oil prices. In recent years, the economy has diversified; several large ski resorts have developed and high-technology industries expanded in the county.

Salt Lake County residents are better educated and have homes with higher values than other residents in the state and the nation (see table 3-1). County residents also have higher incomes than others in the state. While per capita income is lower than in the nation, median family income is higher.

THE NATURE OF SEISMIC HAZARDS ALONG THE WASATCH FRONT

The Wasatch Front counties are subject to a variety of seismic-related natural hazards. They lie along the intermountain seismic belt, an area of active faults running from Montana to southwestern Utah (Christensen 1987). The type of fault exhibited along this belt is considerably different from that experienced in California, and the difference has implications

Table 3.1 Socioeconomic Characteristics of Salt Lake County, Utah, and the United States (1979)

	Salt Lake County	Utah	U.S.
Per capita income	$ 7,013	$ 6,305	$ 7,298
Median family income	21,064	20,024	19,917
Median years of education	12.9	12.8	12.5
Median value of owner-occupied homes	$59,200	$57,300	$47,200

Source: U.S. Census Bureau (1980a, b).

for the kinds of mitigation that are appropriate. The San Andreas fault in California is a "strike-slip" fault, while Utah faults are "normal" or "dip-slip" faults. For strike-slip faulting, movement occurs horizontally, and the zone of deformation is generally symmetrical and uniform on both sides of the fault line. For normal or dip-slip faults, movement is more vertical, and the zone of deformation is less uniform and symmetrical (see fig. 3-1). The zone of deformation tends to be considerably wider, with the widest portion on the down-dropped side.

Low-magnitude earthquakes are common along the Wasatch Front, but a major earthquake has not occurred since settlement of the region in the 1840s. Large-magnitude earthquakes, however, have recently occurred in Idaho and Montana. The most recent incident was the 1983 Borah Peak (Idaho) earthquake (7.3 magnitude). While Utah did not sustain serious damage, Salt Lake County experienced ground shaking from this event. Findings from a postevent seismic study commissioned by the U.S. Geological Survey (USGS) indicate that the faulting characteristics in Idaho exemplify those in Utah (Meek 1988). Vertical displacement was as much as ten feet, with the zone of deformation about three-hundred feet— substantially wider than would be the case in a strike-slip or California-type earthquake.

In addition to the fault-rupture hazard, the Wasatch Front counties are subject to other earthquake-generated forces, including liquefaction,

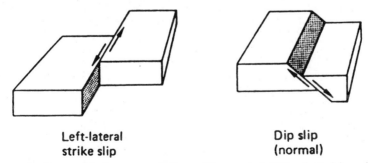

Left-lateral strike slip

Dip slip (normal)

Figure 3.1 Types of fault movement. *Source:* Wesson et al. 1975; adapted from figure 6.15, p. 169.

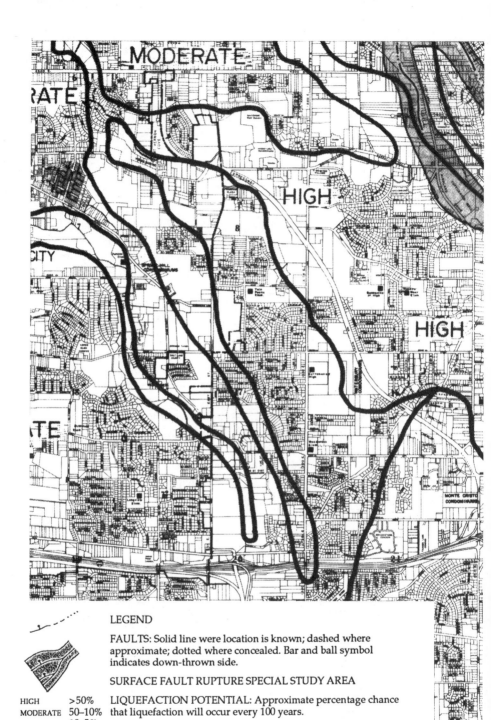

MODERATE

RATE

HIGH

CITY

ATE

HIGH

LEGEND

FAULTS: Solid line were location is known; dashed where approximate; dotted where concealed. Bar and ball symbol indicates down-thrown side.

SURFACE FAULT RUPTURE SPECIAL STUDY AREA

HIGH	>50%	LIQUEFACTION POTENTIAL: Approximate percentage chance
MODERATE	50–10%	that liquefaction will occur every 100 years.
LOW	10–5%	
VERY LOW	<5%	

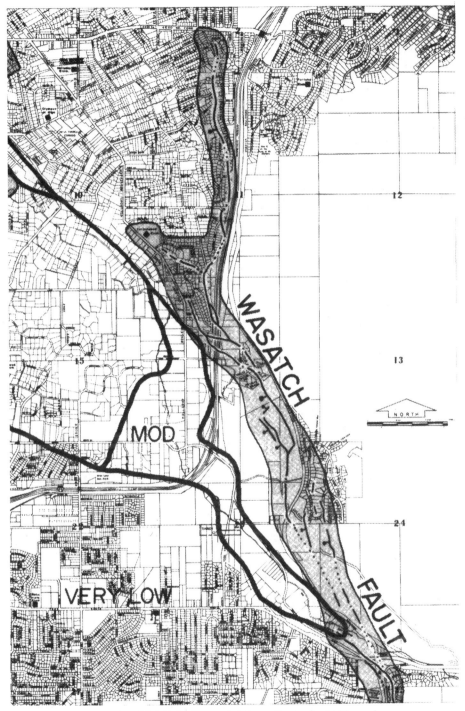

Figure 3.2 A portion of Salt Lake County's interpretive geological hazards map.
Source: Salt Lake County 1989.

Figure 3.3 New housing development along a dip-slip (normal) fault with a steep, unstable slope in Salt Lake County, Utah. Photograph by Philip R. Berke, 1988.

ground shaking, and seismically induced slope failure. Liquefaction is a considerable problem because Salt Lake County rests on loosely consolidated lakebed materials and has a relatively high water table. Fault-rupture hazard zones and liquefaction areas have been identified and placed on a detailed composite hazards map prepared for the region (see fig. 3-2).

Recently, slope failure has been a serious problem along the Wasatch Front, though not as a result of seismic activity. From 1982 to 1985 the region experienced a severe "wet cycle" with abnormally high precipitation, resulting in serious landsliding. In 1983 a landslide, purported to be the most expensive in U.S. history, occurred near Thistle, Utah (Christensen 1987). The wet cycle also caused flooding from historically high water levels in Great Salt Lake during the springs of 1986 and 1987.

A considerable amount of people and property are at risk from earthquake hazards in the Wasatch Front counties. A 1976 USGS study concluded that a major earthquake in the Wasatch Front area would cause 14,000 deaths, and leave 30,000 people homeless (USGS 1976). Undoubtedly the risks posed by earthquakes have increased since the USGS study. In particular, development along and on top of fault lines has been substantial (see figs. 3-3 and 3-4). The new structures are typically expensive; many of the fault zones contain prime homesites with impressive views of the valley.

Figure 3.4 New development is promoted despite its location along a dip-slip (normal) fault in Salt Lake County, Utah. Photograph by Philip R. Berke, 1988.

Numerous critical facilities and high-occupancy structures such as hospitals and schools have also been constructed on top of or very near fault traces. South High School in Salt Lake City, for instance, lies directly on top of a fault line; it is attended by some 2,000 students (see fig. 3-5). A seismic vulnerability assessment of West Valley City, located in the western portion of the county, found that most of the critical facilities examined could not sustain significant seismic forces and were in need of substantial retrofit (West Valley, Utah 1988). Among the deficient facilities were civil defense shelters, bridges and highway overpasses, power substations, water and sewer lines, and water storage tanks. Many facilities throughout the Salt Lake County area are equally deficient (Reaveley 1988).

MITIGATION POLICY IN SALT LAKE COUNTY

Evolution of Mitigation Policy

Salt Lake County has slowly acknowledged the need to address natural hazards in its land use and planning decisions. Since 1965, the County Planning Commission has periodically required geological site investigations through zoning and subdivision permit requests (Barnes 1988). Under the county's zoning ordinance, most uses other than single-family,

Figure 3.5 South High School in Salt Lake City, Utah, was built astride an active fault. Photograph by Philip R. Berke, 1988.

detached residential units require a conditional use permit. When a natural hazard is suspected, a developer or property owner may be required to prepare a geological hazard study. Depending on the study results, site design or building requirements may be imposed.[1] Under the county's subdivision ordinance, geological studies have been required if active faults were suspected on a proposed development site. Some subdivisions have been approved only after a fault setback zone has been legally incorporated in the plat.[2]

In the late 1970s, however, county planners determined that such permit review procedures were inadequate. Their inadequacy stemmed from the institutional division in the county's planning department between the advance planning activities of the Planning Division and the day-to-day permit administration activities of the Development Services Divi-

1. The proposed Dresdin Lane apartments is an instance of how seismic considerations can be integrated into a conditional use permit review. In this case, in 1983 Salt Lake City required a geological study in a suspected fault zone. Trenching undertaken in preparing the study indicated an active fault. To avoid straddling the fault line meant reducing the land available for development. This limitation prevented the project from proceeding at the density originally planned. A large apartment complex was no longer possible, and the site has since remained vacant.

2. The recently approved Prospector Hills subdivision exemplifies the positive results of such a requirement. The subdivision plat was approved conditionally on the inclusion of a fifty-foot setback from the fault line. Construction of homes on the portion of the lots covered by the setback was not permitted.

sion.[3] All development review occurred in the latter division, but seismic hazards were considered in the former. While Development Services Division staff were aware of seismic hazards, they generally did not consider them in development reviews because, as one staffer observed, "there is no uniform standard for review." Consideration of seismic hazards was only "optional" and "discretionary." In almost all instances, reviews were conducted because Planning Division staff had spot-checked development reviews of the Development Services Division. As a result, consideration of seismic safety has been hit-and-miss at best.

Through strong support of planning staff, the county expanded its consideration of geological hazards over the next ten years. In 1980 the county adopted a special Hillside Protection Ordinance to regulate development in the mountainous eastern portion of the county (Salt Lake City, Utah 1988a).[4] While there is no officially adopted countywide comprehensive plan, the county in 1986 adopted a set of planning goals and policies. One key goal indicates that the county will protect the health and well-being of residents and the physical safety of property "by identifying and avoiding areas of physical or geologic hazard or mitigating the hazards . . . based on 'State of the Art' design" (Salt Lake City, Utah 1986, 3). Seismic hazards are also considered in a draft environmental plan for the Wasatch Canyon ski resort area (Salt Lake City, Utah 1988c). Key mitigation policies under consideration include, for example, public acquisition of high-hazard lands and limited development densities in hazardous locations.

The county is currently incorporating seismic concerns into the preparation of land use plans for twenty-two community districts within its jurisdiction. The land use plan for the Millcreek community district, for example, considers seismic hazards in its discussion of development suitability. As figures 3-6 and 3-7 indicate, the plan displays fault-rupture and liquefaction zones among its development constraint maps. Like other district plans, however, the Millcreek plan does not propose changes in use, or reductions in density, in high-hazard seismic zones (Salt Lake City, Utah 1988b).

While the county has made some limited improvements in its seismic mitigation program, in December 1988 county planners deemed them

---

3. The Development Services Division administers the conditional use permit procedure. It also has responsibility for administering subdivision regulations along with other departments of county government, such as health and public works. None of these other departments have direct responsibility to assure consideration of seismic hazards for proposed developments.

4. In 1980 the Hillside Protection Ordinance was designed to prohibit development of slopes of 40 percent or greater. In 1986 the county made the ordinance more stringent by prohibiting development on 30 percent slopes.

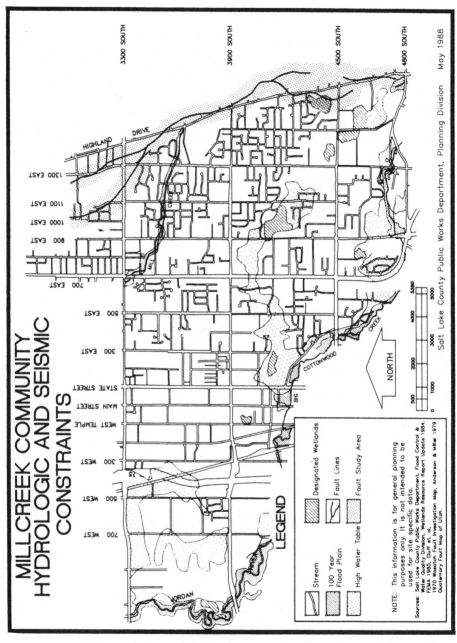

Figure 3.6 This map shows the hydrological and seismic constraints in the Millcreek community, Salt Lake County, Utah.

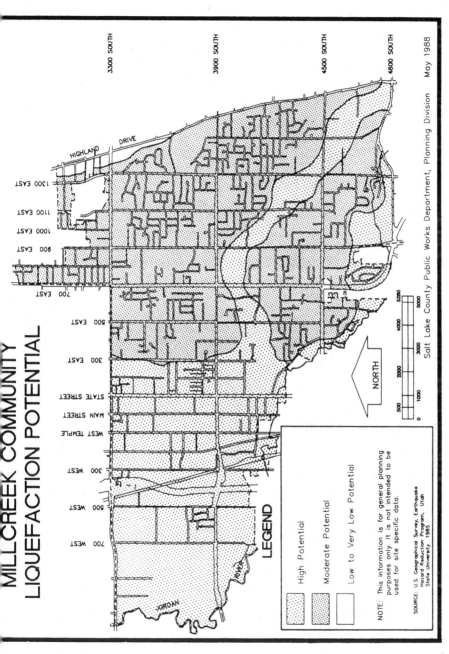

Figure 3.7 This map shows the liquefaction potential in the Millcreek community, Salt Lake County, Utah. *Source:* Salt Lake County 1988b.

inadequate for two reasons. First, with the exception of the Hillside Protection Ordinance, none of the recent county mitigation activities resulted in policies that regulate development in seismically hazardous areas. Second, permit reviews for most development projects in potentially hazardous locations did not consider seismic hazards due to the hit-and-miss pattern of the Development Services Division.

The Natural Hazards Ordinance

In an attempt to correct problems related to permitting and to expand the scope of seismic regulatory activities, the county adopted the Natural Hazards Ordinance in 1989. The ordinance requires the most explicit consideration of seismic hazards to date in Salt Lake County. The objectives of the ordinance are "to promote the health, safety and general welfare of the citizens of Salt Lake County and minimize the potential effects of natural hazards to public health, safety and property by encouraging wise use of hazardous areas" (Salt Lake City, Utah 1989, 1).

The ordinance is based on a series of overlay hazard zones that are coterminous with liquefaction and surface fault-rupture hazard maps prepared for the county with funds from the National Earthquake Hazards Reduction Program through the USGS (see fig. 3-2). While seismic risks are the most significant emphasis of the ordinance, other hazards, such as avalanches and landslides, are also addressed.

If a development project were proposed in one of these hazard zones, the developer could be required to prepare a special engineering geology study. This study is to be prepared by an "experienced engineering geologist" and is to "identify all known or suspected natural hazards, originating on site or off site, affecting the particular property and present an assessment of the hazards as they relate to the intended land use. Recommendations and conclusions shall be presented to insure that the hazards are avoided or integrated so that the purposes . . . in section 19.75010 [goals] are met" (Salt Lake City, Utah 1989, 3). Table 3-2 indicates the two criteria for determining if a geology study should be required. They are the type of hazardous conditions, if any, on a given site and the land use intensity of a proposed project. In low-liquefaction zones, for instance, a developer would be required to prepare a geological study only if "essential facilities" and "high-occupancy buildings" are proposed. The definitions of essential facilities and high-occupancy buildings are obtained from the Uniform Building Code. High-occupancy buildings include schools, hotels, and offices, while essential facilities include police and fire stations, hospitals, communication centers, and disaster response facilities.

Before development can be approved, the geological study must be submitted for review to the county geologist, the Utah Geological Mineral

Table 3.2 Guidelines for Determining Whether an Engineering Geology Study Is Needed

Land Use (Type of Facility)	Liquefaction Area			
	High	Moderate	Low	Very Low
Essential facilities [(UBC 2312(k)] and high-occupancy buildings (UBC A-1, A-2, A-2.1)	Yes	Yes	Yes	Yes
Industrial and commercial buildings (>2 stories or >5,000 square feet)	Yes	Yes	No	No
Multifamily residential (4 or more units/acre) and other industrial and commercial	Yes	Yes	No	No
Residential subdivisions	No*	No*	No	No
Residential single lots and multifamily developments (less than 4 units/acre)	No*	No*	No	No

Source: Nelson 1987.
*Disclosure of potential hazard to buyers/residents is recommended.

Survey (UGMS), and the Forest Service (in the case of an avalanche threat). The adequacy of the report is ultimately determined by the Planning Commission (with advisory assistance from the Development Services Division), in the case of conditional use projects, and the Development Services Division, in the case of permitted uses.

Once a geological study has been prepared, the ordinance does little in stipulating specific mitigation requirements. The only specific performance standard is prohibition against building any structure designed for human occupancy astride an active fault.

County planning staff noted that the success of the ordinance in mitigating risks depends upon flexibility, as opposed to explicit performance standards, which must be satisfied by any proposed development in a hazard overlay zone. Staff planners suggested two reasons for the need for flexibility. One is that the ordinance provides an applicant with the responsibility of specifying mitigation options. The flexible approach acknowledges that others, namely developers and experts they may hire, may know more than county staff does about mitigation measures.

A second reason is related to the seismic hazard characteristics of Utah. Such characteristics are not well suited to performance-based approaches, particularly for the most obvious performance standard—the fault line setback. As mentioned, the faults in Utah are of the "normal" or "dip-slip" type, and the zone of deformation is much less uniform than in the case of the "strike-slip" type of fault existing in California (e.g., the San Andreas fault). In these situations a uniform setback, like the one used under California's Alquist Priolo Act, is not appropriate. Rather, the zone of deformation astride different segments of fault line tends to vary in width, suggesting different setback distances.

An additional aspect of the Salt Lake County ordinance is a hazard disclosure provision for new development. The ordinance states that where the required geological study "shows [that] a natural hazard affects a particular parcel, the type and severity of the hazard shall be recorded as a deed covenant running with the land" (Salt Lake City, Utah 1989, 5). The intention is to inform potential home buyers and property owners about the hazard. In principal this provision should lead to changes in real estate investment decisions of consumers, financial institutions, and developers, who may take alternative actions to avoid hazardous locations.

A controversial issue surrounding the disclosure provision dealt with its application to existing development. Two particularly vocal elected officials representing affluent areas of the county expressed concern that the ordinance might be applied retroactively to existing homes. Such an application, according to these officials, might result in the creation of "blighted areas" where property values could be dramatically lowered. While county planning staff gave some consideration to applying the disclosure provision to existing development, the current ordinance is politically crafted to avoid this issue.

INTERNAL FACTORS AFFECTING POLICY RESPONSE

Interorganization Coordination and Communication Activities

An important explanation for the advancement of the Natural Hazards Ordinance as well as other mitigation activities in Salt Lake County was the presence of two key interorganizational coordination and communication activities. First, locally elected officials who belonged to the United Association of Community Councils (UACC) and county planning staff communicated continually about the nature of the seismic problem and possible solutions. UACC is a membership organization of locally elected officials from the community districts in Salt Lake County.[5] Through regular monthly meetings, county planners used UACC as a forum for introducing the latest results of geological studies in the county and for reviewing the

5. UACC is an advisory group to the county board. Its membership consists of two elected council persons from each community district in the county. UACC votes on county ordinances, and council members approve conditional use permits and proposed zoning changes within their own districts. UACC has given the councils a strong, unified voice in county affairs. Its endorsement of a legislative proposal carries substantial political influence and a high level of recognition of council concerns.

various mitigation activities of individual community districts. Interviews with UACC members revealed a high level of familiarity with a range of seismic activities—for example, the seismic mapping project for the Millcreek community district comprehensive plan.

Second, initial communication and coordination efforts about seismic problems and their potential solutions stemmed from the presence of the Utah Seismic Safety Advisory Council. The council was established by the state legislature in 1977 to (1) assess the magnitude of the risks posed by earthquakes in Utah, (2) promote public education on earthquake hazards, and (3) make recommendations for statewide seismic safety policy.

Council membership was dominated by state and local officials (including several representatives from Salt Lake County) who were to be instrumental in pushing seismic policy.[6] During its four-year existence (it dissolved as a result of a sunset clause), council members met three to four times annually to assess available information on seismic issues and to arrive at a set of recommendations for consideration by state and local governments. While few recommendations were implemented, the long-term impact of the council was significant in the state and particularly in Salt Lake County. Because the council was the first state activity to assess seismic safety policy issues in Utah, it had become a highly visible focal point for many stakeholders and was instrumental in bringing together and establishing a core group of seismic safety advocates. As one informed observer notes, "With its demise in 1981, a core group of 'true believers' had been developed" (Sprinkel 1988, 89).

The Role of Advocates

The Natural Hazards Ordinance as well as other mitigation activities would not likely have been originated or elevated to the public agenda without the strong interest and advocacy of certain key individuals. In particular, the ordinance is the brainchild of the director of one of the county planning divisions and former member of the Utah Seismic Safety Advisory Council. This advocate has worked behind the scenes for many years to bring attention to natural hazards in the planning process. The particular ordinance adopted is, in this informant's words, "something I've been working on for some ten years, in one way or another." The political success of the ordinance can be attributed in large part to his credibility and perceived competence among both public officials and citizens.

The mere presence of an advocate, however, is not sufficient. To com-

6. Membership consisted of elected and appointed officials from state and local government, several federal agency representatives, and several consultants with engineering and geological expertise.

mand attention and make an impact, the advocate must possess a high level of credibility in the eyes of public officials. This was certainly true of the planning director, who was often described as a dedicated and technically competent professional planner.

The availability of credible technical expertise from another advocate—the county geologist—has also had a positive influence on development of the ordinance. This informant has been a strong proponent of mitigation and has supported the ordinance from a scientific and technical viewpoint. During a brief three-year period of employment (1986–89) by Salt Lake County, the geologist developed the confidence of elected officials and the general public. The geologist's slide-show presentations had considerable impact in convincing others of the need for mitigation.

Two other advocates of the Salt Lake County mitigation efforts deserve mention. One was a geologist and high-level administrator for UGMS. This advocate's efforts at the state level have done much to create a more supportive climate for the mitigation initiatives of localities like Salt Lake County. At the state level, this informant created the Utah Seismic Safety Advisory Council in 1977 and pushed for a statewide Geological Hazard Information Act while serving in the legislature. Although the proposed act was never adopted, it would have required that UGMS collect and map hazard information for each locality by a certain deadline. This person was also politically active at the local level; for example, testifying in March 1988 before the Salt Lake County Planning Commission to convince commissioners to hire a full-time county geologist.

A local structural engineering consulting firm has been aggressively advocating mitigation upgrading. A Salt Lake County planner maintained that the firm has been so aggressive that it has lost several clients who were not willing to pay for additional structural reinforcement measures. Nevertheless, a representative pointed out that the firm had been involved in numerous development projects incorporating higher levels of structural mitigation than the local building code specified.

Linking Seismic Hazards to Local Planning Activities

Mitigation was advanced in several ways through linkage of seismic hazards to local planning activities. Two recent examples are the Millcreek Community Plan and the proposed Wasatch Canyons Master Plan. While linking seismic hazards to community district and area master planning programs has not directly translated into zoning or land use restrictions, it has heightened community awareness of seismic risks. The effect of linkage is demonstrated by an incident following the sudden appearance of the Natural Hazards Ordinance on a Planning Commission meeting agenda in the fall of 1988. The County Planning Division had not informed community council members about the proposed ordinance.[7] In interviews, several council members maintained that they were surprised, not that the Planning Division was addressing seismic hazards, but that the members were not familiar with the proposed ordinance. They were not surprised, in part, they said, because seismic hazards had been incorporated into several previous and ongoing planning activities—for example, Millcreek and Wasatch Canyon planning programs—undertaken at the community district level.

A third example of linkage involved the limited but effective use of conditional use and subdivision permits. Linking seismic hazards to permit reviews was optional and was done only occasionally. However, when incorporation did occur, seismic safety was accounted for and integrated into the development process. Use of permit reviews to account for hazards over a ten-year period allowed planners and developers to become accustomed to earthquake mitigation. Furthermore, the new Natural Hazards Ordinance does not represent a radical change in the way of doing things because it does not go beyond existing land use regulations. It merely imposes an additional procedural step—the preparation of an engineering geology study—and makes possible the requirement of additional site design or structural features as a condition for development approval.

Availability of Resources

An important explanation for the advancement of earthquake mitigation in the county was the availability of adequate technical resources. Specifically, two key technical activities that were funded under the National Earthquake Hazards Reduction Program (NEHRP) through USGS played a crucial role. First, extensive geological studies were undertaken to prepare detailed composite seismic hazards maps, which were completed in 1988 (see fig. 3-2). Without such maps it would have been impossible to implement the Natural Hazards Ordinance or to prepare development-suitability maps for the Millcreek and Wasatch Canyon plans.

The factual and scientific documentation of seismic hazards also did much to diffuse the arguments of those who dismissed mitigation on the grounds of uncertainty. As one informed observer of Utah's experience notes:

7. The failure to notify council members may have been perceived. The Planning Division director claims that the council members were mailed a notice about the ordinance on the agenda about one month before the planning commission meeting. Several members maintained, however, that they remembered receiving the notice but that the proposed ordinance was mentioned only in a few words as an agenda item. There was no explanation of the content or purpose of the ordinance.

The series of trenches that have been dug across the fault at different locations is the single most important activity that has been conducted. . . . With this hard data, all other influences have followed in a logical manner. Without specific scientific data, the people of Utah would tend to use most of the reasons listed in Table 2 [e.g., public apathy, perceived economic hardship, resistance to change] to make no change in their activities. (Reaveley 1988, 473, 476)

Second, NEHRP influenced Salt Lake County's mitigation efforts through funding of a County Geologist Program over a three-year period (1985–88). A geologist was placed in the Salt Lake County Planning Department to improve in-house expertise for reviewing geological reports submitted during development review. When federal support for this program terminated in 1988, Salt Lake County picked up the geologist's salary and retained the position permanently.

Planning staff indicated that since employment of the geologist the technical quality of the geological studies has markedly improved. They maintained that, previously, developers tended to award contracts for studies to the lowest-bidding consultant. The studies were often of poor quality and had to be resubmitted, often several times, each time with a new charge. The county geologist eventually convinced many developers that it is worthwhile to look beyond the initial bidding price. For example, a developer indicated that, in the long run, it has been less costly to choose a more expensive bid by a consultant who could prepare a study that did not have to be resubmitted.

The ability of county planners to consider seismic hazards was also enhanced through technical assistance from a state agency—Utah Geological Mineral Survey (UGMS). Before the county had a full-time geologist, state geologists reviewed numerous geological studies for proposed developments at the request of the County Planning Division. UGMS staff also helped county planners prepare the Natural Hazards Ordinance and issued guidelines for preparing geological studies (Association of Engineering Geologists 1986).

EXTERNAL FACTORS AFFECTING POLICY RESPONSE

Stakeholder Reaction to the Earthquake Problem

Reactions of stakeholder groups to the seismic problem had a mixed impact on the formulation and adoption of mitigation policy. Interviews revealed that the public was perceived to be apathetic and thus has had little influence on policy development. Most informants acknowledged that while events like the Borah Peak earthquake and the wet cycle raised awareness about the potential for natural disasters, awareness has not translated into citizen action. Others maintained that the public had never experienced a major earthquake and that citizens consider their chances of being seriously affected by an earthquake too remote to require hazard reduction actions.

Support for mitigation primarily came from local planning staff and seismic professionals. These informants understood the causes of earthquake risk, particularly from the recent studies on mapping faults and liquefaction zones, and the need for mitigation policy.

Elected officials also acknowledge earthquakes as a significant problem. As exemplified by community council members, once elected officials became well informed about the problem, most were supportive. In the case of the Natural Hazards Ordinance, several council members repeatedly mentioned during interviews that they supported the ordinance because of concerns over liability and consumer protection. As one council member observed, "Now that public officials know the location of hazardous areas, would the county not be open to legal challenges if development is permitted in these areas without at least informing potential homebuyers and property owners of the risks?" Two council members even translated the county liability issue into personal liability. They believed that lawsuits won against the county would be paid for by average taxpayers.[8] Others expressed concern that it was unfair for developers to sell homes without making some reasonable effort to divulge geological hazards to potential homebuyers. Thus, liability and consumer protection arguments carried considerable political and popular appeal.

As mentioned, two dissenting council members expressed concern that if the hazard disclosure provision were applied to existing development, property values would decline dramatically. To avoid political conflict over this concern, the provision was not applied to existing development.

Surprisingly, developers did not oppose the ordinance. Interviews revealed that they did not object because the new regulations allayed their concern that additional costs would cut into profits. Representatives of the real estate industry indicated that while engineering geology studies can be expensive (typically between $3,000 and $4,000 each), the cost in most cases appears small in view of the overall expenses of developing.

8. In making the liability case, council members frequently cited trends and decisions in the California courts as evidence. The county geologist sought to raise the liability issue explicitly at his slide presentations by describing a 1984 liability decision in California—a case that actually involves the liability of real estate brokers and does not involve local government. Whether or not the erosion of sovereign immunity is occurring in Utah, the liability argument appears to have had considerable political potency. The case was *Easton* v. *Strassburger*, which found that a real estate broker was negligent for failing to inform a prospective buyer of a landslide hazard (see Davenport and Smith 1985).

In fact, some developers expressed support for the ordinance because the geological study requirements would be uniformly applied to all proposed development projects in potentially hazardous locations. This approach was considered to be fairer and more equitable than the hit-and-miss approach used previously.

Political Culture

The general political culture of Utah had some influence on the formulation of hazard mitigation policy in Salt Lake County. Owing largely to the historical Mormon influence, Utah is a politically conservative state with strong traditions of "home rule" and support of individual property rights. A state planner with the Department of Comprehensive Emergency Management suggested that Utah's citizens are not receptive to government regulation of private actions generally, and particularly not from "big and distant" government. Other observers added that there are strong beliefs in a free market and local political autonomy.

Most informants interviewed who expressed strong support for private property rights and limited government intervention also supported the Salt Lake County ordinance. A key reason is that the ordinance is well suited to the political culture of Utah.[9] As discussed, it is perceived primarily as a consumer protection and liability-avoiding strategy that imposes limited restrictions on developers and landowners. Additionally, it is primarily a local initiative, rather than one imposed by state government. The ordinance is also consistent with the general view expressed in interviews that the private market system is best suited to making land and development decisions. The ordinance does not prevent but, in fact, facilitates the system. It is an information-generating approach consistent with the conservative Utah climate.

Socioeconomic Conditions

Socioeconomic conditions in Salt Lake County had mixed effects on development of seismic mitigation policy. Due to a poorly performing state economy, much attention in Salt Lake County has been given to issues of economic growth and unemployment. These issues loomed large in importance relative to seismic safety and thus constrained efforts to advance mitigation.

---

9. While the Mormon church and doctrine clearly have a significant influence on virtually all aspects of daily life in Utah, we were never able, despite considerable probing, to find a direct and discernible influence on the development and adoption of the Salt Lake County mitigation ordinance. We recognize that some studies (Natural Research Council 1984 and Oaks 1987) have attributed to the Mormon culture a significant positive influence on local hazard reduction responses. However, at least in our study, this was not the case.

Surprisingly, however, poor economic conditions had a positive influence on mitigation policy. Interviews with representatives of development interests revealed that the poorly performing economy caused many developers to leave the area for other markets. It was believed that most went "back to California" and left behind a less organized, less powerful real estate lobby to oppose new development regulations.

These representatives also believed that the economic downturn in the region changed developers' perception of what is at stake. Comments like "just staying alive" or "holding our own" suggest that developers were preoccupied with surviving in a stagnating market. They had little concern, time, or energy to oppose new development regulations that address "growth"-oriented issues.

Windows of Opportunity

Within the past ten years, two crises—windows of opportunity—suddenly occurred near the Wasatch Front. While the 1983 Borah Peak earthquake raised awareness of earthquake hazards and caused a series of geological studies to be sponsored, no seismic mitigation policies were adopted in Salt Lake County during the disaster aftermath. Similarly, the 1983–85 wet cycle raised awareness of local geological hazards, but follow-up efforts to push for adoption of a policy were not taken.

County planning staff maintained that a key reason for not taking action was that adequate data about fault locations and liquefaction zones were not readily available when these windows opened. Without such information, practical methods for integrating seismic concerns into land use controls were unknown. Many informants, however, said in interviews that although seismic mitigation policy was not adopted, these disasters did much to raise awareness and keep the seismic issue on the public agenda until adoption of the Natural Hazards Ordinance.

IMPACT AND ADEQUACY OF THE SALT LAKE COUNTY PROGRAM

To date the potential hazard reduction of the county's mitigation efforts is only moderate. Although the geological review provision of the Natural Hazards Ordinance requires site design and construction mitigation measures, development can still occur in hazardous locations. Thus, no attempt has been made to regulate density of growth in seismic areas directly. Other mitigation activities, like the Millcreek community district and Wasatch Canyon plans have not yet resulted in direct regulation of land use and development.

County planners were well aware that in some areas, particularly in the vicinity of active fault lines, development should be severely restricted. They suggested that the most effective option might be for the county to

Figure 3.8 Faultline Park is situated astride an active fault near downtown Salt Lake City, Utah. Photograph by Philip R. Berke, 1988.

purchase land around fault lines and convert these dangerous areas into public parks, building on the example of Salt Lake City's Faultline Park (see fig. 3-8). Given the poorly performing local economy, however, they maintained that this option was not financially feasible in the near future.

Another limitation is that the Natural Hazard Ordinance only affects future development and does not address existing structures. A hazard disclosure provision for real estate transactions involving existing development was discussed but not adopted.

Recent examples suggest that buildings can be designed to provide considerable protection from earthquake forces. Two are the renovation of the historic city and county building and a new building housing a computer facility in the University of Utah Research Park (see fig. 3-9). The computer facility has incorporated "base isolation" technology, which involves placing energy-dissipating shock absorbers between the ground and the structure and results in substantial reduction in damages caused by ground motion. While extensive structural modifications, such as base isolation, will not result from all site investigations, some form of mitigative building design will be incorporated into all new developments in hazardous areas.

Some criticism has been leveled at the proposed ordinance because it does not address some natural hazards, particularly ground shaking. Of all hazards associated with earthquakes, ground shaking is probably the

Figure 3.9 This new building at the University of Utah Research Park in Salt Lake City houses computer facilities with base isolation technology. Photograph by Philip R. Berke, 1988.

most significant and the least understood. To date, detailed maps that delineate the spatial severity of ground shaking have not been produced. Until such maps become available, measures affecting ground shaking cannot be incorporated into the ordinance.[10]

The implementation prospects of the county program are encouraging, particularly because developers have complied with geological reviews. Moreover, the technical quality of the geological studies has considerably improved with the hiring of a full-time county geologist.

The disclosure provision of the Natural Hazards Ordinance might meet some implementation problems, however. A California study (Palm 1981) suggests that the provision will not appreciably change the decision-making patterns of housing consumers and others involved in real estate. This study found that disclosure requirements had little influence on the decisions of homeowners or on market performance (i.e., it did not have any discernible price effects). The study concluded that the lack of impact is caused by several factors. For example, homebuyers give low importance to environmental hazards, and real estate agents inform buyers of hazards late in the home-buying process, after buyers are psychologically committed. The general ineffectiveness of the California disclosure requirement calls into question the ability of the Salt Lake County disclosure provisions to lead to appreciable changes in development patterns.

10. The county, however, is moving forward in studying and preparing maps for other hazards. The county geologist has recently completed a preliminary study and map delineating rock-fall hazards in the county (Nelson 1988).

Another implementation problem could be that unlike other similar geological study ordinances, such as the one under consideration in Utah County, the Salt Lake County ordinance does not incorporate specific performance criteria. Such criteria would provide detailed building and design standards. For example, with respect to surface fault-rupture areas, the Utah County ordinance specifies performance standards that indicate circumstances in which trenching must be undertaken and the minimal setback line beyond which trenching is not required. Compared to the Utah County approach, successful implementation of the Salt Lake County ordinance would be more dependent upon the technical capability and level of personal commitment of those overseeing it. While there is general agreement that the current Salt Lake County geologist is well qualified and highly committed to seismic safety, if this person were to leave, effective implementation of performance standards would be in greater jeopardy.

4 • SEISMIC SAFETY IN CALIFORNIA
The Palo Alto Seismic Hazard Identification Program

The city of Palo Alto is located south of San Francisco in the mid-peninsula area. It is home to Stanford University and had a 1980 population of approximately 55,000. The city is highly educated and affluent; its average education and income levels are substantially higher than the averages in both the state and the nation (see table 4-1). Home and property values are also substantially higher. For example, the 1980 median value of owner-occupied homes was $149,000, compared to $84,500 for the state and $47,200 for the nation.

Palo Alto is subject to substantial earthquake hazards. As illustrated in figure 4-1, California and the mid-peninsula area of Palo Alto have frequently experienced significant earthquakes. Moreover, the city's close proximity to the Hayward and San Andreas faults, and the existence of numerous unreinforced masonry, tilt-up, and other susceptible structures, combine to create a serious public safety problem. The city incurred substantial damage from ground shaking during the famous 1906 San Francisco earthquake. The potential for earthquake damage could be much greater, if not for the public acquisition of hazardous areas, primarily for

Table 4.1 Socioeconomic Characteristics of Palo Alto, California, and the United States (1979)

	Palo Alto	California	U.S.
Median per capita income	$ 12,799	$ 8,295	$ 7,298
Median family income	31,796	21,537	19,917
Median years of education	16.2	12.7	12.5
Median value of owner-occupied homes	$149,000	$84,500	$47,200

Source: U.S. Census Bureau (1980a, b).

Major Faults and Significant Earthquakes of California 1836-1987

Earthquakes

★ Magnitude 8 or greater
● Magnitude 7 to 7.9
■ Magnitude 6 to 6.9
▲ Magnitude 5 to 5.9

Figure 4.1 California has historically been the location for serious earthquakes. This map shows the location of major faults and significant earthquakes in the state from 1836 to 1987. *Source:* Spangle and Associates, Inc., 1988b, 3.

nonseismic safety reasons. Specifically, a public agency—Mid-Peninsula Open Space District—acquired major portions of the landslide-prone foothills in the southern portion of the community (see fig. 4-2), while the city acquired liquefaction-prone baylands to the north (see fig. 4-3). These acquisitions permitted the city to focus its mitigation activities in the downtown area, where the bulk of older, seismically vulnerable structures are located (see fig. 4-3).

Figure 4.2 These foothills in Palo Alto, California, are prone to landslides and were purchased for open space preservation. Photograph by Timothy Beatley, 1988.

MITIGATION PROGRAM IN PALO ALTO

The Progression of Seismic Policy Making

Palo Alto's current seismic safety program is the result of many years of public policy activity. In interviews, most people pointed to the city's 1976 comprehensive plan as the genesis of its most recent seismic planning efforts. As required by state law, a provision of the plan's seismic safety element addressed the problem of existing structurally inadequate buildings. The provision stated the city's intention to "contract with a structural engineer to inspect and evaluate all high-occupancy buildings and all buildings of more than two stories [and to] review city codes to ensure that a mechanism exists to require that public safety deficiencies are corrected by those responsible for the buildings."[1]

Efforts were made in 1977 to secure $10,000 to implement this recommendation and specifically to finance an engineering study to identify seismically deficient structures in the city. After initial review, however, building inspection staff realized that this funding level was inadequate.

1. In 1971 the California legislature mandated that all local jurisdictions in seismic zone 4 should add a seismic safety element to their general plans. The upshot of this legislation was that when Palo Alto's 1976 general plan was adopted, a seismic safety element was included. The structural evaluation provision was included in this plan as well as the 1981 general plan (see Palo Alto, California 1981, 70).

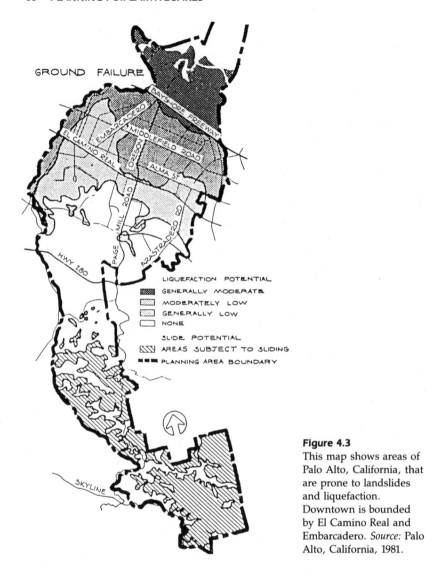

Figure 4.3
This map shows areas of
Palo Alto, California, that
are prone to landslides
and liquefaction.
Downtown is bounded
by El Camino Real and
Embarcadero. *Source:* Palo
Alto, California, 1981.

Through the strong support of the planning director, the building department was able to argue for and receive from the city council in 1981 $115,000. An outside structural engineering consultant was also hired, and efforts to develop a seismic retrofit ordinance were initiated. The consultant and the city's chief building official together drafted and advocated to the city council in 1982 a strong ordinance that required mandatory retrofit of 250 seismically deficient structures.

The ordinance received considerable political opposition, particularly from affected building owners and their tenants. Subsequently the city council killed the bill. It accomplished, however, what the chief building official and the consultant intended: it gave support to the concept of seismic retrofit. In particular, the council called for the formation of a citizens' committee to carefully consider the options to the city. This action also responded to the criticism leveled by many that the mandatory ordinance came out of the blue and that there was little effort to solicit citizen input on the ordinance before it was drafted and submitted for council action.

The citizens' Seismic Hazard Committee represented a diversity of public and private community interests. Most informants interviewed who were on the committee commented on the learning process that occurred during a year of committee meetings. They maintained that committee members, even those with initial skepticism about the need for seismic safety policies, developed a strong appreciation of the local earthquake problem and the need for a solution. This educational process was reflected in a new seismic ordinance proposed by the committee in 1983. This ordinance was even more ambitious than the 1982 proposal; it mandated the investigation and possible repair of about 1,000 buildings within a fifteen-year period. Opposition to this ordinance was also vehement, again largely from property owners and tenants.

At the heart of the opposition was the perceived impracticality of the mandatory approach and its attendant fifteen-year deadline. A citizens' committee memorandum to the city council indicated that this approach did not acknowledge that many owners had tenants with long-term leases, and that better opportunities for retrofit occur, in particular when buildings are sold, when their use changes, or when leases expire (Palo Alto, California 1984a, 5). The memorandum further indicated that for some building owners, the costs of retrofit would far outweigh any economic benefits and that if retrofit were required, some buildings would likely be torn down or taken out of commission (Palo Alto 1984a, 6).

A second objection related to the lack of information about structural deficiencies in buildings and about the economic impact of the ordinance. In response to this objection, the citizens' committee memorandum indicated, "It became clear that without this information committee support and community support for an ordinance requiring repair work would be impossible" (Palo Alto, California 1984a, 2). In interviews, many informants reinforced this position. They believed that because of such uncertainties, it would be unfair to use a mandatory approach. Most also pointed out that because each building was different, it would be nearly impossible to estimate the costs to the building owner before detailed evaluations were made.

The seismic committee took note of these objections and went back to the drawing board. Several members of the committee, in particular an influential developer who was a former mayor, opposed a mandatory approach. They argued for a voluntary program that would allow each property owner to decide when and how to retrofit, and whether retrofit investments were economically justifiable. In May of 1984 the committee issued a final report that recommended adoption of the voluntary approach (Palo Alto, California 1984b). Specifically, this approach required the preparation of engineering studies to determine the seismic adequacy of structures and the public disclosure of study findings. The voluntary program was to apply to six categories of buildings, comprising 350 structures. In June of 1984, the council unanimously approved the committee recommendation and directed city staff to prepare an ordinance.

The city council unanimously adopted the voluntary ordinance in 1986 but not before making a series of modifications that were responsive to constituency concerns. Among other things, the council substantially reduced the number of structures to which the ordinance would apply (reducing the six categories of buildings to the three categories with the highest-risk buildings). The council also exempted unreinforced masonry buildings with six or fewer occupants or less than 1,900 square feet. This action was intended to exclude several properties from the requirements and thus to alleviate the potentially negative impact on the "little guy" with limited financial resources.

One council member was particularly concerned with the potential impact of the ordinance on historic structures. As a result, the council allowed owners of historic buildings an additional eighteen months to submit engineering studies. An exemption to the engineering study requirement was also added by the council for structures under an amortization schedule (i.e., nonconforming uses permitted to continue only a specified number of years). The perception was that it was neither fair nor practical to require an engineering study for a building under a nonconforming use when in a short time the building might be demolished or undergo serious modifications as a result of required changes in use.

In adopting the voluntary approach, the council and Seismic Hazard Committee acknowledged the political and practical importance of allowing building owners flexibility in correcting earthquake hazards. A convincing argument for the voluntary approach during council debate was that if it did not result in seismic retrofit, the city could then adopt mandatory requirements. Furthermore, the city would be in a better position to adopt a mandatory program because precise information about the nature and extent of structural problems would then be available. No time would be lost because the engineering studies would already have been prepared. The council was assured during these discussions that property

Figure 4.4 This view of downtown Palo Alto, California, shows the site of the largest concentration of unreinforced masonry structures in the area. Photograph by Timothy Beatley, 1988.

owners would make the necessary seismic improvements but that they needed the flexibility of a voluntary program.

The Policy Outcome: A Seismic Hazard Identification Program

Palo Alto's solution to the seismic safety issue is unique in two ways. Unlike the mandatory retrofit approach taken in other California communities (e.g., Los Angeles, Long Beach, and Santa Rosa), the Palo Alto ordinance implements a voluntary approach—one that relies on the generation and disclosure of information about seismic risks and on the creation of incentives to retrofit voluntarily. Secondly, unlike most programs, which focus almost exclusively on unreinforced masonry buildings, the Palo Alto ordinance applies to other types of structures at risk, particularly high-occupancy ones (see figs. 4-4 and 4-5).

The Palo Alto ordinance imposes mitigation requirements on 99 structures in three building categories (see table 4-2). Once notified by the city, owners of these structures are required to contract with a structural engineer to evaluate the seismic adequacy of the buildings and to determine the structural measures needed to assure that the buildings meet seismic standards of the 1973 Uniform Building Code (UBC) (Palo Alto, California 1986). Building owners are given a specified time period in

Figure 4.5 A typical unreinforced masonry structure in downtown Palo Alto, California. Photograph by Timothy Beatley, 1988.

Table 4.2 Affected Buildings and Schedule of Compliance

| | | | Time Period (Months) |
Building Category	Type of Building	Number of Buildings	Submittal of Engineering Report[a,b]
I	All unreinforced	49	18
II	All pre-1935 buildings other than URM with 100 or more occupants	29	24
III	All buildings with 300 or more occupants constructed between 1 January, 1935 and August 1976	21	30

Source: Modified from Palo Alto (1986).

a. Time period measure from postmark date on letter of notification sent to a building owner from the city indicating that an engineering report is required. Building owners must submit letter indicating what, if anything, they intend to do about structural deficiencies one year from the date the engineering report is submitted.

b. An additional eighteen months was provided for historic structures within each building category.

which to conduct these studies, according to the category of the building. The highest-priority buildings—unreinforced masonry structures—are required to submit engineering reports no later than eighteen months after the city notified the owner, while buildings in the lowest-priority category are given thirty months. As mentioned, historic structures are given an additional eighteen months to comply. Once submitted to the city, the engineering reports are then reviewed by the city building official (with the assistance of outside consultant engineers) for compliance with the ordinance.

In addition to submitting the engineering report, the building owner must inform building occupants in writing that an engineering study has been prepared and that it is available for review at the office of the city Building Inspection Division. Building owners must then submit a letter to the city indicating their intentions regarding correction of seismic deficiencies. These letters must be submitted within one year after the engineering report is submitted. Failure to submit either the engineering report or the letter of intent can result in injunctive relief and criminal prosecution.

As mentioned, there is no requirement that building owners take corrective action. The only requirement is that owners submit a letter to the city stating their intentions. While retrofit is not imposed, it was believed that the reporting requirements would create sufficient concern about liability in the event of building collapse during an earthquake and about decline in market value of earthquake-deficient structures that improvements would be made voluntarily.

Developers viewed the pressures the program created to retrofit based on disclosure and concern about liability and market value decline as serious side effects. In testimony and council discussion of the ordinance, they voiced considerable worry about the impact of the reporting requirement on the availability of liability insurance for businesses (Palo Alto, California 1984d). They argued that requiring engineering studies that document serious structural problems would lead insurance companies to cancel liability policies. To many this possibility meant that the program was mandatory rather than voluntary because no business could operate without liability insurance. The council was not persuaded by these arguments. In interviews, several council members pointed out that unreinforced masonry buildings were not currently denied liability insurance even though the risk is well known. In fact, to date there are no documented cases of businesses losing insurance or failing to obtain insurance because of the reporting requirement (Herman et al. 1988). Insurance rates may have gone up as a result of the studies, but to date there is no documentation that they have. The arguments about losing liability insurance were strong enough, however, that the city council chose to use the

1973 UBC as the standard for preparing the engineering reports as opposed to the more stringent 1985 UBC, which was originally proposed by the staff and the citizens' seismic committee.[2]

An additional component of the Palo Alto retrofit program is the downtown density and parking incentive. Due to long-standing concerns about traffic congestion, visual scale, and other growth-related problems, the city in the early 1980s placed a substantial limitation on downtown commercial growth. Specifically, in most parts of the Palo Alto downtown the floor area ratio (FAR) cap of 3:1 was reduced to 1:1.[3] That is, under the new limitation the total square footage of a building cannot exceed the square footage of the development site. However, for buildings falling into seismic categories I, II, or III (see table 4-2), a building footage increase of 25 percent over the base FAR, or an additional floor area of 2,500 square feet—whichever is greater—is given as a bonus if a building is seismically upgraded (Palo Alto, California 1987). An additional bonus is provided in that this floor area increase is exempt from parking requirements. Typically an increase in building size requires a proportionate increase in on-site parking space.

INTERNAL FACTORS AFFECTING POLICY RESPONSE

Interorganization Coordination and Communication Activities

A high level of interaction among key stakeholder groups was an important factor in the advancement of Palo Alto's seismic hazard program. Such interaction was created by the citizens' Seismic Hazard Committee. This committee was formed by the city council to respond to the perceived lack of stakeholder input in the formulation of the initial seismic ordinance proposals. Its membership comprised twelve representatives, with a predominate representation of local business interests (Chamber of Commerce, Downtown Merchants Association, and Board of Realtors).

2. Use of the 1973 UBC represented a compromise on the part of the city council. The concern was that all buildings in the city would be inadequate if the 1985 UBC were used. The idea behind use of the 1985 UBC was to base evaluations of collapse potential on the current state of buildings, as opposed to their state twelve years earlier. The 1973 UBC, however, provides an adequate requirement for life safety design, whereas the 1985 UBC also requires property damage control, which was not the intention of the retrofit ordinance.

3. Floor area ratio (FAR) refers to a zoning formula for regulating the size of a structure. A FAR of 1:1 means, for example, that total square footage of the building cannot exceed the square footage of the parcel of land. A FAR of 2:1 means that total square footage of the building cannot exceed the square footage of the parcel by two times. There are three downtown commercial districts. The 1:1 FAR cap applies to the largest district, CD-C; two other districts, CD-5 and CD-N, impose more stringent FAR limitations (Palo Alto, California 1987).

As mentioned, during its two-year existence (1982–84) it gathered and reviewed much information on seismic safety. Many informants interviewed who either were committee members or were involved with committee activities commented on the learning process that occurred during the committee's regular meetings. Even members with initial skepticism about the need for strong seismic policies developed a strong appreciation for the seriousness of seismic hazards and the need for solutions.

Furthermore, once committee members reached consensus on the voluntary retrofit ordinance, it was difficult to dismiss this highly credible group politically. In interviews city council members, developers, and city staff repeatedly cited several reasons for their high credibility. First, although representatives of businesses were extensively involved, recommendations were not perceived to be in their financial interests. Thus potential opponents—building owners and downtown businesses—found it difficult to discredit committee recommendations. Second, the committee chairman—a noted local architect and former chairman of the city's Planning Commission—and two structural engineering consultants were highly respected in the community. Third, because committee members had met frequently and were considered to have carefully studied the issues, elected officials were willing to trust their judgment. Indeed, several local politicians cited the committee's work and energy as a reason for city council support of the ordinance and the resistance to technical and other objections.

Importance of Seismic Safety Advocates

The fact that an advocate of the seismic retrofit ordinance served as a policy catalyst was an important reason why the measure was adopted. In Palo Alto the chief building official served this function. For more than a decade this official consistently pushed the seismic safety issue and kept it alive when it might have disappeared from view. The official strongly believed in a building inspector's responsibility to promote public safety.

The mere presence of an advocate is not enough, however. Commanding attention and making an impact requires that the advocate possess a high level of credibility in the eyes of public officials. This was certainly true in the building official's case; the official was repeatedly described in interviews as one of the best building officials in the state. The chief building official has a reputation in the building and development community as one who stringently interprets the building code, and most informants appear to respect his technical competence.

The chief building official was not, however, the only seismic safety advocate. The official was assisted by a structural engineering consultant. In interviews, informants repeatedly indicated that the consultant was both a catalyst and a credible authority on seismic issues. This person proved to be effective in dealing with the citizens' Seismic Hazard Committee. A city planning staffer in the mid-1970s also has a keen interest in earthquake safety. This advocate produced background reports that identified geological hazards in Palo Alto and pushed for city action regarding building hazards. The 1976 seismic safety element provision, which indicated that the city should evaluate hazardous buildings, was a direct result of the planner's efforts. In addition, the city's former planning director exercised considerable influence in support of repeated budget requests by the building official in the late 1970s and early 1980s to carry out the recommendation. Together, the actions of these advocates had much to do with the attention the seismic issue received and, ultimately, with the adoption of a seismic program.

Availability of Resources

The availability of resources had an important impact on the advancement of seismic safety policy. Specifically, two technical activities that were of key importance were funded. First, the city council appropriated funding in 1977 and 1981 for a seismic safety study. As discussed, study results consisted of structural evaluations of all high-occupancy buildings and all buildings of more than two stories in the city. Without this information it would have been impossible to identify structures the proposed retrofit ordinance should target as of greatest risk to occupants.

Second, mitigation efforts were positively influenced by the city's hiring of a structural engineering consultant under a long-term contract. The consultant provided technical assistance to the citizens' seismic committee in drafting the retrofit proposal. The key activity the consultant undertook, according to many informants, was to collect and translate technical information about local building retrofit and disaster experiences for committee members. Indeed, when the proposal was being formulated references to other community efforts repeatedly appeared in the minutes of committee meetings (see Palo Alto, California 1984c, 4, 6, 7). In interviews, comments like, "The specter of a retrofit program would not be believable if it were not for Santa Rosa [a nearby bay area community]," or, "If they could do it, so can we," highlighted the political function of this information.

Furthermore, when the Coalinga earthquake occurred in 1983, the consultant along with the chief building official conducted a quick response study of the disaster. They presented a slide show on the types and magnitude of damages to the citizens' committee. This work, according to several committee members, motivated the committee to conclude its work.

Linking Seismic Issues with Conventional Community Issues

A critical factor that helped advance the building retrofit policy was the linkage of the seismic problem to a well-established activity in the policymaking arena of urban planning. During the early stages of policy formulation in the mid-1970s, advocates of seismic safety consistently pointed to the state requirement that communities like Palo Alto had to address the problem of existing structurally inadequate buildings as part of the city's ongoing comprehensive planning activities. As one of a group of issues centered on comprehensive planning, the seismic problem was consistently brought up and discussed at city council and at planning and building department staff meetings. Thus the seismic problem was gradually accounted for and integrated into local planning activities.

Linkage of seismic issues to conventional and other growth management issues had little influence on the formulation of mitigation policy. Some informants, particularly those with real estate interests, perceived a direct political connection between support for retrofit and the antigrowth or slow-growth attitudes that led to the downtown growth cap regulation discussed previously. To them the retrofit requirements were considered to be one among many antigrowth measures.

However, there is little evidence that antigrowth attitudes influenced the retrofit effort. Instead, all informants, who were actively involved in promoting and preparing the retrofit proposal indicated that they were primarily, if not exclusively, concerned with seismic safety. One elected official, for instance, adamantly maintained that "no attempt to sneak in growth restrictions under the guise of earthquake mitigation went on in this town—we took the high road on this one."

EXTERNAL FACTORS AFFECTING POLICY RESPONSE

Stakeholder Reaction to the Earthquake Problem

Reactions of stakeholders to the seismic problem varied widely and had an important influence on the retrofit ordinance. Most informants perceived public concern about earthquake safety to be low and thus to have little impact on the development of the retrofit ordinance. While many indicated that the recent Coalinga (1983) and Mexico City (1985) earthquake disasters raised awareness of seismic events, they also maintained that such awareness has not translated into active popular support for mitigation. Others suggested that almost all Palo Alto residents have never experienced a damaging earthquake and thus consider earthquakes as too remote to require mitigation actions. Still others reported that concerns related to the city's rapid urban growth, such as traffic congestion, noise, and degradation of community amenities, divert attention away from seismic safety.

Elected officials (city council members) supported the seismic retrofit ordinance. They appropriated funds for a structural evaluation study and for hiring a structural engineering consultant, formed the citizens' seismic committee, and ultimately adopted the seismic retrofit ordinance. In interviews, council members expressed a conviction that seismic retrofit was a necessary and valuable activity. They also maintained that their awareness of the earthquake problem and the attention they gave to the retrofit solution were largely due to efforts of the local building inspection and planning staff.

City building and planning staff viewed earthquakes as a significant public problem and thus gave strong support for the retrofit ordinance. To this group, building collapse during an earthquake was unacceptable, almost irrespective of the costs of retrofit.

Developers and building owners generally did not consider seismic safety a serious public problem. One developer, for example, suggested that the local building code department was pushing for a "zero-risk world," which he considered totally impractical. Another maintained that compared to other common risks, such as driving on the freeway, the risk posed by earthquakes was small. Of greater concern to this stakeholder group was the cost of retrofit proposals. Moreover, most people interviewed from this group believed that the safety provided by seismic retrofit does not justify the cost.

An additional cost-related concern dealt with liability insurance for businesses. Developers and property owners repeatedly expressed concern that the impact of the structural evaluation reports would lead insurance companies to cancel liability policies. To many, this possibility meant the retrofit ordinance was not voluntary but mandatory because no business could operate without such insurance.

In sum, the Palo Alto retrofit ordinance was designed to address the principal concerns of the stakeholders. On the one hand, the concerns of both city staff and elected officials were accounted for in that a legitimate risk-reducing activity was instituted. On the other hand, the voluntary approach taken by the program responded to the concerns of real estate interests by allowing building owners to determine the feasibility of retrofit for their businesses. Furthermore, restricting the scope of the program from six building categories to three (from 350 to 99 buildings) and following the 1973 Uniform Building Code instead of the more stringent 1985 code further reduced both the economic impact of and political opposition to the ordinance. Other modifications, such as the exemption of amortized structures and small-square-footage, low-occupancy, unreinforced masonry buildings, also accommodated the concerns of building owners.

Local Economic Conditions

Adoption of the seismic retrofit ordinance was strongly influenced by local market conditions. Palo Alto's downtown has had a strong business climate. The profitability of downtown development projects has been high, and demand for downtown space tremendous; as a result, rents are relatively high and vacancy rates low. Working in combination with this strong market is the development cap currently in place downtown. As mentioned, in response to perceived overdevelopment downtown during the early 1980s, the city reduced the allowable ratio of building floor area to lot size from 3:1 to 1:1. This reduction in commercial development fueled an already strong downtown market. Together these forces have resulted in a climate in which the negative economic impact of additional seismic restrictions on development is very small. In this climate, developers and building owners can obtain the rents necessary to cover the costs of seismic engineering studies and, ultimately, the costs of retrofit.

Windows of Opportunity

Most informants indicated that two recent earthquake events—windows of opportunity—had an effect on seismic policy making in Palo Alto. In 1983 the Coalinga earthquake struck. While Palo Alto did not incur damage, the event raised awareness about local geological hazards. In fact, in interviews, two citizens' Seismic Hazard Committee members reported that they felt ground shaking while on their way to a committee meeting. They indicated that the Coalinga incident motivated the committee to conclude their work on the 1983 version of the seismic retrofit proposal. Furthermore, as discussed, the engineering consultant and chief building official took advantage of this opportunity to inspect the damage at Coalinga and prepare a slide show for presentation in Palo Alto.

Because no politically acceptable solution was available when this window opened, attempts to adopt the 1983 proposal failed. As mentioned, the proposal was rejected due to opposition by real estate interests and building tenants. Nevertheless, the event helped to assure that the seismic safety issue remained on the public agenda. Similarly, several people commented that although no viable solution was readily available immediately after the 1985 Mexico City earthquake, this event temporarily raised local awareness of geological hazards. A higher level of awareness helped keep the seismic issue on the agenda until the retrofit ordinance was adopted in 1986.

Progressive Political Culture

An important reason for advancement of the retrofit program is a supportive political culture. In many ways, Palo Alto is not a typical American

community. It is well educated and highly civic minded and has a partici-
pative populace with a history of instigating innovative and progressive
programs (Herman et al. 1987). The presence of Stanford University also
has a substantial influence on the community. The city manager, for
example, suggested that the policy solution adopted by Palo Alto was
"uniquely suited to the Stanford setting, because it required the generation
of much information. . . . It fit into the academic approach and is difficult
to argue against in this university town."

Furthermore, while elected officials had some reservations about mandating seismic upgrades, they reported that it was their responsibility to
support mitigation. In a public policy area like earthquake mitigation,
which typically does not engender citizen demand for political action,
taking on such a responsibility can be viewed, in part, as a result of a
highly educated, civic-minded community.

In California, activities at the state level also helped shape a supportive
political culture. In particular, the state legislature has recently been aggressive in mandating that localities plan adequately for earthquake hazards. The unreinforced masonry building law of 1986, for example, requires all localities in seismic zone 4 to identify unreinforced masonry
buildings and to develop a program for dealing with them. (It does not,
however, mandate any form of retrofit.)

Such state activities have served to keep earthquake hazard mitigation
visible. When questioned about the impact of state seismic requirements,
both city staff and elected officials maintained that the mandates helped
keep earthquakes on their minds. They also indicated that the mandates
are symbolically significant because they convey the importance and legitimacy of the earthquake risk. Additionally, interviews revealed that state
activities are supportive in that local officials perceived that Palo Alto
would eventually have to adopt some type of mitigation program. The
perception, true or otherwise, that the city must take action, and that the
seismic hazard identification and retrofit program was a way of satisfying
this requirement, was helpful in creating a supportive political climate.

IMPACT AND ADEQUACY OF THE PALO ALTO RETROFIT PROGRAM

The retrofit ordinance makes damage reduction to existing development
highly probable because it targets unreinforced masonry buildings and
older, high-occupancy buildings. These building types account for much
of the existing risk. Yet the ordinance has several limitations. First, it
does not address future development. While development in the publicly
owned liquefaction-prone baylands and landslide-prone hillside areas will
not occur, it still could occur in hazardous areas subject to strong ground

Figure 4.6 A small unreinforced masonry gas station. Buildings of this size were exempted under the Palo Alto seismic hazard identification program. Photograph by Timothy Beatley, 1988.

motion. The hazard in these latter areas would be extremely difficult to map, however.

Second, the ordinance does not cover all potential high-risk buildings. As mentioned, the 1983 version of the ordinance targeted six categories of high-risk buildings for retrofit, but the final version targeted only the three highest-risk categories. Also, all unreinforced masonry buildings with one or some combination of the following characteristics are exempted: six or fewer occupants; less than 1900 square feet; and nonconforming use designation (see fig. 4-6). Third, the ordinance uses the 1973 UBC as the standard code for assessing suitability of structures, as opposed to the more stringent 1985 UBC.

The implementation prospects for the ordinance are encouraging. The chief building official has indicated in several progress reports to the city council that property owners are generally complying with the study and disclosure requirements. The most recent report (31 March 1988) indicated that of the thirty-six nonhistoric buildings in seismic category I, only ten had not submitted reports to the city by the November 1987 deadline, and of these most were in the process of completing the report (Palo Alto, California 1988).

A number of seismic upgrades have already taken place, and most

Figure 4.7 This masonry structure in downtown Palo Alto, California, once unreinforced, is newly renovated. Photograph by Timothy Beatley, 1988.

informants believed that the engineering reports and public disclosure requirements of the program were serving as strong incentives. The March 1988 report to the city council cited six buildings (mostly unreinforced masonry structures in category I) that had either completed seismic upgrades or were in the process of doing so (see fig. 4-7).

Property owners are also taking advantage of the flexibility to retrofit under the voluntary approach. Recently, for example, a building owner was able to incorporate seismic retrofit into a lease agreement with tenants. Specifically, the tenant agreed to vacate the building in the event of future seismic improvements and to return after the improvements. The tenant has also agreed to help fund the building upgrade with a lump-sum payment when seismic improvements are made.

Much of the success of the program can be attributed to innovative developers who, instead of being discouraged by the new requirements, have found ways to capitalize on them. Specifically, the parking and floor area incentives are being used in several ongoing projects. The planned renovation of the Stanford Theater is an example (see fig. 4-8). Here the owners will undertake a seismic upgrade in exchange for an increase in square footage. In fact, according to the chief building official, some owners of structures not included in the three building categories have sought to submit seismic engineering studies to earn the bonus but have been prevented from doing so.

Figure 4.8 Developers took advantage of the seismic retrofit density bonus when they renovated the historic Stanford Theater in Palo Alto, California. Photograph by Timothy Beatley, 1988.

Several developers and an elected official argued that, in addition to the desired effect of encouraging seismic upgrades, the ordinance has had negative side effects in that it has forced development to locate in other jurisdictions. One often-cited case is the Ford Aerospace Building. Several developers believe that the cost of retrofit identified in the engineering study would have been prohibitively high and that this caused the company to purchase a newer building in a different city (in southern California) and to move much of its operation out of Palo Alto. According to the chief building official, despite accusations of such economic impacts, few if any of these effects have been recorded. City planning staff, for example, were quick to point out that the need for a larger building was the key factor for relocating Ford Aerospace. Furthermore, while concerns about liability and public disclosure will encourage gradual retrofit, the absence of a mandatory provision will make it unlikely that property owners will be forced into dramatic actions (i.e., closing down and moving to another city).

5 • SEISMIC HAZARDS IN SOUTH CAROLINA
An Emerging Mitigation Program

Historically, seismic risks on the East Coast have received substantially less attention than those on the West Coast, where the communities discussed in chapters 3 and 4, are located. However, as noted in chapter 1, the East Coast is seismically active and has a substantial potential for disaster. The 1886 earthquake that rocked the Charleston, South Carolina, area dramatically illustrated this potential. Killing sixty people and causing more than $5 million in property damage (the equivalent of $460 to $560 million in 1985 dollars), this earthquake was one of the strongest and most devastating to occur in the United States in known history. The potential risk in the Charleston area has not gone unnoticed, however, and efforts are being made to plan for and mitigate the risk.

Charleston is an old and historic city founded in 1670. It lies on a peninsula at the intersection of the Ashley and Cooper rivers. Frequently referred to as the Low Country, the Charleston area developed as a thriving seaport. The city has relied heavily in recent years on tourism, which was stimulated by successful efforts to preserve and protect the historic district. Charleston contained (in 1980) a population of approximately 70,000, while the Charleston–North Charleston Standard Metropolitan Statistical Area (SMSA) had a population of more than 430,000 (U.S. Census Bureau 1980a). As table 5-1 indicates, South Carolina generally lags behind the nation as a whole in income and education. By South Carolina standards, Charleston is a relatively prosperous community; its per capita and median family income levels are higher; and its median home values considerably higher, than those of other communities in the state.

Table 5.1 Socioeconomic Characteristics of Charleston, South Carolina, and the United States (1979)

	Charleston City	South Carolina	U.S.
Median per capita income	$ 6,906	$ 5,886	$ 7,198
Median family income	17,041	16,978	19,917
Median years of education	12.6	12.3	12.5
Median value of owner-occupied homes	$47,900	35,100	47,200

Source: U.S. Census Bureau (1980a, b).

THE NATURE OF SEISMIC HAZARDS IN THE LOW COUNTRY

About 300 years of documented earthquake history is available for South Carolina. The earliest recorded quake occurred in Charleston in 1698 (Visvanathan 1980). By far the most powerful and damaging earthquake to strike South Carolina was the one that shook Charleston on 31 August, 1886. This was the third largest earthquake to strike North America; its estimated magnitude was between 6.6 and 6.9 and its estimated intensity (Modified Mercalli Intensity) X at its epicenter and IX in the city of Charleston. It was felt as far away as Wisconsin and caused damage in New York City. Within Charleston, nearly 1,300 buildings were damaged, representing 66 percent of the city's existing building stock, the majority constructed of brick. Figure 5-1 depicts the damage patterns for the 1886 earthquake and shows a strong correspondence between high damage levels and brick construction. Other factors found to have contributed to the Charleston damage include: areas of high water table and resulting liquefaction; building type (commercial and public buildings received the greatest damages); and the quality of construction (e.g., the type of mortar used).[1]

The nature of the earthquake threat in Charleston, and the East generally, is different from the threat in California and the West. The frequency of large and damaging earthquakes in the East is obviously much lower than in the West, but earthquakes in the East affect a much larger geographical area. As figure 5-2 illustrates, for earthquakes of roughly equivalent magnitudes, the distances affected are much greater in the East. The 1886 Charleston earthquake was felt hundreds of miles away from its epicenter. In comparison, the energy from a similar earthquake in California would have dissipated quickly and would have affected a much more localized area.

1. Knowledge of past earthquake history can be used to calculate likely recurrence intervals for different magnitudes of events. Talwani and Collinsworth (1988), summarizing historical earthquake data, conclude that the recurrence interval for a moderate earthquake of MMI VI or larger is about 100 years for South Carolina and 20 years for the southeastern region as a whole. The chances are considerably lower for a MMI X, like the Charleston 1886 event; the recurrence interval is between 1,500 and 1,800 years (Talwani and Cox 1985).

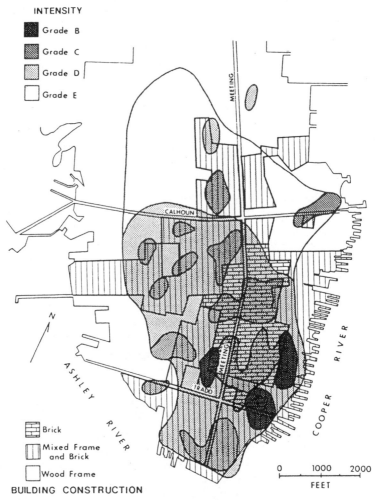

Figure 5.1 This map of Charleston, South Carolina, compares the damage intensity with the type of building construction to illustrate the effect of building type on observed damage. *Source:* Robinson and Talwani 1983.

Certain types of hazards typically associated with earthquakes in the West are not present in South Carolina. Surface faulting does not generally occur in the East, whereas it is a serious problem, as we have seen, in the West. Tsunamis also do not generally occur in the East and did not occur after the 1886 Charleston earthquake.[2]

2. Tsunamis in the East are very rare. Along the Atlantic Coast only one tsunami has been recorded—a very small one experienced from an earthquake off the coast of Newfoundland.

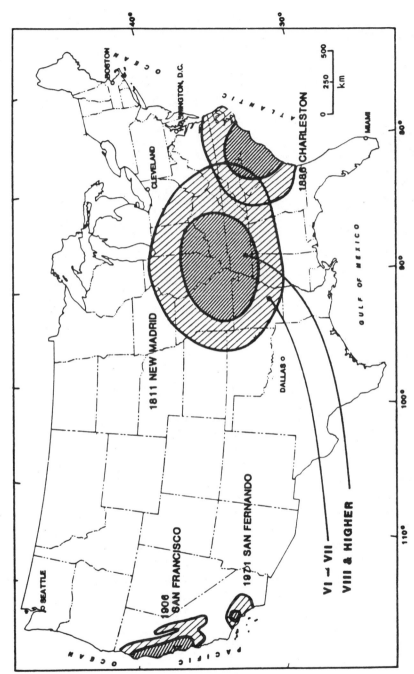

Figure 5.2 This map shows a comparison of isoseismal contours for the following famous earthquakes: New Madrid (1811–12), Charleston (1886), San Francisco (1906), and San Fernando (1971). *Source:* Lindbergh 1986.

Figure 5.3 Typical unreinforced masonry structures in historic downtown Charleston, South Carolina. Photograph by Philip R. Berke, 1989.

It is clear that the risk to people and property of future earthquakes in Charleston is substantial. Little effort was made after the 1886 earthquake to ensure that rebuilt structures, many of which are in use today, would be better able to withstand earthquake forces. Many structures built in more recent periods are also constructed of similarly vulnerable, unreinforced masonry. Until very recently, buildings have not been constructed to account for seismic forces (see figs. 5-3 and 5-4). In particular, many key public buildings and most existing schools are constructed of unreinforced masonry (Lindbergh undated).

A group of engineers at the Citadel in Charleston have conducted a vulnerability analysis of the Charleston area (Charleston, Berkeley, and Dorchester counties) that quantitatively documents the existing risk. A key study finding was that a severe event (MMI IX) would cause more than 2,100 fatalities, with about half occurring in schools (Harlan and Lindbergh 1988). Maximal property damage could approach $5 billion. Moreover, 136,000 people could be homeless for between five and thirty days, and nearly 20,000 for more than a month.

Figure 5.4 A typical unreinforced brick structure in historic downtown Charleston, South Carolina. Photograph by Philip R. Berke, 1989.

MITIGATION POLICY IN SOUTH CAROLINA

An Emerging Mitigation Program

Many current seismic activities in Charleston, and South Carolina generally, are intended to lay the foundation for future policy making. Planning and mitigation efforts are in the early stages of development, with emphasis on educating citizens, building and design professionals, and public officials about the risks and risk reduction actions. Emphasis has also been placed on developing professional networks within and outside the state to facilitate such efforts.

The South Carolina seismic program, which has largely been initiated by activities in Charleston, can be viewed as a collection of ongoing activities broadly grouped into three somewhat overlapping areas. One set of activities, beginning in a concerted way in the early 1980s and spearheaded by faculty at the Citadel and the Baptist College at Charleston, has focused on technology transfer, institution building, and public education. These activities have included the creation of the South Carolina Seismic Safety Consortium, the Technology Transfer and Development Council, and the Earthquake Education Center at Baptist College.

A second set of activities is centered around efforts to understand better the nature of the earthquake threat. Considerable emphasis has focused on research and theory building in an effort to explain the causes and dynamics of the 1886 Charleston earthquake. A third activity area involves development and adoption of seismic building standards. Charleston has been a leader in the state (South Carolina does not require localities to adopt building standards) in establishing seismic building design requirements.

Technology Transfer and Awareness Building: An Emphasis on Creating New Institutions

Many of the activities involved with creating new institutions stem from a 1981 national earthquake conference held in Knoxville, Tennessee.[3] This conference focused on the earthquake problem in the eastern United States. Conference participants concluded that awareness of, and planning for, earthquakes in the East was relatively low. During this conference, the idea of the South Carolina Seismic Safety Consortium (SCSSC) was formulated. The initiative for forming this group came largely from an engineering faculty member of the Citadel and a geology professor of Baptist College in Charleston, who were strongly encouraged by a USGS geologist. The group held an organizational meeting at the Citadel in February of 1982 (see Lindbergh 1986).

South Carolina Seismic Safety Consortium The formation of the South Carolina Seismic Safety Consortium (SCSSC) has been one of the most significant actions taken to promote earthquake planning in South Carolina. Two key objectives of the consortium are: (1) to promote cooperation among geologists, engineers, government officials, and the public and (2) to ensure that federal and state seismic research and development programs adequately address the needs of South Carolina (Lindbergh 1986).

The consortium membership largely consists of academicians and professionals involved in geology and engineering. Some representatives of businesses and public service agencies are also included, as well as local government officials. The consortium is co-chaired by two faculty members, one from the Citadel and one from Baptist College. A key activity of the consortium has been conducting conferences focusing on issues related to earthquake prediction, planning and mitigation strategies, and public awareness. Considerable attention has been given to bringing in outside experts during the conferences to provide information on strate-

3. The 1981 Knoxville Conference was entitled "A Workshop on Preparing for and Responding to a Damaging Earthquake in the Eastern United States."

gies and technologies that might be applicable to South Carolina. The conferences were largely organized by faculty at the Citadel and Baptist College.

Another key activity of the consortium was the completion of the Charleston Vulnerability Study (Harlan and Lindbergh 1988). As mentioned, the study was prepared by faculty of the Department of Civil Engineering at the Citadel. It was conducted with FEMA funds provided under the National Earthquake Hazards Reduction Program. The study will serve as an important educational tool because it is the first to document quantitatively a problem that public officials and the general citizenry have given limited attention.

The consortium has also focused on raising support outside of the state. A co-chairperson of the consortium has testified before Congress on several occasions, stressing the importance of planning for earthquakes in the Southeast and the potential for disaster. This testimony has emphasized as well the need to reorient some resources and funding under the National Earthquake Hazard Reduction Program to the Southeast, in addition to California and the West.[4]

Technology Transfer and Development Councils. A Technology Transfer and Development Council (TTDC) has also been established to facilitate development of regionally applicable engineering technology. Consisting of engineers and scientists from the Southeast, its objectives are "(1) to establish and maintain a technology baseline; (2) to disseminate technical information pertaining to earthquake effects; (3) to develop technical information pertaining to earthquake effects; and (4) to review, analyze, and provide technical support for applicable building code requirements and standards" (Lindbergh 1986, 92). In addition to engineers and scientists from within the region, the TTDC also includes representatives from the Applied Technology Council, Inc., and the Earthquake Engineering Research Center of California. The TTDC is a relatively recent creation, meeting for the first time in January 1986.

Among the recent activities of the TTDC is a collaboration with ABK Joint Venture of California to develop a methodology for retrofitting URM buildings in South Carolina and to prepare appropriate retrofit code provisions. The TTDC has also been active in promoting the installation of strong-motion seismic monitoring instrumentation in certain Charleston buildings and in advocating stronger building code standards for seismic

4. In addition to the South Carolina Seismic Safety Consortium, a Southeast Seismic Safety Consortium was also established, drawing membership from the broader southeastern region. This group has to date accomplished little. It is primarily intended to serve as a coordinating body, should other states adopt similar state consortiums.

hazards, including seismic design standards for all schools. The council also intends to develop appropriate continuing education courses in seismic and wind design.

The TTDC has so far advanced its key objective of technology transfer in several ways. A primary strategy has been to conduct workshops on important technological issues related to seismic safety and to invite experts from other parts of the country to South Carolina to share experiences and research. Financial assistance for conducting the workshops came from NSF, FEMA, and the Citadel. The TTDC also conducts engineering research and produces educational materials of direct utility to engineers and building professionals. Two members of the Citadel's civil engineering department are currently preparing, for example, a seismic and wind masonry building design handbook, which is funded jointly through NSF and the National Center for Earthquake Engineering Research.

Earthquake Education Center. Most educational activities directed at the general public have been undertaken by the Earthquake Education Center (EEC) at Baptist College in Charleston, under the part-time directorship of a college geology faculty member. The center was established in the fall of 1986. FEMA pays 70 percent of its costs, and Baptist College provides for 30 percent, in the form of the professor's salary. The center, primarily through the efforts of the geologist, has had considerable impact in enhancing awareness of the seismic threat in the Charleston area. It has attempted to target certain subgroups within the general public, including: "special need groups (elderly, disabled, non-English-speaking), youth groups, school populations, neighborhoods, public officials, hospital, fire and other emergency response personnel, business and industry, volunteer agencies, community service groups, and the media" (Bagwell 1988, 107). Numerous members of these groups have attended EEC workshops and conferences. Between 1983 and 1987, the EEC sponsored some 495 workshops and programs involving some 40,000 individuals (Bagwell 1986, 1988).[5]

Much of the center's energy has been focused on educational programs for Charleston area schools. Training programs have been given on appropriate preparedness actions for schools, and extensive earthquake drills have been undertaken.[6] The EEC has encouraged and assisted commer-

5. One of the most interesting and innovative strategies was the Saturday Shopping Mall Earthquake Preparedness Display and Puppet Show (Bagwell 1988). While organizers initially believed this program was not successful because acoustics in the mall were poor, extensive television coverage of the event greatly expanded the audience.

6. A particularly good example of a school that has taken significant actions as a result of the center's work is the Newington Elementary School in Charleston. As a result of

cial establishments in undertaking earthquake preparedness[7] and has emerged as a regional clearinghouse for seismic information.[8] The center has also been actively involved in recording earthquake events. It now operates a system of seismographs covering approximately an eight-mile radius.

Advancing the Science and Understanding of Regional Seismology

Much of the research and debate about Charleston seismicity, and South Carolina seismicity in general, has been a direct result of the requirements of the Nuclear Regulatory Commission (NRC). South Carolina has the mixed blessing of five nuclear power facilities within its border. Under NRC licensing requirements, proposals for such facilities must undergo stringent site and design considerations, including consideration of seismic threat. Because of concern about the potential impact of seismic events, the NRC has been active in promoting and sponsoring seismological research. It sponsored the first significant studies of earthquake seismicity for the Charleston area in 1974 (commonly referred to as the Charleston question, see Talwani 1986). Conducted by USGS scientists and university faculty, these and subsequent studies sought to explain the 1886 Charleston earthquake and the causes and dynamics of seismicity in the Charleston area. Since then, there has been an active and ongoing debate in the scientific community on the nature of the earthquake threat.

Much of the debate has centered around alternative models for explaining the 1886 earthquake. Some models suggest that earthquakes in the East are the result of movements of large geological and subsurface blocks (backslipping of certain areas due to gravity). The implication is that earthquakes similar to the 1886 Charleston earthquake could occur anywhere along the East Coast. Other quakes are local in character. That is, they are the product of certain conditions thought to occur only in the Charleston region. However, as geologist Talwani notes, "All proposed models have one feature in common: none of them has been universally accepted by the scientific community" (1986, 25).

---

the center's training program, the school principal initiated a series of earthquake preparedness measures. Included among these were moving the school's air conditioners and certain light fixtures to safer locations and anchoring bookshelves. The school also requires its students to undergo earthquake preparedness drills (like the "drop and cover" routine) periodically.

7. A training program conducted for Westvaco Industries, for example, lead to the preparation of an earthquake preparedness plan. The EEC's efforts have also facilitated the upgrading of preparedness plans for the Charleston Naval Base.

8. It has received numerous phone calls from citizens, many immediately after felt seismic events, which occur often in the Charleston area. Even local police and fire departments have on occasion contacted the center for information concerning earthquake events. The center also operates a lending library that offers audiovisual and other materials on earthquakes and earthquake safety.

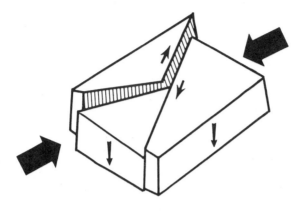

Figure 5.5
This schematic diagram shows the relative motion of blocks joined along two intersecting faults. If the main fault undergoes strike-slip motion, then the adjoining block moves down due to kinematic adjustment. Here, the large arrows indicate the direction of maximal horizontal compression. *Source:* Talwani 1989.

Despite disagreement, in 1982 the USGS issued an influential position paper acknowledging that the cause of the 1886 earthquake was as yet unconfirmed, but concluding that such an event could occur at any location in the eastern United States.[9] In response, and at the encouragement of the NRC, an industry-funded research group called the Electric Power Research Institute (EPRI) initiated a research project to analyze East Coast seismicity in greater depth. A number of technical studies generated by EPRI have substantially enhanced scientific understanding and consensus.

The 1982 USGS position has in recent years been strongly challenged by some seismologists, notably a faculty member at the University of South Carolina. This scientist and others have argued that the occurrence of the 1886 Charleston earthquake was not completely random but can be explained by local geological structures. Specifically, this person has argued that the existence of two intersecting faults—the Woodstock fault and the Ashley River fault—explains much of the seismicity of the Charleston area. Figure 5.5 shows how the intersecting fault system operates (Talwani 1988, 1989). Simultaneous movement along the faults is thought to explain the 1886 earthquake. According to the University of South Carolina seismologist, the bulk of scientific opinion has shifted toward the local intersecting fault theory. The USGS has not retracted its position but is apparently not pushing it either.

Another important activity has been the installation and upgrading of a seismic monitoring system. A joint USGS and NRC seismic monitoring program began in 1974 and has continued since. Additional seismic monitoring instruments have been added over the years, as in the case of the

9. For a thorough discussion of the USGS position paper, refer to Talwani (1986).

Baptist College network. Another seismic monitoring initiative, which is only in its early stages, is the installation of strong-motion instrumentation. In July 1986, a strong-motion instrumentation system was installed in Charleston Place, a convention and commercial center in the historic downtown area. This is the first such system installed outside of California and is important for better understanding how buildings perform during strong-motion events.[10]

In sum, research and scientific debate among seismologists concerning the Charleston question has done much to advance understanding of earthquake dynamics in South Carolina, as well as the rest of the eastern United States. Prompted by NRC requirements, and fueled with NRC and industry research monies, these scientific activities are laying the foundation for future seismic planning and policy making.

Seismic Building Standards

One area where South Carolina, and Charleston in particular, have made significant advances is in seismic building standards. Under current South Carolina law, local jurisdictions are not required to adopt building codes or construction standards. However, if a locality chooses to adopt a building code, it is required to adopt the latest version of the Standard Building Code issued by the Southern Building Code Congress International. While only about 50 percent of the localities in South Carolina have adopted the code, these jurisdictions together contain about 70 percent of the state's population (Lindbergh (1988)). Most urban and heavily populated areas have adopted the code.

The standard code incorporates design for seismic forces. Until recently, the seismic provisions were contained as an appendix to the code and had to be specifically adopted by each individual locality. That is, localities adopting the code were not required to adopt the seismic provisions. In 1988, the Southern Building Code Congress International chose to move the seismic provisions from the appendix to the regular text of the code, thus making them mandatory for localities adopting the code.

Efforts to make the Standard Building Code mandatory for all South Carolina jurisdictions are in progress. Such a proposal, currently under consideration by the South Carolina legislature, was largely the initiative of the South Carolina Seismic Safety Consortium and the Technology

10. The request to Taubman Companies, the owners of Charleston Place, was made by engineering faculty at the Citadel and was a joint proposal of the Technology Transfer and Development Council and the USGS, with USGS providing the funds. The hope is to eventually expand the network to include other important buildings in strategic locations in Charleston. USGS and the council have formed an advisory committee to guide this program, and the committee has already prepared a priority list of future sites for strong-motion instrumentation sites.

Transfer and Development Council. Proposed companion legislation would mandate certification for code enforcement personnel, as well as certain minimum continuing education requirements. According to a high-level building official in state government, this companion proposal addresses a basic problem regarding implementation of seismic building provisions in many jurisdictions, particularly rural ones, in South Carolina. Specifically, building officials are generally poorly trained and do not have the skills to monitor builders and engineers adequately.

These building code proposals are currently heating up politically. A coalition group called COMBS (Citizens and Organizations for Minimum Building Standards) strongly supports them. The principal organized opponents are the Municipal Association of South Carolina and the South Carolina Association of Counties, who appear strongly concerned that the bill will take away local autonomy.

Charleston was one of the first localities in South Carolina to adopt and enforce the optional seismic component. By special bulletin in June of 1981, the city council imposed the seismic standards on all new construction; renovations and restorations of historic buildings are exempt. Existing structures are not required to meet the seismic standards; however, renovations must not reduce a structure's seismic capacity. The adoption of this bulletin was largely the initiative of the chief city building official, who had just been hired. This person, who was uncertain as to whether the seismic provisions were in force, aggressively lobbied for a clarification in favor of their enforcement.

INTERNAL FACTORS AFFECTING POLICY RESPONSE

Interorganization Coordination and Communication Activities

Most activities related to development of the Charleston and South Carolina mitigation programs have attempted to facilitate interorganizational coordination and communication. These activities have lead to the creation of three new organizations concerned with promoting seismic issues. Specifically, the South Carolina Seismic Safety Consortium was established to promote cooperation among scientists, engineers, building code personnel, and public officials in general. The consortium represented a wide range of technical disciplines, as well as private interest groups. Its activities, including workshops and risk assessment studies, have enhanced awareness, involvement, and cooperation among technical specialists and government leaders.

The Technology Transfer and Development Council is the second primary new institution. More technical and specialized in focus than the consortium, the council has undertaken several activities, such as producing educational materials for building inspectors and bringing in expertise from other parts of the country, that have disseminated earthquake engineering technology in South Carolina, and Charleston in particular. In addition, there has been a substantial degree of networking between the council and the consortium. That is, many people participate in the activities of both groups.

The third new institution established to promote seismic safety is the Earthquake Education Center at Baptist College. Activities of this organization are educational and directed at the general public. The center has conducted numerous workshops and conferences, and it serves as a regional clearinghouse for seismic information in the Charleston area. In interviews, several informants, including scientists, building code officials, and government leaders in Charleston, reported that the center has enhanced awareness about earthquakes in the region.

The Presence of Advocates

As in other case studies presented in this book, the emergence of the Charleston and state level programs can be attributed to the unwavering interest and enthusiasm of seismic mitigation advocates. Of particular importance are the engineering faculty members at the Citadel, the geology faculty member at Baptist College, and a high-level USGS staffer, who together are responsible for the formation of the South Carolina Seismic Safety Consortium. The engineering faculty member has been the driving force behind the consortium and the Technology Transfer and Development Council and has exercised tremendous personal initiative in organizing technical and engineering conferences and in obtaining grant funds for such activities as the preparation of the wind and seismic design handbook. This person has testified before Congress twice concerning the need for greater earthquake planning in the East and is largely responsible for the proposal made to the state to make the Standard Building Code mandatory for all South Carolina localities. The same person was also instrumental in putting before the Southern Building Code Congress International a proposal that strengthened the seismic components of the Standard Building Code.

This faculty member has aggressively rebuked the arguments of some of the seismic community that the risks of another great earthquake are low and that seismic planning and mitigation activities should be given low priority (Cox 1989). After traveling to Armenia following the devastating earthquake event in December of 1988, he brought back an extensive slide collection that has been effectively used to make the point that South Carolina is equally at risk to such a catastrophe (Lindbergh 1989). This person has been involved more than any other in South Carolina with efforts to coordinate and communicate with engineers and building officials in other parts of the country. He is also actively involved with groups like Applied Technology Corporation and with various national professional and code groups, always searching for ways to transfer knowledge and technology to South Carolina.

The director of the Earthquake Education Center in Charleston has also been an important advocate, spearheading the effort to educate the public and to encourage preparedness in the schools and elsewhere. This geologist has appeared numerous times on local television and radio shows and assumes a high public profile.

Within Charleston, the chief building official was also an important advocate. This official's initiative led the city to adopt the optional seismic provisions. Without him, it is unlikely that the city would have adopted the standards. Moreover, he is aggressively enforcing the code, as well as promoting seismic design in the renovation of existing structures. A background in engineering permits the official to challenge designs with more technical expertise than most building officials have.

The early phase of development of the programs in Charleston and South Carolina generally has produced some public disagreements between the scientific community, which tends to be relatively conservative concerning involvement in public policy, and seismic advocates. The advocates are sometimes criticized for overstating the seismic risks and for unduly alarming the public (Cox 1989). Several informants noted an important distinction between the basic perspectives of the advocates, who tended to be drawn from engineering and other professional backgrounds, and those in the scientific community. The advocates were more likely to focus on the need for some minimum level of public safety and to plan for a 1886 magnitude earthquake, at least for critical facilities and high-occupancy structures. Geologists and seismologists, on the other hand, tend to take a more detached view, focusing on the improbability of such large events and minimizing such concepts as risk and public safety.

Availability of Resources

Compared with the large amounts of outside resources directed toward the earthquake problem in western states like California and Utah, those available in South Carolina have been relatively small. However, many of the start-up activities would not have been possible without outside funding. As noted earlier, outside funds have been provided by NSF, USGS, FEMA, and NRC for a variety of activities, including public education programs, professional and technical workshops and conferences, and basic scientific research. Much of this has been funding provided under the National Earthquake Hazard Reduction Act. The SCSSC and TTDC have been funded also through the Citadel Development Foundation, and the Earthquake Education Center has received additional funding from the Baptist College Development Board. The EEC is an excellent example of the potential long-term benefits of small, strategically placed seed monies.

A kind of psychological boost accompanies such resources. Several informants interviewed stressed the importance of redirecting federal emphasis to the East. The Citadel engineer noted that the South Carolina contingent does not wish to impede the progress of seismic mitigation efforts in the West, but strongly argues for a need to view earthquakes as a national phenomenon and threat. Informants attributed much of the progress to date to an increasingly national earthquake program.

With respect to efforts to advance scientific understanding of South Carolina seismicity, the role of nuclear power and nuclear facilities cannot be overstated. Federal seismic safety standards imposed by the Nuclear Regulatory Commission (NRC) have spurred much of the scientific research. The NRC has funded much of this work, as has the Electric Power Research Institute. Beavers (1988) argues that the nuclear power industry is responsible for earthquake planning in the East as a whole and that "a better understanding of the earthquake threat in the eastern U.S. may be the number one indirect benefit of nuclear power" (427). While this effect may indeed be true for the eastern United States, it is especially the case in South Carolina, primarily because of the large number of nuclear facilities and the seismicity of the region.

Linkage with Other Policy Issues

Several issues that have influenced mitigation responses were identified. The most significant of these issues relates to the presence of other hazards, particularly hurricanes and severe coastal storms. For most people, particularly architects, engineers, and builders, hurricanes are more frequent and of greater concern than earthquakes. Seismic strengthening of buildings has occurred as a direct side effect of designing for hurricane windloads in coastal areas. Most informants who had engineering backgrounds agreed that for smaller structures, designing for coastal windloads also provides adequate protection from earthquakes. However, for larger structures, designing for windloads does not necessarily provide such protection. A point made by several engineers is that it makes sense to link design for seismic building stresses to wind stresses, rather than undertaking separate designs for each hazard. This linkage could enhance the political acceptability of hazards construction standards and lessen resistance to the idea of designing for earthquakes. The Citadel engineering faculty member took this linkage strategy in proposing to the Southern Building Code Congress International that the seismic and wind design provisions of the Standard Building Code be strengthened. A seismic and wind design handbook currently being prepared at the Citadel is also a reflection of this unified approach.

A second issue uncovered was the relationship between seismic hazard mitigation and protection of historic structures. In a city such as Charleston, the economy is heavily dependent upon the tourism generated by its historic downtown. Indeed, historic structures are the very identity and lifeblood of the city. Because few buildings were strengthened after the 1886 earthquake, it appears that the most important economic and cultural resources of the city are in jeopardy of being destroyed or severely diminished by future earthquakes. The chief building official has argued that seismic design measures are good for historic preservation; that is, they ensure that historic structures will survive the next earthquake. This argument has met only marginal success, partly because some property owners believe that strengthening would diminish the historic nature of the buildings.

EXTERNAL FACTORS AFFECTING POLICY RESPONSES

Stakeholder Response to the Earthquake Problem

Because seismic mitigation programs in Charleston and South Carolina generally are only in the emerging stages, there have been few explicit policy proposals for stakeholder groups to react to. As we have seen, most activities have involved organization building, technology transfer, and information dissemination. These activities are, however, laying the groundwork for subsequent policy debates in which the response of stakeholder groups will likely be much more positive than it would be without these activities. Moreover, while citizens and elected officials may already have a general awareness of the seismic risk (or at least of the 1886 earthquake), the current and future activities of the SCSSC and the Earthquake Education Center will likely have an impact in enhancing the perceived importance of seismic mitigation. As the Citadel faculty member notes, while the public is generally aware of the earthquake threat, and particularly of the occurrence of the 1886 earthquake, such awareness has not translated into a groundswell of demand for planning and mitigation.

Several specific mitigation actions offer some insight into the reaction of stakeholders. First, the current proposal in the South Carolina legislature to make the adoption of building codes mandatory statewide has generated some political conflict. Its potential for adoption is uncertain, but if it is adopted, an effective political coalition called COMBS, or Citizens and Organizations for Minimum Building Standards, is likely to be responsible. This coalition consists largely of professional and trade organizations, including such groups as the Homebuilders Association of South Carolina, the State Board of Architectural Examiners, and the Building Officials Association of South Carolina. The membership list conveys the impression that the force of technical and professional opinion is on the side of adopting the code requirements. On the other hand, the two principal organizations opposing the proposal are the Municipal Association of South Carolina and the South Carolina Association of Counties. They have argued strongly that such a mandate unduly takes away the autonomy of localities. According to one municipal association staffer, "If a locality deems a building code necessary it will adopt one, but it should be left the freedom to decide." This position has been actively supported by several state legislators representing rural counties who have expressed concern about placing too heavy a regulatory burden on the average establishment.

A second example of a mitigation action was Charleston's adoption in 1981 of the seismic element of the Standard Building Code. While there was little involvement or conflict by organized stakeholder groups, support from local elected officials was the crucial factor. Specifically, the current chief building official indicated in an interview that adoption of the seismic provisions was made possible by council members who saw the need to prepare for the earthquake threat and by a supportive mayor. Furthermore, the official indicated that the building inspection staff would probably not be able to enforce the seismic code without on-going support from the council (and the mayor, who is still in office).

The case analysis also suggests the potential importance of the insurance industry and lending institutions as stakeholders pushing for more stringent mitigation measures. Several informants suggested that insurance and lending institutions are increasingly demanding that new buildings in the Charleston area be constructed to seismic standards. The feeling was that such demands were still fairly rare, but that a few prominent examples had arisen. The chief building official discussed the case of the Marriott Hotel, on the north side of Charleston. While under construction, the hotel changed hands, and as a condition of financing for the second owner, the lender required that the building be redesigned to withstand seismic forces (see fig. 5.6).

Political Culture

The city of Charleston, and the state of South Carolina, are unmistakably a part of the South, where the political culture is conservative and oriented toward property rights. Moreover, the proper role of government is typically seen as limited. These attitudes have surfaced, for instance, in the reactions of some state legislators to the proposal to make the Standard Building Code mandatory for all localities. Concerns are being raised about the fairness of telling localities what they should do (in a home-rule

Figure 5.6 This hotel in Charleston, South Carolina, is designed to withstand seismic forces. Photograph by Philip R. Berke, 1989.

state) and the effects such requirements would have on small businesses. More generally, South Carolina is conservative concerning most issues of land use and development regulation. Many localities, particularly rural jurisdictions, still have not adopted even the most rudimentary of zoning or subdivision ordinances. As in the current case of the statewide building code proposal, this relatively conservative political culture tends to place certain parameters on future mitigation and planning.

There have been some indications in recent years that attitudes toward development regulations have liberalized somewhat. The state legislature recently passed, for instance, the fairly stringent (at least by South Carolina standards) Beachfront Management Act, which has the potential of significantly restricting the rights of coastal property owners.[11] However, even in this case, it was suggested in interviews that efforts are in the works to substantially weaken the law. Nevertheless, because most activi-

11. Signed into law in 1988, the South Carolina Beachfront Management Act imposes significant new restrictions on coastal development. Specifically, a new setback line is based on average annual erosion rates. Habitable structures located seaward of the line can be no larger than 5,000 square feet. A "no construction zone" is also created in which only beach access structures are permitted (twenty feet landward of the baseline). The act also bans all future permanent shore-hardening structures (e.g., seawalls) and imposes in advance certain restrictions on the rebuilding of structures damaged beyond repair (such damaged buildings cannot be rebuilt in the no construction zone.)

ties of the Charleston and South Carolina programs have focused on education, technology transfer, and institution building, and not on government mandates or regulations, the full importance of the conservative political culture has not yet been felt. As the state continues to feel increased growth and development pressures, particularly in its coastal region, it may be increasingly inclined to control development, and the political prospects of earthquake mitigation policy may, in turn, improve.

Earthquake History and Windows of Opportunity

The great 1886 Charleston earthquake has had an important influence on seismic policy making in Charleston and in the state generally. While seismic mitigation was not a part of reconstruction, this event represents an important point in the city's chronology. As a consequence, many people said in interviews, citizens and public officials are more likely to be aware of the seismic threat. One local official maintained that such a large and damaging event "changed the complexion of public debate about the earthquake threat." Another suggested that "the 1886 catastrophe has made it more difficult to argue that an earthquake in South Carolina is impossible or inconceivable."

During the 1980s the Charleston area has experienced numerous small earthquakes and tremors. Although these tremors did not lead to adoption of seismic policies, they raised public awareness, as indicated by the many phone calls to the Earthquake Education Center after each event (Bagwell 1988).

Similarly, the Armenian earthquake elevated seismic issues in South Carolina. The Citadel engineering faculty member, as mentioned, was part of an eight-member technical team sent from the United States to Armenia to inspect building damage. Upon returning home, he issued a report that drew strong comparisons between Armenian buildings and construction practices and those in South Carolina. As quoted in the Charleston *News and Courier*, his plea is a compelling one, particularly in view of the vulnerability of schools:

> I will never forget the profound feeling of remorse I felt as I examined the litter of unfinished class notes and wasted textbooks that reflected the many lives left unfulfilled, and realized that the majority of the suffering and loss could have been mitigated through reasonable measures. My feeling of remorse was mixed with that of commitment that our public not allow it to happen to our community. (Findlay 1989, 7A)

While this disaster has not led to adoption of seismic policy, the resulting engineering report and numerous Armenian slide presentations have contributed to the perceived need to plan for and mitigate seismic hazards in South Carolina.

IMPACT AND ADEQUACY OF THE SOUTH CAROLINA PROGRAM

Because the Charleston and South Carolina programs are in the early stages of development, it is somewhat premature to evaluate their success. Nevertheless, the general direction of the programs, and their accomplishments to date, can be evaluated. A general conclusion is that seismic mitigation concerns have been significantly advanced in a relatively short period of time. The most impressive activities are institution building and networking, and specifically the creation of the South Carolina Seismic Safety Consortium, Technology Transfer Development Council, and the Earthquake Education Center. The most significant accomplishments of these organizations have been education—both of engineers and design professionals and of the general public. The variety of workshops and training programs for these groups has been impressive. While it is difficult to document the results of such efforts, these organizations have had a positive impact, including raising awareness and effectively laying the groundwork for subsequent earthquake planning and mitigation activities.

It is also evident that significant advancements have been made, again in a relatively short period of time, in understanding the nature of the seismic hazard. USGS and University of South Carolina research teams have made substantial progress, for instance, in estimating earthquake recurrence intervals. The Charleston vulnerability analysis has provided additional insight into the magnitude of damages and loss of life that may be generated by earthquakes, and the installation of strong-motion instrumentation (e.g., the Charleston Place project) will provide new data on seismic characteristics in the region.

There are, however, significant scientific disagreements. Some effort needs to be made to reconcile different technical perspectives toward the earthquake issue. While the engineering and building design community has stressed the potential collapse of structures during earthquakes, the geological and seismological community appears to stress the infrequency of such large events. The two communities inevitably reach somewhat different policy conclusions.

One of the areas in which considerable progress is being made is in the expansion of seismic building standards. Under South Carolina law, if a locality chooses to adopt a building code, it must adopt the Standard Building Code, which now includes a mandatory seismic design component. While most informants believed the seismic provisions of the Standard Building Code were good, several problems tend to undermine the extent to which new buildings are seismically strengthened. The first is that the building code is optional; about half of the state's localities have not adopted it. Furthermore, under South Carolina law, localities that have adopted the code are only required to implement the code standards that were current at the time of adoption. Thus, some localities are enforcing older versions that contain only optional seismic design standards. Finally, many localities lack the expertise, personnel, and political fortitude to enforce the seismic provision adequately, even where it has been adopted. The state, however, is attempting to correct this problem with the current proposal to mandate certification, and continuing education, of local building officials.

An equally serious problem is that many critical facilities and high-occupancy structures are not designed to withstand seismic forces. The Charleston vulnerability study (Harlan and Lindbergh 1988) estimates that half of the daytime deaths from a large earthquake would occur in schools. Yet, the state Department of Education, although it encourages seismic design, leaves the decision about seismic design up to local school districts. Some school districts impose seismic standards on new school construction, but many do not. Unlike California, South Carolina has few state laws mandating seismic design for such facilities as schools, hospitals, dams, and highway interchanges.

It is also clear that little effort is currently being made to ensure that older buildings, which are often historic, are equally safe from earthquake damages. While many informants interviewed mentioned the need for some form of retrofit program, none has been undertaken anywhere in South Carolina. Under Charleston's building standards, renovations must not reduce the building's ability to withstand an earthquake, but structural strengthening is not required. Moreover, historic structures are specifically exempted from the seismic provisions. This is troubling in that many historic buildings are unreinforced masonry—the construction most vulnerable to seismic destruction. In Charleston, the chief building official indicated that, during renovations, he often tried to encourage seismic strengthening on a case-by-case basis, but results were mixed. Part of the difficulty in promoting retrofit is a lack of clear technological standards. Some of the current and planned activities of the TTDC and SCSSC, mentioned earlier, may help to fill this void in the future.

When asked about the possibility of a seismic retrofit program in Charleston, the chief building official was pessimistic. From this official's perspective, a mandatory retrofit requirement like that of Los Angeles would simply be unworkable. Part of the problem is the high proportion of city buildings that are historic and would fall under such requirements. Such a program would, in the official's view, simply create large numbers of vacant structures and seriously undermine the city's tax base and economic viability. Mandatory retrofit would accordingly not be politically feasible in Charleston. It is possible, however, that a voluntary, incentive-based program, such as that used in Palo Alto, might work. Also of concern to many informants was that development of a seismic retrofit program does not appear to be high on any local politician's agenda.

Most of the technical experts interviewed also did not feel that liquefaction hazards were generally being considered at the local level. Many pointed to the need for accurate and available mapping of liquefaction hazard zones. To our knowledge, such maps have been prepared only for Charleston. And even here, liquefaction is not a major design consideration. In Charleston, for instance, the city's building code does not require design for liquefaction.

6 • ALTERNATIVE MEASURES FOR REDUCING SEISMIC HAZARDS

This chapter provides an overview of planning measures that are currently in use or could be used by local governments to mitigate seismic hazards. It also provides a comparative analysis of the overall effectiveness of these measures. The analysis is based on a set of evaluative criteria that includes effectiveness at reducing vulnerability, political acceptability, public cost, private cost, administrative cost and complexity, and ease of enforcement.

The planning measures described here are grouped into three broad categories: (1) managing land use; (2) strengthening buildings and facilities; and (3) planning for reconstruction. These categories provide a practical means for planners, building inspection personnel, and other practitioners of identifying the broad range of planning measures for various mitigation objectives. While the categories do not coincide with the theoretical typology of planning measures discussed in chapter 2, reference is made to the appropriate class of measure in the typology for each measure described here.

Much of this chapter examines the potential role of *managing land use* in reducing seismic risks. The central idea behind a land use approach is one of hazard avoidance. Risk to life and property does not exist until human activities and structures are located in hazardous areas. Identifying these areas and directing growth and development away from them can be a highly effective mitigation strategy.

A second category of measures deals with *strengthening buildings and facilities* constructed in seismic hazard zones. New buildings, particularly in states like California, are required to incorporate stringent seismic-resistant construction standards. Such standards are not typically required for older buildings, which are often unreinforced masonry structures. Thus, given the extreme vulnerability of such structures, much of the discussion of building construction focuses on programs intended to mandate or encourage retrofit of older, seismically vulnerable buildings.

Land use management and construction standards intersect in some important ways. In particular, the increasingly sophisticated mapping of earthquake hazard zones (e.g., liquefaction zones, ground-shake intensity zones) is now often used as a screening device for determining when and if certain types of building design and construction standards are necessary. If, for instance, during the local development review process, a proposed project is found to be located in a liquefaction zone, special construction standards might then be dictated.

A final category of measures examined here are those used to manage the *reconstruction process* after an earthquake disaster. Given the likelihood of a future earthquake disaster, one strategy is to be prepared, with plans and policies in place, to guide the reconstruction process in ways that mitigate future risks. From a land use perspective, such a strategy may be the only one available in localities that are fully developed.

While individual mitigation measures are discussed in detail below, it should be remembered that a locality's overall mitigation strategy consists of a "package" of measures. Each locality's unique physical, social, and political circumstances require a unique combination of measures.

LAND USE MANAGEMENT

Six broad categories of land use management measures are presented here. They include (1) comprehensive or general plans; (2) development regulations; (3) land acquisition; (4) capital facilities and public investment policy; (5) taxation and financial incentives; and (6) information dissemination.

Comprehensive Plans

Most localities in the United States now engage in some form of local planning. Usually a locality prepares a "comprehensive plan," frequently referred to as a "general plan" or a "master plan." While such plans vary in detail and scope, the general intent is to provide a framework for guiding future growth and development of the community, typically with a time frame of twenty years. Key components of a local comprehensive plan include: an inventory of environmental features and resources; an analysis of demographic trends and projections of future population; an inventory and mapping of existing land uses; an identification of important community problems and issues; a set of community goals and objectives; identification and consideration of different growth and development scenarios, and the choosing of an appropriate scenario or development concept; identification of a desired pattern of future land use types and intensities, usually displayed in the form of a plan diagram; and an implementation program (see, for example, Chapin and Kaiser 1979).

A key function of a comprehensive plan is to provide a jurisdictionwide vision of the future—identifying desirable patterns of development and growth, and activities and uses appropriate to different geographical sectors of the community. More general and less geographically specific than zoning, a local comprehensive plan may establish, for instance, that high-hazard seismic areas should be reserved for recreational uses or for low-density development. The comprehensive plan provides the potential of incorporating natural hazards into the broader growth management and development scheme. It may be possible, for instance, to shift the overall direction of future growth to reduce pressures to build in seismic zones.[1]

The status of local comprehensive planning varies from state to state. In some states the preparation of local plans is mandatory, while in others it is optional. In states such as Oregon and Florida, not only must localities prepare plans, but the issues they must address are specified in great detail, and the plans must be consistent with certain statewide goals and standards (see, for example, DeGrove 1984). In these states, local plans must be reviewed and approved at the state level.

California has been most strident in requiring local governments to consider seismic hazards in their comprehensive plans (referred to as "general plans" in California). After the 1971 San Fernando earthquake, the state legislature took several key actions requiring local governments to pay more attention to seismic risks. A significant action was the requirement that all local general plans contain a "seismic safety element" (see, e.g., Wyner and Mann 1986).[2] The state legislature also enacted the Alquist-Priolo Special Studies Zones Act, which requires localities to take certain minimum actions to regulate development in fault-rupture zones. This act is discussed further in subsequent sections of this chapter.

Each general plan in California must contain explicit consideration of seismic risks, alongside other natural hazards in the community and many

---

1. Ideally, natural hazards, including earthquake-related hazards, ought to be considered equally alongside a variety of other issues that such plans usually address. Among the substantive issues usually considered in a comprehensive plan are the following: transportation, housing, economic development, surface and groundwater protection, protection of wetlands and riparian areas, farmland and open space preservation, recreational opportunities, public services and facilities, floodplain management, and historic preservation.

2. This requirement has since been changed so that earthquakes must now be considered alongside other hazard and safety issues within a more general "safety" element. Most California localities, however, do not appear to have made the transition to this new safety element yet and are still actively using their seismic safety elements as separate plan elements.

Table 6.1 Seismic Hazard Mitigation and Preparedness Goals—Glendale, California, Seismic Safety Element

---

1. *Prevention of serious injury and loss of life*
The 1933 Long Beach Earthquake and the 1971 Sylmar–San Fernando Earthquake have taught us many lessons in disaster preparedness, building safety, and hazard prevention. The conclusions presented in this report are based, in part, on the knowledge gained from those experiences.

Personal injury and loss of life can be reduced in an earthquake. One of the most obvious ways to reduce earthquake "risk" is to design structures to accept a "reasonable" amount of ground shaking without their incurring structural collapse.

Loss of life and prevention of serious injury is a primary responsibility of local government and should be given highest priority in any Public Safety program.

2. *Prevention of serious structural damage to critical facilities and structures where large numbers of people are apt to congregate at one time*
Hospitals, communcations facilities, public facilities, schools, and other critical facilities should be designed to function after an earthquake. Action to be taken in regard to these structures will depend upon the "acceptable risk" that a community is willing to accept.

3. *Insuring the continuity of vital services and functions*
This goal is most important in any disaster. It is one of the most important functions of government simply because there is unlikely to be any other organized source of leadership in a major disaster.

Emergency preparedness should include provisions of food, water, and shelter in disasters, emergency medical care, police protection, utility services, and disease prevention measures. Responsiveness to secondary hazards in an earthquake may be more important than the actual earthquake damage itself. An example is the potential Van Normal Dam disaster after the initial San Fernando Earthquake in 1971. It is estimated that over 80,000 people were living or working below the dam. Had the dam broken, the disaster would have been far more severe than it was. In order to insure the continuity of vital services, "planning ahead" is essential.

4. *Education of the community*
This goal is a necessary ingredient to the success of any planning effort. It is a role to be played by school districts, public agencies, business firms, and other civic-minded individuals who have any interest in the safety programs of their communities. Each city must assume part of this responsibility along with other public agencies.

Source: Glendale, California 1975, 1–3.

other local issues of concern. Typical seismic safety elements include a series of maps indicating the location and extent of seismic hazards and a series of policy statements related to these hazards. Tables 6-1 and 6-2 present text excerpts from the Seismic Safety Element for the City of Glendale, California. Specifically, these tables illustrate the kinds of goal-setting and policy statements that are typical of such plans.

Unfortunately, the basic problem with plans is that they are frequently placed on a shelf and rarely used in making actual land use decisions.

Table 6.2 Seismic Hazard Policies—Glendale, California, Seismic Safety Element

1. Chapter 70 (Grading) of the Uniform Building Code should be strengthened to require geological and soils engineering investigations in moderate landslide risk areas susceptible to mud and debris flow, potential liquefaction of subsidence areas, and critical seismic zones such as those where ground acceleration values exceed current 1973 UBC Standards. To insure this, the City sould retain on a full or part-time basis a qualified engineering geologist to review reports and assist the Building Section in public projects.
2. The Building Section should use as a guideline the seismic zones and attendant response spectra for modification of the City Building Code to bring it into conformance with expected seismic conditions resulting from future earthquakes.
3. A program of building inspection should be initiated to identify all structures in the City that do not meet modern earthquake standards for construction and conform to design criteria of the modified City Building Code.
4. The Building Section should establish and implement a program for the orderly elimination of hazardous buildings.
5. The Technical Section of the Seismic Safety Element should be made available to developers for review and use when proposing land development.
6. A building strong-motion instrumentation program should be instituted for buildings over four (4) stories in height with an aggregate floor area of 40,000 square feet or more, and every building over six (6) stories in height regardless of floor area, if such buildings are anticipated.
7. A review committee should be established by the City Council to consider criteria for unsafe building abatement and feasibility of initiating abatement proceedings against structures found to be unsafe.
8. Emergency communication centers, fire stations, and other emergency service facilities should be examined as to their earthquake-resistant capacities.
9. All critical facilities constructed prior to 1948 should be reviewed by a structural engineer for potential hazards. Since many of these structures have regional impact, the source of funding for the inspection program ought to be at the regional level. High-pressure natural gas, petroleum, electrical power transmission lines should be reviewed for safety and land use compatibility.
10. New construction directly astride or across known active faults, or fault zones, should be prohibited. Nonstructural land uses, however, should be permitted.
11. A geological program to comprehensively evaluate the Sierra Madre, Verdugo, and Sycamore Canyon faults in terms of recency of movement and location should be initiated.
12. A program to effectively lower the groundwater in the potential liquefaction areas to at least thirty feet below the surface should be evaluated as to feasibility.
13. Community programs that train volunteers to assist police, fire, and civil defense personnel following an earthquake should be supported.
14. Divisions 1 and 2 of Part 2 of Title 7 of the Government Code relating to subdivisions require that all developments be submitted for governmental review. The City should enforce this provision, taking into account recommendations from the Seismic Safety Element.
15. The City should develop an information release program to familiarize the citizens of the region with the Seismic Safety Element. School districts and agencies serving the aged, handicapped, and seismically susceptible industries should be encouraged to develop education programs relative to seismic awareness.

continued

Table 6.2 *continued*

16. Upon adoption of this Element, the City should establish a Seismic Safety Review Committee to oversee the implementation of this element. This committee should be composed of the Director of Planning, the Superintendent of Buildings, and at least one representative from each of police and fire protection service agencies.
17. Establish a priority system of evacuation routes and critical services to be provided in the event of an earthquake disaster.
18. Evaluate land use impacts resulting from "stacking" of multiple hazard zones.
19. Continue to support the Emergency Plan for the City of Glendale. Objectives of this program are:
    a. to save lives and protect property
    b. to provide a basis for direction and control of emergency operations
    c. to provide for the continuity of government
    d. to repair and restore essential systems and services
    e. to coordinate operations with the civil defense emergency operations or other jurisdictions
20. State, Federal, and other governmental agencies should be encouraged to intensify research of seismic and other geological hazards.
21. The Seismic Safety Element should be reviewed by the City Planning Division annually and should be comprehensively revised every five years or whenever substantially new scientific evidence becomes available.

Source: Glendale, California 1975, 13–14.

They are in most cases advisory in nature and depend on other actions for their implementation (e.g., the enactment of zoning and subdivision ordinances). These problems are overcome to some extent in states such as Oregon and California, where specific implementation measures must be consistent with adopted plans.

Development Regulations

Seismic Zone Density Reductions; Zoning and Subdivision Ordinances. Historically zoning has been the primary measure by which localities regulate land use. Conventional zoning ordinances control the types of land uses permitted in particular parts of a community (e.g., residential, commercial, industrial), as well as their intensity (e.g., bulk, height, floor area ratio). As a result, zoning provisions can control the extent of risk to people and property from earthquake hazards. For instance, open space and recreational uses may be the most appropriate uses to be permitted in high-risk fault-rupture or liquefaction zones.

Conventional zoning has been used for many years and thus has high political and legal acceptability. Most local governments have adopted some form of zoning ordinance, and in some states localities are required to adopt such provisions. The constitutionality of zoning has been consistently upheld in the courts. However, any attempt to regulate the use of land in the United States must still acknowledge and work within the "takings clause" of the Fifth Amendment of the U.S. Constitution. This clause restricts government from regulating land to such an extent that it physically expropriates the land and must compensate for it. Consequently, it would likely be unconstitutional for a local government to designate a dangerous seismic hazard zone (such as a liquefaction area or landslide-prone area) as completely off-limits to private activities. In general, local governments must permit some reasonable economic use of the land (Bosselman et al. 1976).

In most instances, in the absence of land acquisition or some other form of landowner compensation, large-scale prohibition of new development in seismic hazard zones is not likely to be feasible. A more pragmatic approach is to reduce the overall quantity or density of development at risk. While a residential zoning designation in high-hazard seismic zones permits considerable development, this density may still be lower than what the unregulated market would support. Moreover, reducing a zoning designation from relatively dense, multi-family or office developments to single-family uses may reduce substantially the amount of property and number of lives at risk.

San Mateo County, California, located south of San Francisco, is a good example of a jurisdiction using zoning to control density in high-risk locations. This county is subject to a variety of natural hazards, including seismic ground shaking, fault rupturing, and landslides. The county's zoning ordinance specifies a series of resource management districts in which the amount of development that can occur in unstable, high-slope, or seismically dangerous areas is substantially restricted. Three zoning districts—Resource Management District (RM), Timberland Preserve District (TPD), and Planned Agricultural District (PAD)—take these hazards into consideration when calculating permissible density. In these districts, areas susceptible to landslides or active faults are assigned a development density of one dwelling unit per forty acres. Land areas with slopes of 50 percent or greater are also assigned a density of one unit per forty acres, slopes between 30 percent and 50 percent are assigned a density of one unit per twenty acres, and slopes between 15 percent and 30 percent are assigned a density of one unit per ten acres.

Subdivision ordinances also offer the ability to reduce seismic risk. Such regulations govern the conversion of raw land into building sites and the types and extent of improvements required in this conversion. Subdivision regulations can control the density, configuration, and layout of development. They operate in ways similar to zoning to control the amount and density of development on a particular site. They can also establish effective requirements and standards for public improvements, including streets, drainage pipes, sewer outlets, and so forth. The requirement of a minimum lot size can reduce, as with zoning, the amount of new development exposed to seismic risk. Site-plan review and other requirements of subdivision approval can provide the opportunity to orient the layout of development sites in ways that minimize exposure to seismic risks. For instance, subdivision regulations may require that new, single-family dwellings on lots be sited so as to avoid or maximize distance from liquefaction, fault-rupture, or other seismic zones.

Some localities determine permissible density by considering the cumulative effect of a number of environmental factors, including seismic hazards. The Santa Cruz County, California, development code is a good example of this. Specifically, the county has developed a system for basing permissible lot sizes in rural zoning districts on the cumulative effects of different site-specific factors. The county's zoning ordinance includes a series of matrices that assign points to a development site according to the following environmental factors or conditions: type of access available, groundwater quality, proximity to important wildlife habitats, slope and erosion potential, seismic and landslide hazards, and fire hazards. For landslide, seismic, and other hazards, the more hazardous the site, the fewer the points assigned. On the basis of these point matrices, a development site is given a cumulative score, which is then used to determine permissible lot size. For sites that are assigned twenty or fewer points (in rural residential zones), a minimal average parcel size of twenty acres is required. If, on the other hand, a parcel receives more than eighty points, the minimal parcel size drops to 2.5 acres. Thus, in the Santa Cruz system, seismic and related hazards are systematically used in determining allowable density. They are considered in a cumulative fashion alongside other important environmental factors.

Land Use Suitability Matrices. Certain types and intensities of land use are more suitable for seismic hazard zones than others. Some localities have devised suitability matrices that are used in considering whether development proposals are appropriate in seismic and related hazard areas. Usually these matrices are used in considering specific development, such as a proposal to build a hospital or other public facility, or in cases where private parties seek rezonings or special use permits.

In California (e.g., under the California Environmental Quality Act) and other states with strong environmental impact assessment requirements, such matrices have been useful in assessing the impacts and appropriateness of particular projects. Riverside County, California, presents a good example of the use of suitability matrices. These matrices are included within the seismic safety element of the county's general plan and have been extremely useful in the evaluation of public and private development proposals. A matrix is developed for each seismic zone in the county (fault hazard zones, potential liquefaction zones, and ground-shaking zones). Potential uses are divided into four broad categories: critical uses (e.g., nuclear facilities, dams, hospitals); essential uses (e.g., police and fire stations, power plants, sewage treatment plants, major highways, schools and public assembly structures); normal- to high-risk uses (e.g., multifamily residential of 100 or more units); and normal- to low-risk uses (e.g., single-family residential). For example, critical uses are deemed unsuitable for zones of high or moderately high liquefaction potential. Such uses would be provisionally suitable, however, for zones of low liquefaction potential (i.e., requiring site investigation or mitigation to confirm suitability and perhaps requiring some modification of facility design or siting).

Belmont, California, provides another example of the use of suitability matrices. It enacted a special geological hazards ordinance in 1988 to better manage development in its San Juan Hills area. A table in the Belmont ordinance "establishes the land use restrictions based on geologic hazards which will apply in considering applications for building and grading permits, rezonings, formation of assessment districts, and divisions of land within the San Juan Hills Area" (Belmont, California 1988, 3).

Three general categories of uses are considered: residential uses, roads, and intensive and critical uses. Intensive uses include, for instance, schools, churches, and "uses with comparable occupancy characteristics," while critical uses include those functions "critical to the city's ability to respond to a disaster or maintain an acceptable level of public safety, such as fire stations and water tanks" (3). A geological study has divided and mapped the San Juan Hills area into different geological zones. A potential applicant determines which geological zone the project would be located in and then refers to a table to see which types of uses are permitted (see table 6-3). For instance, if the land in question is comprised of the geologi-cal type Sbr (bedrock with thin soil), all types of uses are permitted. In the area classified Md (actively moving deep landslide), none of the uses would be permitted. As table 6-3 indicates, some uses would be permitted when certain conditions are satisfied (e.g., where geological reports indi-cate conditions more favorable than those mapped, or where engineering solutions are favorable). Unlike the Riverside County matrix, the Belmont matrix is actually a working part of the city's zoning and development code and, as a result, may carry more political and legal authority.

Clustering of Development. Subdivision and development layout may provide the opportunity to cluster buildings on a particular portion of the project site, leaving particularly hazardous locations as undeveloped open space. Normally, clustering allows the developer to retain the overall density of the site; the developer may even be permitted to increase overall

Table 6.3 Belmont Geological Suitability Matrix

		Land Use[a]		
Symbol	Geotechnical Parameters	Residential Uses	Roads	Intensive/Critical Uses
Md	Actively moving deep landslide (+10′)	N	N	N
Ms	Actively moving shallow (−10′) landslide failure	N*	N*	N*
Pd	Potential deep (+10′) landslide failure	N*	N*	N*
Pdf	Potential debris flow movement	N	N*	N
Pfs	Potential settlement or failure of fill on a moderate slope	Y*	Y*	N*
Ps	Potential shallow (−10′) landslide failure	Y*	Y*	N*
Sbr	Bedrock with thin soil	Y	Y	Y
Sex	Highly expansive soil	Y*	Y	Y*
Sff	Fill on nearly flat ground	Y*	Y*	Y*
Sun	Unconsolidated sediment	Y	Y	Y*

Source: Belmont, California 1988.
a. Y, Yes (permitted).
    Y*, The land use would be permitted, provided geological date indicate favorable conditions or engineering solutions are favorable.
    N*, The land use would not be permitted unless geological data indicate more favorable conditions than those mapped or engineering solutions will reduce the risk to acceptable levels.
    N, No, the use is not permitted. The map must be changed to show that the hazard does not exist before development can be allowed. The map change must be based on geological data showing that the map was in error or that improvements have removed the hazard.

density as an incentive to cluster. Clustering has been used to protect a variety of different types of land and resources. It has been used extensively to protect farmland and open space, to protect wetlands, and to avoid floodplains and shorelines. Clustering has equal potential for avoiding seismic and other hazard areas.

The town of Portola Valley, California, encourages clustering under its zoning and subdivision ordinances as a way to avoid seismic and landslide hazard areas. While conventional subdivisions are permitted (i.e., where lots are at least as large as the required minimal lot size, and where building sites and roads must be located outside of unstable areas), cluster developments are more common. Clustering has permitted developers to achieve economically viable development densities and at the same time to avoid unstable and hazardous areas. Portola Valley Ranch is a recent example of a clustered project avoiding such hazardous areas (see fig. 6-1). Of the 438 acres on the site, 395 have been left in open space. In all, 205 homes have been organized into small clusters on 43 acres (Spangle and Associates 1988a).

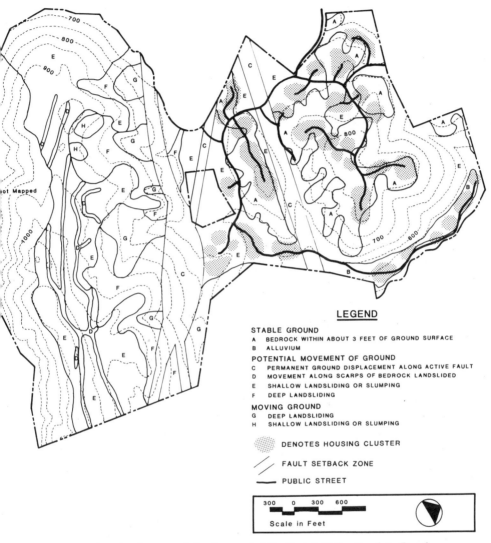

Figure 6.1 This plan for general development of the Portola Valley Ranch in Portola Valley, California, shows the location of housing clusters and streets with respect to geological conditions. *Source:* Spangle and Associates, Inc., 1988a, 46.

Special Studies Zones. A common approach to seismic hazards at the local level is to require a special geological study of a proposed development in a particularly hazardous location. This approach is widely used, particularly in California, which has mandated such requirements under the

Alquist-Priolo Special Studies Zones Act. Under the act, the California legislature directed the state geologist to prepare maps that delineate "special studies zones" for four specific fault systems (San Andreas, Calaveras, Hayward, and San Jacinto), as well as for other potentially dangerous faults. The state Mining and Geology Board was given the task of preparing guidelines to be followed by cities and counties in reviewing and regulating proposed developments in these special studies zones. All development proposals, with the exception of single-family wood frame structures (not part of a development of four or more units), must be accompanied by a geological study. This study must analyze soil and geological conditions, locate fault traces, and so on. Where geological hazards are present, appropriate mitigation and building design measures must be incorporated.

Special studies requirements vary in procedures and content specified and in mitigation and design requirements. Some, like the Salt Lake County, Utah, natural hazards ordinance, provide much flexibility to the engineering geologist and developer and stipulate few specific performance requirements. Others, like the Utah County, Utah, natural hazards ordinance, provide more detailed direction, for instance, by specifying detailed requirements for setting back development from fault traces. (Fault line setbacks are further described in a subsequent section.)

A notable case is the Los Angeles Hillside Area Grading Requirements (Los Angeles, California 1986). These requirements stipulate that a developer must have surface and subsurface exploratory studies performed by a city-approved soils engineer and engineering geologist for all proposed hillside grading work in locations considered susceptible to landslide, slump, and settlement failures. Detailed performance standards, including height and slope limitations for fills and excavations, planting standards promoting growth of ground vegetation to reduce soil erosion, and load-bearing wall requirements, assure hillside and structural stability. Moreover, the requirements include a detailed monitoring timetable that stipulates when a grading operation is ready for each of seven city inspections, such as initial operations, excavation, fill, rough grading, and final review.

Sensitive-Area Ordinances. An increasingly common approach to managing development in seismic and other environmentally sensitive areas is through the use of special overlay zones and special sensitive-area ordinances. The restrictions or requirements of these overlay zones typically apply to land development activities within the boundaries of a certain type of resource or hazard area in the community. Overlay zones are often created to cover the following types of areas: wetlands, steep slopes, landslide hazard areas, fault-rupture zones, expansive soils, and

Table 6.4 Maximal Site Disturbance: High-Slope Areas, Bellevue, Washington, Sensistive-Area Ordinance

Slope Categories (%)	Disturbance Allowed (%)
40 and greater	30
25 to 40	45
15 to 25	60

Source: Bellevue, Washington, Development Code.

others. Thus, seismic hazards are often included among other resources and environmental factors in a sensitive-area overlay approach. Such ordinances usually refer to a set of maps or criteria for defining sensitive areas, require that special studies be conducted, and usually stipulate that certain basic performance standards for building in sensitive areas be adhered to.

Among the environmental standards frequently contained in sensitive-area ordinances are restrictions on the amount and type of land and vegetation disturbance permitted. The Bellevue, Washington, sensitive-area overlay, for instance, places restrictions on the amount of disturbance permissible in high-slope areas. Specifically, development on property that includes slopes equal to or greater than 15 percent must do the following: consolidate on areas of least slope; minimize changes in grade, cleared area, and volume of cut and fill on the site; and limit the area of disturbance according to a disturbance chart contained in the code (table 6-4). For instance, if a site contained 100 acres of more than 40 percent slope, the developer would be permitted to disturb a maximum of 30 percent, or 30 acres, of this land.

An important issue is how such sensitive-area overlay zones influence permissible development density. Under the Bellevue regulations, for example, much of the sensitive land is designated as "protected" and thus is considered undevelopable (e.g., landslide areas and areas of high slope). A developer can use some, but not all, of the density allowed in these areas on remaining developable portions of the parcel. The greater the percentage of undevelopable land in a parcel, the smaller the credit given for unusable density. For instance, for a parcel in which 45 percent of the area (including mandatory buffers) is undevelopable, the developer can receive an 18 percent density credit (i.e., can utilize 18 percent of the development rights formerly allowed on the undevelopable portion of the site).

Setbacks and Buffers. The concept of a development setback has long been part of traditional zoning and land use controls. Setbacks are typically used in urban settings to ensure that sufficient land is available for future roads and other improvements and to ensure adequate light, access, and separation of structures. In coastal areas, building setbacks are frequently mandated to protect against shoreline erosion and to reduce nonpoint water pollution. The use of setbacks to reduce seismic hazards relates primarily to fault-rupture zones. Setbacks are mandated in such zones to prevent building astride or in close proximity to areas of potential displacement.

Such fault line setbacks are required under California's Alquist-Priolo Special Studies Zones Act, mentioned earlier. Specifically, the special studies zone guidelines stipulate that a structure shall not be located across the trace of an active fault. Furthermore, the guidelines stipulate that, unless proven otherwise by a site-specific geological study, active branches of the trace are assumed to extend 50 feet out on both sides of the fault. Consequently, a uniform 50-foot setback from the fault line is required unless the geological study shows that no such branches exist.

Most local jurisdictions in California appear to have adopted this standard setback. However, some localities have imposed fault line setbacks greater than this minimum 50 feet. For example, the town of Portola Valley, California, has imposed two different setbacks, depending upon whether the fault trace location is known or simply inferred (see fig. 6-2). For known fault traces, no building intended for human occupancy is permitted within 50 feet of the trace. In addition, single-family wood frame structures or structures made of other earthquake-resistant materials are the only types of structures permitted in the zone extending 50 to 125 feet on each side of the fault. When these faults are mapped as "inferred," each of these zones is extended an additional 50 feet (Spangle and Associates 1988a).

Some localities have used setbacks to restrict the proximity of development to seismic-related hazard areas. In Washington, King County's proposed revisions to its sensitive-area ordinance include specific detailed setback and buffer requirements for several key environmental areas, including steep slopes and landslide hazard areas. Under the steep-slope provisions, areas with slope of 40 percent or greater are generally prohibited from being developed. A 50-foot buffer zone must then be established from the top and the toe and along the sides of the 40 percent slopes (see fig. 6-3). A 15-foot building setback is then imposed around these buffer areas. Similar buffer and setback requirements are imposed for landslide hazard areas as well.

Planned Unit Developments. The concept of planned unit development, or PUD, combines elements of zoning and subdivision regulation to permit flexibility in designing projects planned as an entire unit. This is an alternative to the conventional lot-by-lot subdivision or by-right develop-

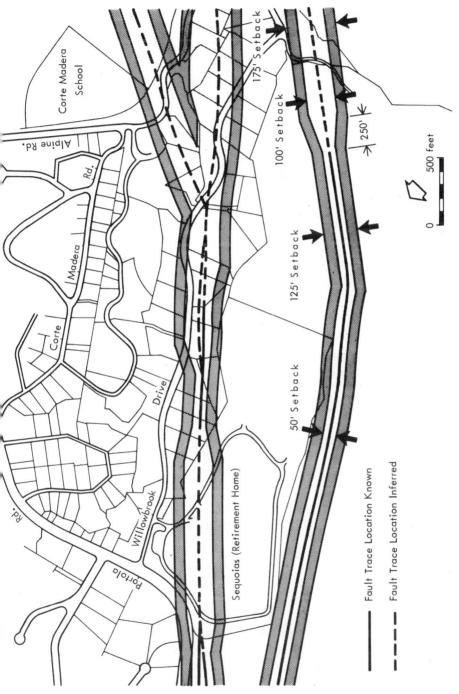

Figure 6.2 This map of simplified zoning indicates earthquake fault setback lines for Portola Valley, California. *Source:* Spangle and Associates, Inc., 1988a, 15.

119

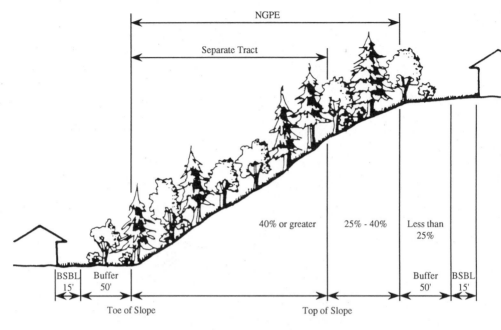

Figure 6.3 King County, Washington, provides the following hazard setback and buffer requirements: no development in areas with 40 percent or greater slope and a buffer zone of 50 feet at the toe, top, and sides of slopes of 40 percent or greater. *Source:* King County, Washington, 1988.

ment, that allows a developer to circumvent otherwise inflexible zoning rules and standards. PUDs often involve creative mixing of uses (e.g., residential and commercial) and typically involve clustering and other creative site designs. The final design is typically a matter of negotiation between the developer and local officials.

PUD projects may provide excellent opportunities to plan for seismic hazards in a way conventional projects might not. Buildings and other investments can be located so as to avoid earthquake hazard zones, designating fault-rupture or high-hazard steep slopes as undeveloped open space. The PUD mechanism offers tremendous potential for promoting creative clustering and layout. For instance, a more effective internal road layout may be designed in order to ensure adequate access after an earthquake event. Relief from conventional zoning and subdivision requirements may also provide a significant carrot that local officials can use to bargain for other forms of seismic mitigation, for instance more stringent building designs.

Land Acquisition. Public acquisition of seismically hazardous lands is perhaps the most effective hazard mitigation measure. By taking private lands off the development market, this measure prevents exposure to future development. Two primary categories of acquisition programs can be identified: fee-simple acquisition; and less than fee-simple acquisition.

Under fee-simple acquisition, the public obtains the full "bundle of rights" associated with a parcel of land. Fee-simple acquisition has the advantage of providing the public with full title and complete control of the land. In the case of purchasing and setting aside seismically hazardous lands, these areas could be converted to public parks or other uses permitting the public direct access.

There are only a few examples of the use of fee-simple acquisition explicitly intended to set aside seismic hazard zones. Palo Alto, for example, has over the years acquired a significant portion of its foothills and bay lands (potential liquefaction areas). While the result of these actions has been a safer pattern of land development, the city made the acquisition for reasons unrelated to earthquakes (the Palo Alto case is discussed in chapter 4). Several communities have purchased land around and along fault lines and have turned these areas into parks that not only prevent hazardous development but also serve to educate the public about earthquakes. Salt Lake City, Utah, for instance, has created a Faultline Park that preserves an undeveloped segment of the Wasatch Fault. Santa Clara County, California, has created a one-mile-long San Andreas Fault Trail as part of the 274-acre Trancos Open Space Preserve (part of the Midpeninsula Regional Open Space District; see Spangle and Associates 1988b).

In less than fee-simple acquisition, the public purchases a portion of the rights associated with the land, typically the rights to development. Under this arrangement, a local government would pay the landowner the fair market value of the development right in exchange for an agreement to leave the land in an undeveloped state, usually in perpetuity. This transaction is usually accomplished through the conveyance of an easement or a restrictive covenant that runs with the property. The underlying ownership of the land would remain in private hands, and the land might continue to be used for nondevelopment activities such as agriculture, forestry, or recreation. Less than fee-simple acquisitions, or purchase of development rights (PDR), has several advantages over fee-simple acquisition. First, it may be considerably less expensive, although in areas subject to metropolitan growth pressures, the development value may constitute the largest portion of the value of the land (Coughlin and Plant 1978). Second, management costs are reduced because the land remains in private hands. Finally, the impact on the local tax base is reduced because the land remains on the tax rolls.

Acquisition, whether fee-simple or less than fee-simple, remains a difficult approach to mitigating seismic hazards, however. Acquisition can be extremely expensive,[3] and considering the typically large expanse of seismically hazardous land, only a relatively small portion of the risk can be mitigated. For most jurisdictions it is infeasible to secure an entire liquefaction area, or landslide-prone area, or dam-failure flood zone. Land use controls and building standards often hold greater promise for this reason. Perhaps a more practical view of acquisition is to look for opportunities to incorporate seismic hazard reduction when considering the purchase of lands for other reasons (e.g., for parks and open spaces, or to preserve natural areas). For instance, the Midpeninsula Regional Open Space District, in the San Francisco area, has acquired substantial acreage in high-slope areas and in areas with high faulting potential. While these lands were acquired essentially for their scenic and recreational potential, the result nonetheless has been a reduction in the extent of development placed at risk. Thus there may often be opportunities to combine open space and hazard reduction goals.

Taxation and Financial Incentives

The types and patterns of land uses occurring in the community can also be influenced by taxation policies and other financial incentives. Measures in this category are intended to influence land use and the extent of seismic risk in the community in more indirect ways. In contrast to, for example, public acquisition of seismically hazardous lands, a taxation policy might seek to reduce development in risky locations by decreasing the holding costs of such lands, in turn reducing the pressures to convert these lands to more intensive developed uses. Several specific taxation and financial measures are discussed here, including: differential property taxation; exactions and development conditions; transfer of development rights; and density bonuses.

Differential Property Taxation. Differential property taxation is based on the concept that reducing the property tax burden on undeveloped parcels

3. Land acquisition can be financed in a variety of ways. Some communities, such as Boulder, Colorado, have used a sales tax to fund open space acquisition. There, voters approved a one-cent sales tax, 40 percent of which was specifically earmarked for open space acquisition (see Beatley et al. 1988). There is increasing interest in the use of real estate transfer taxes. The Nantucket Land Bank (Massachusetts) is perhaps the most notable example of the use of a transfer tax. As a result of the booming land market there, the tax has generated tremendous income, approximately $80,000 per week. Some $6 million had been raised from about 3,000 transfers as of July 1986 (see Phillips 1985). Other localities have funded land acquisition through general revenues, impact fees, and grants from other public and private entities (e.g., the federal Land and Water Conservation Fund. Both fee-simple and less than fee-simple interests in land are also frequently acquired through mandatory dedication as a condition of development approval and through voluntary donation (e.g., scenic easements).

of land reduces pressures to convert the parcels to more intensive uses (i.e., holding costs are decreased). Almost every state now has special provisions for some form of preferential assessment for certain desired land uses (Coughlin and Keene 1981; Keene et al. 1976). The key element of such provisions is the assessment of land at its current "use value" (e.g., its value in farming or forest production) rather than its fair market or development value. The uses that are typically eligible for such preferential assessments are agricultural lands, forests, recreational lands, and open space. Such areas sometimes incorporate seismic risk zones.

Three basic variations of differential assessment are currently in use: pure preferential assessment, deferred taxation, and restrictive agreements (Keene et al. 1976). Pure preferential assessment provides the "use value" assessment to qualifying landowners with no strings attached, while the deferred taxation approach seeks to recoup a portion of lost taxes should the land be converted to urban or developed uses. The recapture period under deferred taxation averages around five years, but some states have imposed ten-year recapture periods. If the land should be developed, the landowner or developer is then required to pay back the difference between the assessed use value and the fair market value for the specific recapture period. In addition, most states using this approach require the landowner to pay interest on the recaptured funds, usually at a below-market rate. A third approach, the use of restrictive agreements, is best exemplified by California's Williamson Act (see Couglin et al. 1977). To obtain the lower tax assessment, landowners must be willing to enter into written agreements to keep their land in its current use for a minimum of ten years. The contract is a "rolling-front" agreement, which is self-renewing each year unless the landowner notifies the locality of an intention to change the use. In this way, the restrictive agreement approach provides greater legal protection for the land and greater certainty that the public gets something for its tax expenditures.

It is difficult to assess the potential effectiveness of such differential taxation programs in reducing seismic hazards. First, there are no examples of efforts to directly orient such a program to seismically hazardous lands. The concept developed primarily out of a perceived need to protect farmland and rural open space. Large amounts of land typically qualify, and some of it could contain significant hazardous areas. Perhaps more important, even though differential taxation has been used widely, its effectiveness has generally been found to be low (Keene et al. 1976; Coughlin and Keene 1981).[4] Preferential assessment may indeed reduce holding

4. Preferential assessments also create significant "tax shifts." That is, because assessments are reduced for some properties, the overall tax rate must often be raised to make up the difference (or expenditures must be reduced, and such a course is unlikely). Nonlandowners and owners of nonqualifying land often view this as an inequity. The

costs somewhat or even substantially, but in the face of high market prices, and thus high opportunity costs of maintaining land in open space or resource uses, the pressures to develop generally far outweigh the tax incentives. This is particularly true in rapidly urbanizing areas like the San Francisco Bay area or the Los Angeles metropolitan area. Consequently, preferential assessment is likely to be most successful in situations where development pressures are slight to moderate, and where landowners are actively interested in maintaining the present undeveloped use of their land. Also, for many seismically hazardous lands, such as high-slope landslide areas, there may be few other economically profitable uses besides some form of development (e.g., where farming is not possible).

Preferential assessment may be a more effective tool when used in combination with other approaches, such as land use regulation or transfer of development rights. For instance, reducing permissible development density through zoning changes, in combination with use-value assessment, may significantly reduce the pressures to develop. Also, to maximize the effects of such tax benefits, localities could consider establishing mechanisms for funneling tax benefits to lands with the greatest hazard reduction potential, for instance by providing even lower assessments for high-hazard areas. In most states, however, this would require special enabling legislation (perhaps even modifications to state constitutions).

Bonus or Incentive Zoning. Bonus or incentive zoning allows developers to exceed limitations—usually height or density restrictions—imposed by conventional zoning in exchange for certain project amenities or concessions. For example, a builder may be permitted to exceed a preexisting height restriction by providing additional open space adjacent to the building (over and above what would otherwise be required). Incentive zoning has been used for some time in large urban areas. In New York City, for example, developers can obtain 20 percent increases in permissible floor area for projects that incorporate a legitimate theater. Density bonuses have also been used extensively to encourage the construction of low- and moderate-income housing (Beatley et al. 1988; Merriam et al. 1985).

Density bonuses can be used to promote seismic hazard mitigation in several ways. One way is to provide additional density for projects that

---

sense of inequity is heightened further when it appears that such tax breaks are being given primarily to land speculators and not to people interested in preserving their land in open and undeveloped uses. On the other hand, preferential assessment programs are often much more feasible politically than other types of incentive programs because the actual public costs are largely hidden (i.e., the locality is not required to expend monies directly).

incorporate extra seismic engineering or that in some way promote stronger and safer buildings. As mentioned in chapter 4, Palo Alto, provides a bonus in the form of a 25 percent increase in FAR (or an additional floor area of 2,500 square feet, whichever is greater) for redevelopment projects in which buildings are seismically upgraded. An additional incentive is provided in that developers are exempt from providing on-site parking for this additional density.

Density bonuses might also be provided for proposed developments that effectively avoid high-hazard areas. Localities commonly provide bonuses for projects that cluster, for example. Clustering, described earlier, allows avoidance of hazardous or environmentally sensitive areas while maintaining or exceeding (with bonuses) the base density.

Transfer of Development Rights. A potentially effective strategy for reducing seismic hazards is to permit the transfer of development rights (TDR) from high-hazard seismic areas to less hazardous areas. The concept underlying TDRs is that the right to develop land can be severed from the other rights of land ownership. These severed rights can be transferred and used in another location. As part of such a system a locality designates one or more "sending zones," or areas from which rights can be transferred, and one or more "receiving zones," or areas where transferred development rights can be used to increase project density. In receiving zones, the transfer of development rights allows the developer to increase density above what would otherwise be allowed. To mitigate seismic hazards the sending zones would theoretically include those areas that should remain undeveloped.

A TDR system can be either voluntary or mandatory. Under a mandatory program the locality would "downzone" the sending zones, prohibiting or severely reducing the amount of development allowable on site. The landowner would have no other option but to transfer the development rights. The landowner could either transfer and use the rights directly or sell them on the open market to another landowner or developer in the receiving zone. A voluntary approach would provide landowners in the sending zones the option of transferring or selling rights if they wished to maintain their land in an undeveloped or less developed state.

While localities do not commonly use TDR, it is no longer the radical concept it once was. There are a number of examples of its use over a relatively long period of time (see Pizor 1986). Florida localities have used it to protect wetlands and sensitive coastal lands. Some localities have used TDRs to preserve farmland, historic districts, and important views (Beatley et al. 1988). A significant advantage of TDR is its ability to provide some level of compensation to landowners who have been downzoned. It consequently enhances the political feasibility of land use controls that severely restrict development in seismic and other sensitive areas. It also reduces the perceived inequity of these regulations.

Despite its increasing use over the years, TDR has a number of practical difficulties. Perhaps most significantly, it often requires strong development pressures—that is, strong demand to increase densities in the receiving zones—to assure adequate compensation. This is less of a problem where full fair market compensation is not intended. The local government can also correct this problem somewhat by actively involving itself in the development rights market. It can, for instance, act as a development rights broker, ensuring that a minimum price is paid to those selling rights. Another controversial question is whether residents and landowners in and around receiving zones are willing to accept increased density. In some communities, residents of adjoining neighborhoods have become enraged by the added traffic, noise, and other negative side effects of increased development. A variety of other specific technical issues must also be resolved, including how to assign development rights (e.g., based on acreage or on market value of the property), how these rights can be used in receiving zones, and how to determine the size and configuration of receiving and sending zones.

Exactions and Development Conditions. Traditionally, subdivision and development approval are made contingent upon developers dedicating land or facilities, or making monetary contributions in lieu of such dedications. Referred to broadly as "exactions," these conditions require developers either to construct or to pay for construction of facilities such as sewer and water lines, curbs and gutters, and roads. Exactions can also require developers to contribute land for open space, parks and recreation facilities, and future school sites. Such facilities and lands are directly related to the needs of the new development.

The exactions process offers potential for earthquake hazard mitigation in several ways. One is to require that dedicated public facilities be earthquake resistant. Another way is to require that dedicated lands be the most hazardous portion of the area to be developed. Finally, the community could establish an in-lieu land acquisition fund to be used to acquire hazardous lands.

Two recent exaction approaches have potential for application in earthquake mitigation. One is the increasing use of impact fees. Impact fees are an extension of the concept of fees in lieu of dedication and are now in use in almost every state. They represent a flexible and effective means for the public to charge for the public services and facilities required by new development (Snyder and Stegman 1986; Alterman 1988; Nelson 1988). The general trend is in the direction of charging new development a much greater share of these costs. A portion of these impact fees could be used to fund seismic mitigation activities, such as acquiring hazardous lands, conducting vulnerability assessments, and retrofitting public structures.[5]

A second trend is the increase in the use of "linkage" programs in downtown areas (Keating 1986). Linkage requirements are exactions typically assessed on proposed downtown office projects, usually to help pay for low-income and affordable housing, public transit improvements, and parks and open space. Such linkage measures are currently in use in San Francisco, Santa Monica, Boston, Chicago, and Washington, D.C. Linkage assessments, as a form of impact fee, could fund a variety of seismic mitigation and preparedness activities. For instance, developers of downtown office projects could contribute to funding of seismic retrofit of public structures.

Capital Facilities and Public Investment Policies

The location, density, and timing of urban development is highly influenced by decisions about capital facilities and other public investments. These decisions deal with sewer and water treatment distribution systems, roads and highways, bridges, airports, public structures, and other matters.

According to Nugent (1976), two primary dimensions of capital facilities have implications for mitigating seismic hazards. One is geographical (where capital facilities are placed), and the other is temporal (when they are put in place). With respect to the first dimension, a locality can develop capital facilities extension policies designed to avoid high-risk seismic areas, thus reducing the amount of development attracted to such areas as well as the amount of public investment placed directly at risk to seismic hazards. The use of capital facilities decisions as a deterrent to development in high-risk areas is effective, however, only if the facilities are seen as essential. If, for instance, developers can obtain water through on-site wells and dispose of wastewater through on-site septic tanks, then redirecting sewer and water facilities does little to impede growth in hazardous zones.

Redirecting capital facilities, and the development that accompanies

---

5. One legal limitation is the so-called rational nexus test. This judicial standard generally requires that it is shown that development created the needs for which it is paying, that the amount of the fee be related to the extent of need created, and that the benefits from expenditure of the fee monies flow toward the development (see e.g. Stroud 1988). An impact fee on new development to pay for seismic retrofit of existing public structures might be questioned, for instance, because the new development has done nothing to create the hazardous condition.

them, into "safer" areas of the locality can be facilitated by several means. One is the clear delineation of an urban services area or district in which the jurisdiction agrees to provide certain facilities or services. The service district might also entail a temporal dimension by including sufficient land to accommodate ten or twenty years of future growth. Localities often have urban growth boundaries to separate urban and rural areas (Beatley et al. 1988). The state of Oregon, for example, mandates that each incorporated municipality must establish and implement such a boundary.

The establishment of an urban growth boundary or service area has several advantages. It provides a long-term perspective on growth and development and permits developers, residents, and the local government to visualize where and when public facilities will become available in the future and where they cannot be expected. This perspective modifies long-term expectations about where future development will and will not be acceptable. Development pressures may tend to shift naturally as a result of these designations, as developers, landowners, and others realize that certain facilities will not be made available outside of specific areas.

In more intermediate terms, localities need a policy instrument to systematically identify, finance, and sequence specific capital improvements. This is generally the function of a capital improvements program (CIP). Ideally, the CIP follows closely designated service boundaries, as well as the comprehensive plan, zoning, and other regulatory and planning provisions. The CIP provides a specific framework for making short-term (annual) decisions about the type and location of improvements that are to be made. Avoidance of seismic hazard zones can easily be incorporated into this instrument as a specific CIP policy.

A close connection among the designation of service areas, capital improvement programs, and the overall planning process in a jurisdiction (including the local comprehensive plan) is essential. Such a connection will tend to enhance the combined effectiveness of the measures in advancing overall local objectives. From a practical standpoint, the concept of guiding growth through capital facilities should be closely linked to the objective of reducing the public costs of such facilities and the extent of public investment at risk in high-hazard areas. The latter consideration is, by itself, a legitimate argument for denying facility extension into seismic hazard areas and may provide a sound legal rational for a hazard-sensitive capital facilities extension policy.[6]

6. Public infrastructure and investments may also be guided away from seismic hazard zones at broader state and even federal levels. Such a trend can be seen in the other natural hazard areas, particularly with respect to hurricane and coastal storm hazards (see e.g. Godschalk et. al. 1989). Florida pioneered this idea with its executive order 81-

Hazard Disclosure and Information Dissemination

Classical economic theory argues that better informed consumers make more rational market decisions. Thus an additional mitigation strategy is to inform and educate consumers about the nature and location of seismic risks. Several types of measures could be used, including "passive" and "active" forms of real estate disclosure.

A key objective of many of these measures is to inform potential buyers of the risks associated with location in a high-hazard district. Hazard information can be provided in several ways. State legislation might require that real estate agents inform prospective buyers about potential dangers from earthquakes. This type of program can be considered an "active" form of disclosure. This approach has been taken in California under the Alquist-Priolo Special Studies Zones Act. Under this act a real estate agent or person selling property must disclose to the prospective buyer that the property lies in a "special studies zone" (earthquake fault zone). A study by Palm (1981) indicates, however, that this requirement has had little measurable effect on the market behavior of housing consumers. Among the problems identified are the issuance of the disclosure in the latter stages of a home purchase, when prospective buyers tend to be psychologically committed to the home under consideration, and a disclosure technique (a single line that says simply "in Alquist-Priolo zone") that conveys little or no real information about the earthquake risk.

The result of Palm's work suggest that the disclosure must be provided early in the sales transaction, preferably during the initial meeting of agent and purchaser, and that it must convey accurate information about the location and nature of the seismic hazard. Not only should the disclosure form clearly state the presence of hazards (i.e., the home is in an "earthquake fault zone" as opposed to an ambiguous "special studies zone"); it must provide a full description of the nature of seismic-related risks. Strong resistance from real estate interests can usually be expected, and efforts to convince them of the utility of disclosure may be essential to its success.

---

105 in 1981, which said that state agencies were not to fund projects in hazardous barrier island locations. The Florida idea has been largely embodied in the 1982 Federal Coastal Barrier Resources Act (CoBRA) which withdraws most federal subsidies for development on designated undeveloped barrier island units (see Kuehn 1984). The act withdraws federal flood insurance, development monies for such things as highways and sewer improvements, and postdisaster assistance. While it is unclear whether this approach will in the long run really retard barrier island development, signs indicate that it is having some effect (see Godschalk 1984). Under its 1985 Growth Management Act, Florida has attempted to restrict even further state subsidies in hazardous shoreline areas. Specifically, its new infrastructure policies prevent the state from funding the construction of bridges to barrier islands not already served by a bridge. State agencies are also prevented from funding improvements in high-hazard zones, as designated in the coastal protection elements of local comprehensive plans (see Godschalk et al. 1989).

Some local ordinances have sought to provide similar forms of disclosure. The Mapleton, Utah, Critical Environmental Zone Ordinance, for instance, includes the following provision:

> It shall be unlawful for any person, directly or indirectly in connection with the sale or offering for sale of any property located within the zone to make any untrue statements of a material fact related to the known geologic condition of the subject property or to omit to state a known material fact regarding a geologic condition which under the conditions, would be misleading. Failure to abide by the terms and conditions of this section shall be punishable as a Class B misdemeanor (Mapleton, Utah 1985, 3).

It is difficult to imagine, however, how a locality would effectively enforce such a requirement. And it would likely suffer from the same limitations as the Alquist-Priolo requirements.

More "passive" types of hazard disclosure are also useful. Included in this category are requirements that hazard zone designations be recorded on deeds and subdivision plats and that public signs be erected indicating the boundaries of seismic hazard areas (and perhaps the location of past earthquake damage). Notation of seismic hazard zones on subdivision plats has become a fairly common requirement. Sensitive-area ordinances often contain such requirements. The Hazard Overlay Ordinance of Washington Terrace, Utah, for example, contains the following provision about the disclosure of hazard information generated from special geological studies:

> Where a report indicates that a hazard affects a particular parcel, a notation shall be made on the recorded plat which indicates that a report has been written concerning the natural conditions and potential hazards to which the parcel is subject, and that said report may be reviewed at the city offices or at the Weber County planning commission [Washington Terrace, Utah 1988, sec. 1(4)(k)].

Some local programs are intended to require the generation of new information about the hazard specifically so that citizens can be informed. As mentioned in chapter 4, Palo Alto, California, has initiated an innovative program that requires owners of seismically vulnerable structures to have engineering studies prepared evaluating the structural integrity of their buildings. The reports must be placed on file with the city, and building tenants must be notified of their existence.

STRENGTHENING BUILDINGS AND FACILITIES

An effective category of mitigation measures is the strengthening of buildings and facilities to withstand seismic forces. Two general types of measures within this strategy are described here: (1) seismic standards for construction of new buildings and facilities; and (2) retrofitting existing hazardous structures and facilities.

Seismic Standards for Construction of New Buildings and Facilities

It is commonly said that earthquakes don't kill people; buildings do. Consequently, an effective mitigation strategy is to ensure that new buildings and public facilities are constructed to certain minimal structural standards. In many high-risk locations in the United States, localities must implement a standard building code that contains seismic construction standards. In California, for instance, localities must enforce the Unified Building Code or UBC, which contains fairly stringent earthquake design standards.

In other parts of the country, other standard codes are used. In South Carolina, for example, the Standard Building Code, which contains seismic standards, has been adopted. In this state, high-risk seismic areas are also subject to hurricanes and coastal storms. Construction standards intended primarily to address these coastal hazards (i.e., standards that require construction to a specified wind speed) can also have the significant side effect of making new structures less vulnerable to earthquake damage. As discussed in chapter 5, localities in South Carolina are unfortunately not required to adopt any form of building code. Rather, the state mandates that if a locality chooses to adopt a building code, it must be the Standard Code.

Special provisions are often made to ensure that certain "critical" structures and facilities are built to adequate seismic standards. Such critical facilities include emergency operation centers, hospitals, fire and police stations, among others. In California, for example, the Hospital Seismic Safety Act of 1972 requires that new hospitals be constructed to certain minimal seismic standards. Minimal construction standards for fire stations, police stations, and emergency operation centers have also been mandated at the state level in California under the Essential Buildings Seismic Safety Act of 1986 (Spangle and Associates 1988b).

Some communities have made special efforts to ensure that high-occupancy structures, such as schools, auditoriums, convention centers, jails, and high-rise office buildings are seismically safe. Palo Alto, for instance, has undertaken substantial seismic improvements to its high-rise city hall. Salt Lake County, Utah, has incorporated state-of-the-art seismic engineering in the design and construction of its new county office building. And, as already discussed, many localities have developed land use policies and suitability matrices to steer critical facilities and high-occupancy structures away from high-risk zones.

Retrofitting Existing Hazardous Structures and Facilities

Building codes and seismic construction standards for new construction reduce future vulnerability but do not affect the condition and safety of existing structures. In many high-risk areas of the country, significant numbers of existing structures fail to meet even the most rudimentary building standards. The most vulnerable type of older structure is the unreinforced masonry (URM) building, but other types of vulnerable structures include: concrete frame buildings built before 1947; certain tilt-up concrete structures; buildings with large spans, irregular shapes, or weak or "soft" first stories; and buildings not properly maintained or weakened through modification (California Seismic Safety Commission 1987). Some 60,000 URM buildings were constructed before 1933 in California alone (California Seismic Safety Commission 1988). Consequently, programs are needed to promote retrofitting these dangerous buildings.

A number of localities have instituted some form of seismic retrofit, primarily in California. In California these retrofit efforts have been boosted substantially as a result of the passage of the Unreinforced Masonry Building Law in 1986. Under this law, each local government in seismic zone 4 is required to develop a program to identify and mitigate hazards associated with URM buildings. Localities had to have completed the following tasks by 1 January 1990: identify all potentially hazardous URM buildings; develop and implement a mitigation program to reduce these hazards; and submit information concerning these buildings and the locality's mitigation program to the Seismic Safety Commission (California Seismic Safety Commission 1987).

Localities have taken a variety of approaches to the retrofit problem. A number of them have undertaken thorough inventories of hazardous existing structures but have gone no further. Some localities view such inventories of hazardous buildings primarily as a form of information distribution. In other localities, the inventory serves as the basis for programs that encourage or mandate the actual retrofit of hazardous buildings. The URM law, while requiring localities to prepare mitigation programs, is vague about what retrofit programs should include. The only requirement is that property owners be notified of potential hazardous conditions in their buildings.

An innovative retrofit incentive program developed by Palo Alto, California, is described in chapter 4. While retrofit is not actually mandated under the Palo Alto ordinance, copies of the engineering reports reviewing potentially hazardous buildings must be placed on file with the city. Building tenants must then be notified of the existence of hazards. The city has also instituted a program for providing a form of density bonus for renovation projects that include retrofit.

Los Angeles has been a leader in the area of mandatory seismic retrofit and has been implementing one of the largest programs in terms of the number of buildings affected. Los Angeles adopted its retrofit ordinance in 1981 after protracted discussion about its possible negative impact on the city's lower-income residents (e.g., displacement, rent increases, and so forth; see Alesch and Petak (1986). The ordinance applies to all pre-1934 unreinforced masonry buildings with the exception of detached residential buildings containing fewer than five dwelling units.

The operation of the Los Angeles program is similar to several mandatory retrofit programs, such as those in Santa Rosa and Long Beach. The Department of Building and Safety notifies building owners that a structural analysis of their building must be prepared and plans submitted outlining alterations to bring the building into compliance (or to demolish the structure). Both the preparation of the plans and the actual improvements must occur within a specified period of time. Compliance periods vary with the type of building and the seriousness of the risk. Essential buildings (e.g., hospitals and fire and police stations) must comply in the shortest period of time, while low-risk, low-occupancy buildings are given the longest time to comply. To ease the burden of compliance, an extension can be obtained by a building owner if wall anchors are installed. Of some 8,000 buildings contained in the city's compliance list in 1981, most have either complied or have initiated compliance with the seismic code. Only about 1,000 buildings have yet to submit plans for compliance. Approximately 1,000 buildings have been demolished under the program.

PLANNING FOR RECONSTRUCTION

While a major earthquake can be tragic, it also offers opportunities to reshape the community in positive ways and to ensure that the community is safer when the next event occurs. Relatively few localities, however, are adequately prepared to take advantage of these opportunities. In this section, we briefly introduce measures to effectively manage rebuilding and recovery after an earthquake.

The extent to which redevelopment opportunities can be capitalized upon in the aftermath of a disaster depends in large part on the nature of damages incurred (Cibrowski 1981) and the predisaster planning that has taken place. If destruction is widespread in terms of the number of structures affected and the extent of damage to each structure, then substantial changes in land use patterns are feasible. Less ambitious mitigation programs (e.g., the purchase of individual damage sites for use as open space) may be more successful when the damaged area is relatively small.

An important point is that in many urbanized earthquake-prone areas, the predisaster land use measures described earlier are relatively ineffective. Cities such as Los Angeles and San Francisco fall into this category. Given the absence of large amounts of vacant and undeveloped land, reconstruction planning may be the only opportunity to achieve seismic hazard mitigation.

Some communities have taken advantage of the opportunities offered by extensive earthquake damage. Santa Rosa, California, was struck by an earthquake in October 1969, when it was undertaking a federally funded downtown urban renewal project. As a consequence of the disaster, and the significant damage done to buildings within and adjacent to the urban renewal area, the city expanded substantially the geographic scope of the renewal project (adding a second phase). As Wyner and Mann (1986, 29) comment:

> The city's successful efforts to secure federal cooperation after the earthquake permitted a dramatic change in the use of the western half of the old downtown area. The second-phase area had been the site of older, small retail businesses and small manufacturing firms, as well as some older housing units. The redevelopment project became the site for construction of a large regional shopping center. If the earthquake had not occurred, this land use change would have been much more difficult. In 1968 the city had essentially given up. Unquestionably the earthquake was itself the agent of change. It provided the opportunity, resources, and motivation that were necessary.

To fully take advantage of such opportunities, however, special reconstruction planning is often required in advance of the event.

Reconstruction Plans and Policies

To counterbalance the inevitable economic and political pressures to rebuild quickly after an earthquake and the inability to envision a different land use outcome, communities can in advance prepare reconstruction plans and policies that would guide the rebuilding process. There are a number of examples of the development of such plans for other types of disasters, especially floods and coastal storms (see Brower et al. 1984, 1987), that are transferable to earthquake reconstruction planning. Increasingly coastal states require their coastal localities to prepare mitigation and reconstruction plans (Godschalk et al. 1989). North Carolina and Florida have been the first states to impose such requirements as part of the normal local land use planning requirements. Under North Carolina's

Coastal Area Management Act (CAMA), for instance, local mitigation or reconstruction plans must consider and include at least the following:

1. a local damage classification scheme consistent with those of federal and state assistance agencies

2. the establishment of local damage assessment teams

3. consideration of the establishment of a recovery task force to oversee the reconstruction process and any policy issues that might arise after a storm disaster

4. the establishment of guidelines for postdisaster repair and reconstruction, including but not limited to

   a. timing and completion of damage assessment

   b. the timing and imposition of temporary development moratoria

   c. the development standards to which repairs and reconstruction must conform

5. the establishment of a schedule for staging and permitting repairs and reconstruction according to established priorities assigned to the restoration of essential services, minor repairs, major repairs, and new development

6. the determination of which local agency is to implement the policies and procedures contained in the postdisaster plan

7. establishment of policies concerning the repair and possible relocation of public utilities and facilities (North Carolina Administrative Code of Statutes 1974, sec. 203(9)(6)).

Localities that have prepared postdisaster reconstruction plans for earthquakes are few in number. An extensive hazard mitigation and preparedness plan was prepared for Aberdeen, Washington, with funding from the Federal Emergency Management Agency (Urban and Regional Research 1982). A key hazard around which the plan was focused was seismic-induced tsunamis. A major portion of this plan addresses how the city should rebuild after a major tsunami. Specifically, a plan for relocating facilities and investment out of high-hazard tsunami zones is developed. Several redevelopment options to implement this objective are presented, including encouraging more intensive redevelopment of existing residential areas (i.e., infilling), adding new residential tracts within the present city limits, and annexation of new lands to the city. Potential relocation sites, as indicated on fig. 6-4, are specifically mapped in the plan; they are based on certain site characteristics (e.g., location outside 100-year floodplain). In addition, the plan specifies how high-risk areas should be used after the disaster. Much of the area would be

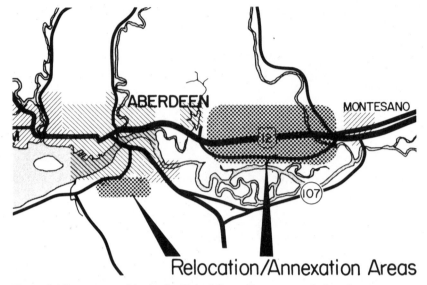

Relocation/Annexation Areas

Figure 6.4 Few communities in the United States have prepared plans for reconstruction after an earthquake. Aberdeen, Washington, is one of those few. Here, areas for relocating facilities outside the city limits after a seismic-related tsunami (tidal wave) are designated. *Source:* Urban and Regional Research 1982, 46.

converted to industrial uses and would incorporate stronger development standards, including protective buffers (e.g., barrier plantings, dikes).

Earthquake reconstruction plans are beginning to be prepared in California. Under new state legislation—the Disaster Recovery Reconstruction Act of 1986 (Senate Bill 1920)—localities are permitted and encouraged to prepare such plans. Specifically, the bill states that each locality is authorized to "prepare, prior to a disaster, plans and ordinances that facilitate orderly reconstruction of damaged areas." These plans and ordinances may include:

1. an evaluation of the vulnerability of specific areas under its jurisdiction to damage from a potential disaster, together with streamlined procedures for the appropriate modification of existing general plans or zoning ordinances affecting those areas after a disaster

2. a contingency plan of action and organization for short-term and long-term recovery and reconstruction to be instituted after a disaster

3. an ordinance, to be adopted before the disaster, that could be invoked as soon as possible after the event and that would provide necessary local authorization for activities designated under subdivisions (California Code of Statutes 1986).

Los Angeles has had the most extensive experience to date with seismic reconstruction planning. Specific reconstruction planning activities include, for example: a review and evaluation of existing city policies and programs; a hazards vulnerability analysis; the determination of an appropriate organizational structure for implementing the plan; development of a streamlined postdisaster permitting process; coordination of postdisaster functions and activities with the private sector and other local jurisdictions (and the crafting in advance of mutual agreements); and a review of how to use volunteers effectively after a disaster (Los Angeles, California 1987, 3–4). A draft version of a comprehensive reconstruction plan was issued in the spring of 1991.

Postearthquake Damage Assessment

Critical to public decisions concerning postearthquake reconstruction is an early understanding of the magnitude, type, and causes of damages. One approach is to form a damage assessment team in advance of a disaster. The team would begin working immediately after an event. Procedures for estimating and documenting the extent and nature of damages would also be established in advance (e.g., damage assessment forms, field guides). The damage assessment team might be assigned the following responsibilities (Brower et al. 1984):

1. to assess the extent and location of earthquake damage to public and private structures and facilities
2. to document the type and location of forces, and the extent to which modifications to the natural environment have occurred (e.g., faulting, ground movement)
3. to determine, to the extent possible, the likely causes of damage (e.g., ground shaking, liquefaction, types and extent of faulty construction).

The damage assessment team could collect this information and present it using a damaged area delineation scheme. The damage team might be asked to compare the actual damages incurred in the community with the seismic hazard maps available before the earthquake.

Recovery Task Force

A task force created to supplement the normal local decision-making process has been used successfully in several postdisaster settings. The North Carolina Coastal Management Program urges localities to consider the creation of such a group. For instance, the Onslow County, North Carolina (1984), hurricane hazard mitigation and postdisaster reconstruction plan proposes a recovery task force with the following responsibilities:

1. to review the nature of damages, identify and evaluate alternate program approaches for repairs and reconstruction, and formulate recommendations for handling community recovery
2. to recommend to the County Commissioners the declaration of a moratorium on repairs and new development
3. to set a calendar of milestones for reconstruction tasks
4. to initiate orders for repairs to critical utilities and facilities
5. to recommend the lifting of a moratorium for minor repairs
6. to recommend the lifting of a moratorium for major repairs to conforming structures
7. to evaluate hazards and the effectiveness of mitigation policies and recommend the amendment of policies, if necessary
8. to initiate negotiations for relocations and acquisitions of property
9. to recommend the lifting of a moratorium on major repairs (with approved changes to conform)
10. to participate in federal hazard mitigation planning
11. to recommend the lifting of a moratorium on new development.

In California, the Disaster Recovery Reconstruction Act described earlier includes specific language authorizing the establishment of a local reconstruction authority, "which would have powers parallel to those of a community redevelopment agency, except that the reconstruction authority would be authorized to operate beyond the confines of designated redevelopment areas and would have financing sources other than tax increment sources" (California Code of Statutes 1986, sect. 8874.5).

Temporary Reconstruction Moratoria

After the disaster a locality may be besieged with requests to rebuild. Typically the pressures to rebuild are great, and local governments are not prepared to deal with either the substance or the number of these requests. One approach to this problem is to declare a temporary moratorium on rebuilding. A moratorium provides sufficient time for the local damage assessment team to do its job, and for the task force and local decision makers to consider appropriate mitigation opportunities. Once the damage assessment is completed, the moratorium can be lifted for less damaged areas. A time limit for the moratorium, such as six months from its initial designation, is advisable.

Reconstruction moratoria have been used after a number of disasters. Such ordinances have been used, for instance, in Galveston, Texas, and Baytown, Texas, to prevent premature rebuilding after Hurricane Alicia

(Godschalk et al. 1989). Moratoria have also been used to prevent rebuilding in landslide and mudslide areas (Kockleman 1985).

Delineation of Damage Zones: The Triage Concept

A primary task of the damage assessment team could be to delineate damaged areas in conjunction with the reconstruction task force. A three-tiered delineation based upon severity of damage has been used in some communities. It functions much as a triage does in emergency medicine. Damaged areas could be designated according to damage criteria such as the following:

1. *major damage areas:* buildings with damages amounting to 50 percent or more of their fair market value
2. *moderate damage areas:* buildings with damages amounting to more than 20 percent but under 50 percent of their fair market value
3. *minor damage areas:* buildings receiving damages of less than 20 percent of their fair market value.

Triage suggests that a community delay reconstruction in major damage areas (at least in the short term), while permitting rebuilding in less damaged areas. The task force's immediate attention should be directed to determining whether structures in moderate damage areas ought to be allowed to rebuild and, if so, under what conditions. In addition, existing local hazard zones (e.g., fault-rupture, landslide hazard areas) should be reviewed and modified to reflect changes in natural processes and topography and new knowledge gained about these processes. The triage damage zone concept, while largely untested, has been incorporated, in one way or another, in a number of local disaster planning programs (Rogers et al. 1981; Onslow County, North Carolina 1984; also see Haas et al. 1977).

EVALUATING MITIGATION MEASURES

The mitigation measures described in this chapter are evaluated on six criteria (1) effectiveness at reducing seismic vulnerability; (2) political acceptability; (3) public cost; (4) private cost; (5) administrative cost and complexity; and (6) ease of enforcement. These criteria are defined in table 6-5.

Table 6-6 summarizes an assessment of the mitigation-planning measures described above. Obviously, any attempt at providing such a measure-by-measure assessment is fraught with limitations. A key limitation is that table 6-6 provides an evaluation only at a general level. The specific

Table 6.5 Criteria for Evaluating Tools and Techniques

1. *Effectiveness at reducing seismic vulnerability*
   • How effective is the measure at reducing seismic risks?
   • How likely is the measure to reduce loss of life and property damage?

2. *Political acceptability*
   • How politically easy will it be to gain adoption of the measure?
   • How politically easy will it be to implement the measure once adopted?
   • Are certain powerful local groups likely to resist strongly the use of such a measure?

3. *Public Costs*
   • Will the measure be costly to the local government to put into use?
   • Will the measure require the local government to raise large amounts of additional funds, such as through the issuance of bonds?

4. *Private Costs*
   • Will the measure require private property owners to expend significant amounts of their own money to comply with local requirements?
   • Will the measure result in significant reductions in the value of land and property?

5. *Administrative cost and complexity*
   • How much administrative effort will be required in using a particular measure?
   • How unique or different is the measure compared with other tools or techniques typically in use?
   • How much staff time will be required to prepare the necessary studies and ordinances before adoption, and to implement the measure once adopted?

6. *Ease of enforcement*
   • How easy will it be to ensure that public and private actors are complying with the measure?
   • How easy will it be to monitor the measure and to determine whether it is having the desired mitigation results?

provisions of an actual ordinance or program can also have a significant influence on effectiveness, political feasibility and so on. Also important, and generally beyond the capability of table 6-6, is an assessment of the extent to which a specific ordinance or program is able to accomplish other important local objectives. While land acquisition may be costly as an approach to seismic hazard mitigation, it may be more appropriate when other local objectives are considered (e.g., the need for open space and recreational facilities). Nevertheless, it is hoped that this evaluative framework will provide the reader with a general approach to assessing local ordinances and programs and a sense of the important questions that should be asked in an evaluation.

Certain general patterns emerge from table 6-6. Some measures are clearly of high effectiveness. Acquiring and setting aside hazardous lands is a highly effective mitigation measure, but it is tremendously costly to the public. Comprehensive plans, on the other hand, do not by themselves

Table 6.6 Evaluation of Alternative Mitigation Measures

Measures	Criteria					
	Effectiveness at Reducing Seismic Vulnerability	Political Acceptability/ Feasibility	Public Cost	Private Cost	Administrative Cost and Complexity	Ease of Enforcement
Building codes/construction standards						
• Standards for new construction	High	High	Moderate	Low–moderate	Moderate	Moderate
• Mandatory retrofit of existing structures	High	Low	Moderate	High	Moderate	Moderate–high
• Voluntary retrofit of existing structures	Moderate	High	Moderate	Moderate	Moderate	N.A.
Capital facilities and public investment policies	Moderate–high	Moderate	Low	Low	Moderate	N.A.
• Comprehensive/land use plans	Low	High	Low–moderate	Low	Low	N.A.
• Hazard disclosure/information dissemination	Low	Moderate–high	Low	Low–moderate	Low	Low–moderate
Land Acquisition	High	Low–moderate	High	Low	Moderate–high	N.A.
Land use regulations						
• Density reductions	High	Low	Moderate	Moderate–high	Moderate	Moderate–high
• Land use suitability	Moderate	Moderate	Low	Low–moderate	Low	N.A.
• Clustering	High	Moderate	Low	Moderate	Low	High
• Special studies zones	Moderate	High	Low	Moderate	Moderate	Moderate–high
• Sensitive-area ordinances/overlays	Moderate	High	Low–moderate	Moderate	Moderate	Moderate–high
• Setbacks and buffers	Moderate–high	High	Low	Low–moderate	Low	High
Reconstruction plans and policies	Moderate	Moderate–high	Low	Low–moderate	Moderate	N.A.
Taxation and other financial incentives						
• Differential property taxation	Low	High	Moderate–high	Low	Low–moderate	N.A.
• Bonus/incentive zoning	Low–moderate	High	Moderate	Low	Moderate	N.A.
• Transfer of development rights	Moderate–high	Low–moderate	Moderate	Moderate	High	N.A.
• Exactions and development conditions	Moderate	Low–moderate	Low	High	Moderate–high	N.A.

tend to involve high public or private costs and do not tend to create significant political opposition, but by the same token their advisory, nonbinding nature leads to a low effectiveness rating.

Most forms of land use regulation are of moderate to high effectiveness. Significant density restrictions are of great effectiveness but often involve substantial private costs (e.g., reductions in the developability and market value of private land). This in turn tends to reduce their political acceptability, particularly in conservative communities where concern about the interference of government with private property rights is high. Those regulatory approaches that tend to focus on performance controls and project design but do little to reduce the overall quantity of permissible development tend to involve fewer private costs and invoke less opposition from local development interests. When these ordinances (e.g., special studies zones, sensitive-area ordinances) involve prohibiting development on extensive portions of a site, with the inability to transfer density, their political acceptability tends to be significantly reduced.

Building codes and construction standards hold relatively high effectiveness at reducing seismic vulnerability, although their effectiveness varies considerably depending upon their stringency. Their public and private costs are low to moderate and tend not to generate significant political opposition. In most cases, building codes and construction standards are seen as a necessary and important form of consumer protection and a normal part of the development process. Mandatory seismic retrofit, on the other hand, may involve significant private costs, and is much more likely to elicit strong political opposition. Voluntary seismic retrofit may be more politically acceptable, but it tends to be less effective.

Measures involving taxation and financial incentives are a mixed bag. Because they tend to be voluntary and market oriented, they are of high political acceptability, yet also of generally lower effectiveness. Preferential or differential property taxation has generally been shown to have little effect in retarding development of sensitive lands, although it tends to be of high political acceptability. Development and density bonuses tend to be of somewhat greater effectiveness, but they rely on voluntary mitigative actions. Transfer of development rights (TDR) has the potential of substantially reducing seismic hazards but is considered a highly complex measure by many localities. Exactions and development conditions are not voluntary and also have great potential for mitigation, depending, of course, on what exaction revenues are actually used for and what specific development conditions are imposed. There appears to be increasing political support around the country for the use of exactions, such as impact fees, to pay for needed public facilities and services associated with urban growth.

The mitigative potential of capital facilities and public investment policy is moderate to high and depends on the specific facilities considered and how critical they are to new development. Where hazard area development can occur without public investments, such policies may have little effectiveness. However, efforts to steer public buildings and facilities out of high-risk areas in order to minimize direct public sector risk are clearly effective. Such capital facilities and public investment decisions are, of course, typically embroiled in politics. When pressures to promote community growth are strong it may be difficult to prevent hazardous public expenditures. However, when adequate low-risk locations exist for public buildings and facilities, it should be easier for politicians to support such a mitigation measure. These measures can be pursued fairly easily with mechanisms that already exist in most localities (e.g., the local CIP), and thus the administrative cost and complexity tend to be low.

While hazard disclosure provisions tend to be of moderate to high political acceptability and low administrative complexity, their effectiveness at reducing vulnerability is questionable. Current experience with the Alquist-Priolo disclosure requirement suggests that such information may have little actual influence on consumer behavior.

Planning for reconstruction in advance of an earthquake offers the possibility of making a community much safer, as well as accomplishing other local land use goals that would simply be unfeasible without the occurrence of a disaster. Reconstruction plans and policies could, moreover, help counteract the tremendous pressures that follow a disaster to rebuild quickly and in essentially the same way. However, effectiveness is considered only moderate because such a measure is usually only advisory and not mandatory. Because the preparation and adoption of such plans in advance of an earthquake involves little immediate political sacrifice (i.e., does not restrict property rights in the short term), their political acceptability is moderate to high. The public and private costs and the administrative complexity of such plans and policies tend to be low, although when the plans are actually implemented, they may be much higher (e.g., if property owners are prevented from rebuilding).

CONCLUSIONS

This chapter has sought to provide greater insight into what local governments are actually doing, or could do, to mitigate seismic hazards. It has focused heavily on land use management as an approach but has also examined building code and structural measures and measures to manage the reconstruction process after an earthquake. It is apparent that localities have available to them a variety of specific mitigation measures, and localities are in fact using a wide spectrum of these measures. Not surprisingly, a predominance of examples are drawn from California, although significant and impressive local programs are also found in Utah and Washington states. Some local measures reduce seismic vulnerability essentially as a side benefit and not as a primary objective (e.g., landslide mitigation and hillside ordinances). Certain measures that are not widely used now could be highly effective at minimizing seismic hazards. Transfer of development rights, for example, is well suited to shifting development away from hazardous areas and into safer locations in the community. Planning for reconstruction in advance of an earthquake is another measure with great potential that is not currently undertaken by most localities. At least in California, the new Disaster Recovery Reconstruction Act may provide a needed boost for this type of planning.

The evaluative criteria indicate that choices about which measures, or combinations of measures, to adopt often involve trade-offs among local values. While one type of measure may be highly effective, it may also be highly costly to the public or to private property owners. Some localities may decide, for instance, to adopt a somewhat less effective technique, recognizing the need to keep such costs down. The more detailed case studies presented in other chapters illustrate how these difficult local trade-offs and compromises are made.

A key conclusion from this chapter is that land use management can play an important role in reducing local seismic risks. The examples presented here demonstrate that local vulnerability can be substantially reduced when seismic risks in conventional land use planning and regulation are adequately considered. Very basic land use regulatory tools, such as reducing density in hazardous areas though existing zoning and subdivision ordinances, or avoiding hazardous areas through mandatory clustering or hazard zone setbacks, can substantially reduce the people and property at risk. The potential of land use management to reduce the seismic risk will continue to increase as our ability to identify and map seismic hazard zones expands.

7 • LOCAL EARTHQUAKE MITIGATION PROGRAMS

Although earthquake risk reduction is a common goal of community mitigation programs, the means of achieving it differ widely. Each program is a result of a political process involving a wide range of both internal and external factors. Variations in the balance of influence among these factors result in mitigation programs that differ in plan policies and implementation measures. Each program is to some extent unique.

Using data from a national survey, this chapter explores the diversity of earthquake mitigation programs by describing a cross section of programs operating in the United States. Following the conceptual framework set forth in chapter 2, the description focuses on three categories of elements: internal factors, external factors, and community responses.[1] Internal factors refer to activities of localities to advance mitigation. These factors include interorganizational relations, program resources, and program operations. External factors consist of the physical, socioeconomic, and political characteristics of a community. The combination of internal and external factors leads to various community responses, including assigning a priority to mitigation on local government agendas, adopting specific land use and development measures, and assuring that measures effectively reduce risk.

1. In some instances the cross-sectional data are not analyzed according to the conceptual framework presented in chapter 2. While two internal factors (advocates and linkage) are presented in the conceptual framework as independent factors that affect local response to earthquakes, they are grouped under one category—program operation. Also, all external factors are grouped under one category, yet they were presented as independent factors in the conceptual framework. These groupings were done to simplify a data reduction strategy presented in chapter 9. Thus we descriptively present program operation and external factors in chapter 8 in order to be consistent with the explanatory analysis in chapter 9.

Throughout the analysis of survey data, local mitigation programs of California are examined separately from those of all other states. While programs of communities throughout the country occupy different points in the evolution process, those of California are far ahead of the others (Scholl 1986). Given this difference in development, analyzing survey communities in two groups allows us to more carefully examine factors associated with local response to the seismic threat than examining pooled data from communities in all states.

COMMUNITY MITIGATION RESPONSES

The survey included three sets of questions about mitigation responses, including mitigation measures adopted, priority of earthquakes on local government agendas, and perceived effectiveness of mitigation measures.

We expected California communities to be more active in earthquake mitigation than communities in other states for two reasons. First, as discussed in the case studies, California is widely recognized as having a progressive political culture that tends to support new and innovative approaches to planning and managing development. Second, earthquakes have received more public attention in California than in other states. This recognition has produced several policy responses, including state legislative mandates for local governments to enact seismic-resistant building standards, seismic plans, and hazard disclosure and fault setback ordinances. While a few other midwestern and western states have shown some response to earthquake hazards, none have approached California's efforts.

Data in tables 7-1 and 7-2 affirm our expectations about greater earthquake mitigation activity in California. The data were derived from a question asking respondents to indicate which of twenty-one building design and planning and management measures their localities have adopted. Five measures listed on the survey, including building codes, zoning and subdivision ordinances, comprehensive plans, and capital improvement programs, are typically enacted for nonhazard reasons but to some extent can be used for earthquake mitigation. The remaining sixteen measures, ranging from planning measures and land use regulation to financial incentives, property acquisition, and hazard disclosure measures, specifically address earthquake hazards, as indicated by wording on the survey.

Table 7-1 shows respondents' indication of measures used by communities in California and other states. California communities use a greater number of measures than communities in other states. For example, the majority of respondents in California (58.6 percent) indicated that their communities used six or more measures, compared to 18.3 percent of

Table 7.1 Number of Mitigation Measures Adopted by
Communities

Measures	California		All Others
0–1	1.2%		19.2%
2–3	19.5		22.5
4–5	20.7		40.0
6 or more	58.6		18.3
No. communities	82		120
	Chi-square	df	Significance
	49.75	3	<.001

respondents in communities outside of California. The difference in number of measures adopted by each group of communities is significant ($p <$ .001).

Table 7-2 provides a more detailed description of respondents' answers regarding the specific measures adopted by their communities. With the exception of capital improvements programs, a majority of communities in both California and all other states have adopted the measures that are typically enacted for nonhazard reasons but can be used for hazard mitigation (building codes, zoning and subdivision ordinances, and plans).

In California, of the sixteen measures that specifically address earthquake hazards, only two—an earthquake component of comprehensive plans and seismic-resistant building standards—were used by a majority of communities.[2] Slightly more than one in three communities used retrofit of existing buildings and public information programs. Location of critical facilities (under critical and public facilities policies) was used by about one in four California communities, and fault setback ordinances (under development regulations) were used by about one in five communities. All five land and property acquisition measures, and both taxation and

2. In fact, we expected a much greater proportion of localities in California to indicate adoption of these measures. For example, all localities in California are required by law to have adopted an earthquake component of comprehensive plans, yet as shown in table 7-2 not all respondents indicated this measure was in use. This can perhaps be explained in several ways. First, some respondents may simply be unaware that mitigation measures exist. Another explanation is that respondents interpreted the question as asking whether these measures were being used to mitigate earthquake risks. While a locality's comprehensive plan may contain a seismic element, the element may be seldom or never, implemented. The respondent, then, may recognize the existence of the provision on paper but see no clear application or use of it (and thus may fail to indicate the measure on the survey). Finally, the existence of a state mandate or requirement does not ensure that localities will adopt these measures. It is entirely possible that some localities have ignored the state mandates.

Table 7.2 Adoption of Planning Measures for Earthquake Hazard Mitigation

Measures	Communities in California	Communities in All Other States
Building standards		
Building code	98%	82%
Special seismic resistance building standards	69	9
Retrofit of existing buildings	35	6
Critical and public facilities policies		
Capital improvements programs	27	33
Location of critical facilities (hospitals, schools) to reduce risk	26	9
Location of capital facilities (street, water) to discourage development in hazardous areas	15	10
Development regulations		
Zoning ordinance	56	66
Subdivision ordinance	52	59
Fault setback ordinance	21	8
Information dissemination		
Public information program	37	13
Hazardous disclosure requirements	17	6
Land and property acquisition		
Transfer of development potential from hazardous to nonhazardous sites	15	4
Acquisition of undeveloped lands	2	3
Acquisition of development rights	5	2
Building relocation	2	1
Acquisition of damaged buildings	0	1
Planning		
Comprehensive or land use plan	94	60
Earthquake component of comprehensive plan	73	11
Recovery/reconstruction plan	12	7
Taxation and fiscal policies		
Impact tax to cover additional public costs of building in hazardous areas	0	2
Reduced or below-market taxation for open space or nonintensive uses in hazardous areas	0	5

Source: List of planning measures adapted from Godschalk et al. (1989, ch. 7).

fiscal policy measures, were used by a much smaller percentage of California communities.

As expected, compared to California communities, the percentage of communities in all other states using measures specifically designed for earthquake mitigation was smaller. For example, the three most frequently adopted measures—public information programs, an earthquake compo-

Table 7.3 Priority of Earthquake Hazards in the Community

Priority	California		All Others
Very low	20.7%		59.2%
Low	39.0		25.8
Medium	23.2		10.8
High	14.6		3.3
Very high	2.5		0.9
No. communities	82		120
	Chi-square	df	Significance
	32.62	4	<.001

nent of comprehensive plans, and location of capital facilities—were used only by about one in ten communities.

The findings on California's more extensive experience call for a few words of caution. While earthquake mitigation in California is substantially higher than in the rest of the nation, it is considerably lower than mitigation activity for other types of hazards (Burby and French 1985; Godschalk et al. 1989). For example, comparison of data in table 7-2 with results of a national survey of coastal communities by Godschalk and his colleagues reveals that California used planning measures for hurricane mitigation more extensively than for earthquakes.

Responses to a survey question about local priority of earthquake mitigation were consistent with survey findings of other policy studies that examine earthquake hazards (Drabek et al. 1983; Rossi et al. 1982; Wyner and Mann 1986). That is, local priority is low. Table 7-3 shows that a majority of respondents in California (59.7 percent) and all other communities (85 percent) indicated that earthquakes are a low or a very low priority in their communities. The difference between the two groups of communities is significant ($p < .001$). While priority in California is substantially higher than in the rest of the nation, it is still considerably lower than local priority for floods and hurricanes. For example, in a national survey of more than 600 communities, Godschalk et al. (1989) found that 27 percent of the responding officials of coastal communities placed hurricanes at a low or very low priority on their local governments' agendas, while 73 percent gave hurricanes a medium, high, or very high priority.

Respondents were asked to rate on a five-point scale with one as the low, the overall effectiveness of building design and planning and management of development measures in mitigating risk posed by earthquakes in their jurisdiction. Table 7-4 indicates that respondents from California jurisdictions rated the effectiveness of each mitigation approach higher than those from other states. The difference in perceived effective-

Table 7.4 Perceived Effectiveness of Earthquake Mitigation Measures

Measures	Effectiveness (%)					Chi-square (Significance)
	1 (Very ineffective)	2	3	4	5	
Building design and construction measures						
California, n = 82	3.7	7.3	19.5	43.9	25.6	29.02
All others, n = 102	17.6	20.6	28.4	22.6	10.8	(<.001)
Measures for planning and regulating development						
California, n = 80	6.2	23.8	37.5	25.0	7.5	26.84
All others, n = 98	29.6	31.6	25.5	6.1	7.2	(<.001)

ness ratings for each approach was significant (p < .001).

Additionally, building design measures were rated more effective than planning measures by both groups. A majority of California respondents (69.5 percent) indicated that building design measures were effective (four or five on the scale) compared to 32.5 percent for planning measures. About one-third of respondents (33.4 percent) from communities in other states rated building design measures as effective in contrast to 13.3 percent for planning measures.

There are two plausible reasons why building design measures were rated more effective. First, we suspect that many communities are fully built up and have very little, if any, vacant land. Opportunities for significant changes related to land use are more limited than if there were a substantial amount of undeveloped land. Change in land use patterns to mitigate earthquake hazards, therefore, is likely to be more difficult and expensive than instituting building design measures. Second, by comparison with flood-related hazards, there is little information on the spatial delineation of earthquake hazards. When site-specific hazard area delineations are not available, it would be difficult to formulate land use policies and regulations guiding decisions about location, density, and type of development in hazardous areas. Thus, enactment of seismic provisions in building codes that are uniformly applied throughout a community would be considered a more effective mitigation response.

INTERNAL FACTORS AFFECTING ADOPTION

Interorganizational Relationships

Interorganizational relationships are the relationships between the program and its political environment. Earthquake mitigation programs are embedded in a larger political context and, therefore, must acquire political support to be effective. Factors discussed below include the extent of

Table 7.5 Interorganizational Contacts with Community

	No. of Contacts over Last 3 Years (%)				Chi-square (Significance)
	None	1–3	4–8	8 or more	
City/county agencies					
California, *n* = 79	20.3	43.0	19.0	17.7	30.47
All others, *n* = 112	58.9	26.8	5.4	8.9	(<.001)
FEMA					
California, *n* = 76	47.4	38.1	6.6	7.9	8.41
All others, *n* = 110	64.6	30.9	2.7	1.8	(<.05)
Private consultants					
California, *n* = 78	42.3	26.9	12.8	18.0	19.93
All others, *n* = 103	74.7	13.6	4.9	6.8	(<.001)
Professional engineering/construction associations					
California, *n* = 76	48.7	25.0	17.1	9.2	9.98
All others, *n* = 108	66.7	21.3	4.6	7.4	(<.05)
Regional agencies					
California, *n* = 78	24.4	42.3	17.9	15.4	62.62
All others, *n* = 109	80.7	15.6	2.8	.9	(<.001)
State agencies					
California, *n* = 78	15.4	50.0	19.2	15.4	42.64
All others, *n* = 113	62.8	23.9	8.0	5.3	(<.001)
U.S. Army Corps of Engineers					
California, *n* = 76	63.2	32.9	2.6	1.3	5.09
All others, *n* = 109	78.0	20.2	.9	.9	(n.s.)
USGS					
California, *n* = 79	59.5	32.9	7.6	0.0	6.13
All others, *n* = 110	73.6	24.6	1.8	0.0	(<.05)

contact between earthquake mitigation programs and other local, state and federal agencies, and the responsiveness of these agencies to program needs.

The first factor to be examined is the frequency of interorganizational contact. When levels of interaction in a policy-making arena are high, opportunities for sharing information and generating common outlooks and ways of thinking among participating organizations are increased. Participants become more aware of the interests and activities of others. Issues of local concern have a greater chance of being communicated to state and federal agencies. Technical and financial support from higher levels of government are more likely to fit the specific needs of local programs. Opportunities for bargaining and compromise are also enhanced.

Table 7-5 presents data on the average annual number of contacts respondents' programs had with eight organizations at the local, state, and national levels over three years, 1983 to 1986. As anticipated, the frequency of contact was greater for California programs than for programs in other states. In fact, with the exception of the U.S. Army Corps of Engineers, the difference in frequency of contact between communities in the two survey groups was significant for all organizations ($p < .05$ or $p < .001$).

Organizations that had the most contact with local programs of both groups of communities were other local agencies, followed by state agencies, professional engineering and construction associations, and private consultants. Regional agencies showed relatively high contact with local programs in California, but not in other states. Contact with federal agencies, including USGS, FEMA, and the Corps of Engineers, was relatively low for both survey groups.

Respondents were asked to rate the responsiveness of each of the eight organizations to local mitigation program needs and requirements. Table 7-6 shows that responsiveness ratings were generally higher for respondents from California communities than for those in other states. This finding is expected, given the greater frequency of interorganizational contacts in California communities. With the exception of two federal agencies—USGS and the Corps of Engineers—the difference in responsiveness ratings between the two groups of communities was significant ($p < .05$ or $p < .001$). In addition, organizations with the most frequent contacts with program staff (see table 7-5) tended to be rated the most responsive by both groups of respondents. Thus state and local agencies were generally the most responsive, and federal agencies were the least.

Program Resources

The extent of program resources is also an important factor related to successful local response to earthquake hazards. The forms of program support discussed here include amount of planning staff time devoted to earthquake hazards, amount of planning department budget allocated to earthquake hazards, and change in planning department budget allocations over time.

Those surveyed were asked to report the amount of time per week their local planning staff spent on earthquake issues. As expected, table 7-7 indicates that planning staffs in California spent more time than their counterparts in other states. The difference between the two groups of communities was significant ($p < .05$). However, the table also shows a majority of respondents from both California (74.1 percent) and other states (87.5 percent) reporting that local planning staffs spent less than one hour.

Although results in table 7-7 indicate that efforts directed toward earthquake mitigation are more extensive in California, they are minimal even

Table 7.6 Responsiveness of Organizations to Local Government Needs and Problems

	Responsiveness (%)					
	1 (Not responsive)	2	3	4	5	Chi-square (Significance)
City/county agencies						
California, $n = 52$	1.6	6.5	27.4	35.5	29.0	26.77
All others, $n = 62$	11.5	13.5	23.1	26.9	25.0	(<.001)
FEMA						
California, $n = 42$	2.4	2.4	45.2	23.8	26.2	6.02
All others, $n = 46$	6.5	10.9	39.1	23.9	19.6	(<.05)
Private consultants						
California, $n = 45$	6.7	6.7	11.0	37.8	37.8	22.36
All others, $n = 36$	25.0	8.3	25.0	25.0	16.7	(<.001)
Professional engineering/construction associations						
California, $n = 42$	9.5	4.8	23.8	38.1	23.8	7.34
All others, $n = 42$	16.7	9.5	23.8	26.2	23.8	(<.05)
Regional agencies						
California, $n = 58$	1.7	5.2	29.3	34.5	29.3	48.71
All others, $n = 35$	20.0	14.3	37.1	11.4	17.2	(<.001)
State agencies						
California, $n = 64$	1.6	7.8	21.9	35.9	32.8	28.31
All others, $n = 50$	8.0	6.0	38.0	24.0	24.0	(<.001)
U.S. Army Corps of Engineers						
California, $n = 26$	3.4	7.7	46.1	34.6	7.7	1.53
All others, $n = 34$	17.7	5.9	47.0	20.6	8.8	(n.s.)
USGS						
California, $n = 38$	7.9	5.3	36.8	31.6	18.4	5.69
All others, $n = 37$	10.8	5.4	46.0	21.6	16.2	(n.s.)

Note: The five-point seriousness scale was collapsed into three categories by combining values 1 and 2, and 4 and 5. The resulting three-point scale was used for computing chi-squares.

Table 7.7 Time Spent on Earthquake-related Problems

No. Hours	California	All Others
Less than 1	74.1%	87.5%
1–7	18.5	7.5
8–39	2.5	4.2
40 or more	4.9	0.8
TOTALS	81	120
	Chi-square	df	Significance
	9.66	3	<.05

Table 7.8 Percentage of Planning Department Budget Allocated
to Earthquake Problems

% of Budget	California	All Others
Less than 1	79.0%	91.5%
1–5	14.8	3.4
6–20	5.0	5.1
Greater than 20	1.2	0.0
Totals	82	120
	Chi-square	*df*	*Significance*
	10.13	3	<.05

Table 7.9 Difference in Planning Department Budget Allocated
to Earthquake Hazards over Last Five Years

Difference	California	All Others
Much less	0.0%	5.8%
Less	3.7	1.7
No change	76.5	83.3
More	16.1	7.5
Much more	3.7	1.7
Totals	81	120
	Chi-square	*df*	*Significance*
	9.84	3	<.05

there. Another finding from the survey reinforces this interpretation.
Table 7-8 shows the percentage of planning department budget allocated
to mitigation. While California communities allocate more than other
communities (this difference is significant, $p < .05$), the majority of communities from California (79.0 percent) and other states (91.5 percent)
allocate less than 1 percent of their planning departments' budgets to
earthquake problems.

Change in program budget reflects the relative importance of issues on
political agendas over time. Respondents were asked if their communities
currently allocated a greater percentage of their operating budget to earthquake problems than they did five years earlier. Table 7-9 indicates that
the majority of communities in both California and other states spent
about the same percentage of total annual budget on earthquake problems
as they had previously. In California, however, almost one in five (19.8
percent) spent more, compared to less than one in twenty (3.7 percent)
that spent less. Slightly less than one out of ten communities (9.2 percent)
in other states spent more, and about one in fifteen (7.5 percent) spent
less. The difference in budget change between the two groups of commu-

nities is significant ($p < .001$). Thus the trend over the last five years has been a small increase, though larger in California, in the relative amount of funding for earthquake hazards.

Program Operations

Program operation activities are of key importance to successful community response to earthquake hazards. The presence of advocates who promote earthquake hazard mitigation, linkage of earthquake hazards to other local concerns and comprehensive planning programs, and the use of the media are discussed.

Advocates are participants in the planning process who are willing to invest their resources—time, energy, and money—to assure that a particular problem is raised on governmental agendas. Advocates have been found to be a strong moving force in hazards mitigation planning.

Respondents were asked if an individual or group at the local, state, or national level advocating mitigation of earthquake hazards had influenced planning decisions in their jurisdictions. The majority (51.3 percent) of California respondents, compared to 28.2 percent in other states, indicated that an advocate was at work in their communities. This difference was significant (chi-square = 10.64, df = 1, $p < .001$).

An open-ended follow-up question asked those respondents who indicated the presence of an advocate to identify the individual or group. Of the forty-nine California respondents answering this question, two types of advocates were most frequently cited; eleven (22.4 percent) mentioned state emergency management agencies, and ten (20.4 percent) mentioned regional planning agencies. Of the thirty-one respondents in the remaining states, only one type of advocate was cited more than others; eight respondents (25.8 percent) indicated state emergency management agencies. The advocates that were mentioned less often by respondents of both survey groups (10 percent or less) included FEMA, USGS, state geology agencies, and local emergency management agencies.

Another way earthquake mitigation efforts can be advanced is through linkage with traditional planning measures. Application of traditional development measures to seismic issues would enhance the feasibility of hazard mitigation by integrating it with politically acceptable planning measures. Thus, the two activities cease to operate as separate administrative functions.

Because of a greater acceptance of earthquake mitigation in local planning operations, we expected California communities to have integrated mitigation measures into local planning more extensively than communities in other states. Survey findings confirmed our expectations. A majority of respondents from California (57.5 percent) indicated that earthquake hazard concerns in their communities were directly integrated into the

Table 7.10 Local Concerns Linked to Earthquake Hazard Issues

Issues	California	All Others	Chi-square	Significance
Economic development	19.8%	13.2%	1.54	n.s.
Environmental protection	44.4	16.7	18.04	<.001
Location of capital facilities	25.9	15.8	3.04	n.s.
Location of critical facilities	34.6	12.3	13.92	<.001
Open space	19.7	11.4	2.61	n.s.
Recreation	6.2	4.4	0.31	n.s.
Redevelopment	35.8	13.2	13.90	<.001
Not aware of any	21.0	55.4	22.97	<.001
Totals	82	120		

comprehensive planning process, compared to only 8.5 percent from other states. This difference was significant (chi-square = 55.96, df = 1, $p < .001$).

Earthquake hazards can be linked to other issues confronting planners and other decision makers. As one of a group of issues or, in some cases, as a tool to be used for very different goals (e.g., stopping new development for purposes of environmental protection or encouraging renovation of buildings in declining community downtowns), the earthquake issue can be raised on local political agendas.

Table 7-10 shows that earthquake hazards are linked to other local issues more often in California communities than in other states. Twenty-one percent of California respondents were not aware of any linkage in their communities, compared to a majority (55.4 percent) of respondents from other communities. This difference is significant ($p < .001$). More specifically, issues related to environmental protection, redevelopment, and location of capital facilities were generally most frequently linked to earthquake hazards in California communities. These issues also had the greatest percentage difference in occurrence ($p < .001$) between the two survey groups.

The mass media are of fundamental importance to efforts to raise public hazard awareness; any attempt at increasing awareness of issues must involve the communication of information. With rapid advancement in communication technology and high public dependence on the media for information, the role of the media as a means of information transfer and of bringing specific matters to public attention for debate is crucial.

We included two questions to identify the extent and effectiveness of media use in communities. A yes-or-no question asked respondents if the media is used in their communities to heighten public awareness about earthquake hazards. As expected, the difference was significant in media use between the two survey groups (chi-square = 34.15, df = 1, $p < .001$). A majority of California respondents (76.8 percent) and a minority of respondents in other states (35.0 percent) indicated use of the media in their communities. An open-ended follow-up question asked those respondents who indicated use of media in their jurisdictions to identify the most effective sources of information transfer. Of those answering (sixty-three respondents from California and forty-two from other states), 66.7 percent of the California respondents and 59.5 percent of those in other states mentioned television. The next most frequently mentioned source (indicated by 53.9 percent of the California respondents and 40.5 percent of other respondents) was newspaper articles. A small proportion of respondents (10 percent or less) from both survey groups indicated conferences, radio programs, emergency training exercises, literature distribution, and lobbying in state legislatures as effective sources of information transfer.

EXTERNAL FACTORS

The last group of factors in the survey described the characteristics of communities in earthquake-prone areas. These characteristics vary greatly and may have an important impact on local response to earthquake hazards. Factors used to describe a locality's external environment include median home value, population size, seismic zone, past earthquake experience, perceived risk, and presence of hazards.

Table 7-11 shows that California communities have a higher median home value than those in other states. This difference is significant ($p <$ .001). For example, the majority of California communities (57.3 percent) had a 1980 median home value of $80,000 compared to 3.3 percent of communities in other states. Communities in California have larger populations than those in other states. Table 7-12 indicates that this difference is significant ($p <$ .01). Only about one-quarter (26.8 percent) of all responding communities in California had populations between 10,000 and 24,999 (the lowest population category) compared to more than one-half (54.2 percent) of communities in other states.

Table 7.11 Respondent Communities by Home Value

Median Value	California		All Others
Less than $39,999	0.0%		39.2%
$40,000–$59,999	8.5		38.3
$60,000–$79,000	34.2		19.2
More than $80,000	57.3		3.3
Totals	82		120
	Chi-square	*df*	*Significance*
	109.16	3	<.001

Table 7.12 Respondent Communities by Permanent Population
Size

Population	California	All Others
10,000–24,999	26.8%	54.2%
25,000–49,999	39.0	27.5
50,000–99,999	22.0	12.5
100,000 and above	12.2	5.8
Totals	82	120
	Chi-square	df	Significance
	15.47	3	<.01

The severity of hazard can have a strong influence on community mitigation response. Currently the country is divided into four zones of earthquake hazard severity designated 0 (least severe) to 4 (see fig. 1-5). As mentioned in chapter 1, communities in seismic zones 3 and 4 were surveyed. Eighty-one of the 82 communities surveyed in California are in seismic zone 4, while 2 of the 120 in other states are in zone 4.

A disastrous earthquake event alters hazard perceptions and typically serves to enhance mitigation responses during the aftermath of the event. Survey data indicated that a majority of California communities (69.1 percent) had experienced a major earthquake resulting in loss of life or extensive property damage (e.g., fallen building walls and broken underground pipes), or both, within the previous twenty years, compared to 38.7 percent of communities in other states.[3] This difference was significant (chi-square = 33.19, df = 4, $p < .001$).

Two questions were asked to ascertain respondents' perception of the degree of perceived risk from seismic hazards in their communities. One question asked, "What are the chances of a major earthquake occurring in your community?" As indicated in table 7-13, the results were consistent with our expectations. More than half (55.6 percent) of California respondents rated their communities' perception of the chances as high or very high, compared to less than one-third (31.4 percent) of respondents from other states. This difference was significant at the .001 level. However, responses to a second question indicate that the built environment of California communities is better able to withstand seismic forces. That is, 39.5 percent of California respondents rated their communities' perception of the ability of structures to withstand seismic forces as high or very high, in contrast to only 12.9 percent of respondents from other states (see table 7-14). This difference was significant at the .001 level.

3. Past experience was divided into the following categories of years on the survey questionnaire: less than 1; 1 to 5; 5 to 10; 11 to 20; more than 20; and never experienced one.

Table 7.13 Chance of a Major Earthquake

Perceived Chance	California		All Others
Very low	11.0%		28.8%
Low	6.2		15.2
Moderate	27.2		24.6
High	34.6		22.9
Very high	21.0		8.5
Totals	81		118
	Chi-square	df	Significance
	18.43	4	<.001

Table 7.14 Ability of Structures to Withstand Major Earthquake

Perceived Ability	California		All Others
Very low	3.7%		15.4%
Low	11.1		16.1
Moderate	45.7		55.6
High	33.3		10.3
Very high	6.2		2.6
Totals	81		117
	Chi-square	df	Significance
	22.43	4	<.001

Table 7.15 Number of Hazards in Community

No. Hazards	California		All Others
0–1	24.4%		60.0%
2–3	28.0		17.5
4–5	28.1		12.5
6 or more	19.5		10.0
Totals	82		120
	Chi-square	df	Significance
	25.49	3	<.001

The number of earthquake-related hazards within a community requires a greater variety of mitigation measures. Communities that are exposed to only ground shaking, for example, might require a seismic building code ordinance, but communities exposed to ground shaking, landslides, and faults might require both building code and land use controls. Table 7-15 indicates that California communities are exposed to a greater number of seismic hazards than communities in the rest of the country. From a list of nine types of hazards, respondents indicated that

47.6 percent of California communities compared to only 22.5 percent of communities outside of California, were exposed to four or more hazards. This difference was significant at the .001 level.

OBSTACLES TO LOCAL MITIGATION RESPONSE

Respondents were asked to rate on a five-point scale in which one is lowest, the seriousness of a range of obstacles to advancement of earthquake mitigation planning programs. Each obstacle falls under one of three sets of factors that affect mitigation response (see table 7-16): (1) *interorganizational relations* include lack of public interest, opposition by real estate interests, and lack of support from governmental officials; (2) *program support* includes lack of state and federal financial support, inadequately trained personnel, and inadequate maps delineating earth-

Table 7.16 Seriousness of Obstacles to Local Mitigation Response

	Seriousness (%)					
	1 *(Not serious)*	*2*	*3*	*4*	*5*	*Chi-square* *(Significance)*
Lack of state or federal financial support						
California, n = 79	12.7	12.7	25.3	20.3	29.1	1.62
All others, n = 99	9.1	13.1	22.2	27.3	28.3	(n.s.)
Conservative political culture						
California, n = 80	11.2	17.5	27.5	35.0	8.8	1.29
All others, n = 100	12.0	16.0	25.0	33.0	14.0	(n.s.)
Opposition by real estate and development interests						
California, n = 80	17.5	7.5	33.8	18.7	22.5	6.63
All others, n = 96	10.4	10.4	22.9	31.3	25.0	(n.s.)
Lack of support from other local government officials						
California, n = 82	25.6	25.6	17.1	13.4	18.3	5.54
All others, n = 99	20.2	18.2	28.3	19.2	14.1	(n.s.)
Lack of public interest						
California, n = 81	16.0	18.5	34.6	18.5	12.4	15.94
All others, n = 100	9.0	8.0	23.0	36.0	24.0	(<.05)
Inadequately trained personnel						
California, n = 81	37.0	22.2	17.3	16.1	7.4	9.26
All others, n = 98	18.4	21.4	25.5	21.4	13.3	(n.s.)
Inadequate maps delineating earthquake hazard areas						
California, n = 81	37.5	20.0	22.5	11.2	8.8	16.79
All others, n = 98	15.1	18.2	22.2	26.3	18.2	(<.01)
Legal restraints in planning and managing development						
California, n = 78	41.0	24.4	19.2	10.3	5.1	1.31
All others, n = 95	34.7	26.3	25.3	9.5	4.2	(n.s.)

Note: List of obstacles adapted from Godschalk et al. (1989).

quake hazards; and (3) *community context* includes a conservative political culture and legal restraints in planning and managing development.

Table 7-16 shows little difference between respondents from California and other states except on two of the eight obstacles. Lack of public interest and inadequate maps delineating earthquake hazard areas were rated as more serious by respondents outside of California than by those from California. The difference in ratings was significant both for public interest ($p < .05$) and for inadequate maps ($p < .01$). Lack of financial support from higher levels of government was the only obstacle rated as serious (4 or 5 on the scale) by a majority of respondents from both groups of communities. No other obstacles were considered serious by a majority of California respondents. Opposition of real estate interests and developers and lack of public interest were rated as serious by a majority of respondents from other states.

SUMMARY AND CONCLUSIONS

Findings described in this chapter indicate diversity in all aspects of programs both between and within community groups. While survey results demonstrate that programs use a wide variety of planning measures for earthquake mitigation, the frequency of adoption of such measures was greater in California than in other states. The majority of California respondents (58.6 percent), compared to 18.3 percent of respondents outside of California, indicated that their communities use six or more measures. More specifically, the most frequently used measures for both community groups are those not specifically designed for hazard mitigation. Building codes, comprehensive plans, and zoning and subdivision ordinances are the most commonly used measures for each community group. Other measures that explicitly address earthquake hazard mitigation, such as earthquake components of comprehensive plans, reconstruction plans, retrofit of existing buildings, and location of critical facilities are used by both groups, but more frequently in California. Finally, both groups of respondents rated the building design mitigation approach higher in overall effectiveness than the planning and managing of development approach. California respondents, however, rated both mitigation approaches as more effective than respondents from other states.

Caution should be exercised in interpreting survey findings on California's relatively more extensive experience. Earthquake mitigation planning in California communities may not be given much attention by planning staff. Planners are often overwhelmed with daily departmental operations and have little time and resources to devote to earthquake mitigation. Results from a survey question on local priority of earthquake mitigation reinforce this suggestion. While priority for earthquake mitigation was higher in California than in the rest of the country, it was considerably lower than local priority for other types of hazards (see Godschalk et al. 1989).

There is also variation in program operation activities. A majority of respondents in California (51.3 percent) reported the presence of an advocate in their jurisdictions, in contrast to 28.2 percent in other states. Earthquake issues are integrated into traditional planning programs more frequently in California, and they are also linked to other local issues more commonly there. The most frequently cited issue linked to earthquake hazards for both community groups is environmental protection. Recreation was the least frequently linked issue mentioned by both groups. Finally, a majority of California respondents (76.8 percent), but a minority (35 percent) of respondents from other states, indicated that the mass media are used to advance earthquake mitigation planning in their jurisdictions.

Some variation also exists in the level of program resources between the two community groups. California communities allocate more planning staff time and budget to earthquake mitigation than communities in other states. The difference in allocation was not great, however. A majority of respondents from both community groups indicated that their jurisdictions allocated less than one hour per week of staff time and less than 1 percent of departmental budgets to earthquake mitigation. However, survey findings indicate a general trend of allocating more staff time and funds for earthquake mitigation. In California almost one in five communities spend a greater percentage of local planning department budget on earthquake mitigation than they did five years ago, while fewer than one in twenty spend less. The change is not as large for earthquake-prone communities in other states, where slightly less than one in ten spend a greater percentage and about one in fifteen spend less.

There are also differences in relationships between mitigation planning program staff and various participants in the political environment of such programs. Contact between program staff and professional engineering associations, private consultants, and local and state agencies is more frequent in California than in other states. Respondents from both state groups indicated infrequent contact with federal agencies. Both groups also rated federal agencies as less responsive to local program needs and concerns than other organizations.

Community mitigation programs are confronted with a wide range of financial, technical, and political obstacles. Lack of financial support from higher levels of government was rated as a very serious obstacle to advancement of local mitigation programs by respondents from both community groups. The obstacle of inadequate maps delineating earthquake hazard areas was also rated as very serious in other states, but only moderately serious in California. Lack of public interest in earthquake hazards is a more serious obstacle to local programs in communities outside of California, but opposition by real estate interests and lack of support from other local government officials pose equally serious obstacles for both groups of communities. Finally, most respondents from both community groups did not consider inadequately trained local staff to deal with earthquake hazards a serious obstacle.

Finally, survey results show that communities in California have larger populations and higher median home values than those in other states. There is also a difference in previous experience with earthquakes. In California, 81.5 percent of respondents indicated that their communities had experienced a damaging earthquake within the last twenty years, compared to 56.9 percent in other states. A majority of California community respondents (55.6 percent) rated their communities' perception of the risk of a major earthquake as high or very high, compared to 31.4 percent in other states. However, respondents in California rated their communities' perception of the ability of the built environment to withstand earthquake forces higher than did respondents in the rest of the country. That is, 39.5 percent of California respondents rated their communities' perception of seismic strength of the built environment to be high or very high, compared to only 12.9 percent for other states. Additionally, of the California communities, 47.6 percent are exposed to four or more seismic-related hazards (e.g., faults, liquefaction, and landslides), compared to 22.5 percent of communities in other states. Almost all of the California communities in the survey are in seismic zone 4, while almost all communities in other states are in seismic zone 3.

8 • ADOPTING PLANNING MEASURES FOR EARTHQUAKE HAZARD MITIGATION

Chapter 7 described and compared contemporary earthquake mitigation planning programs in California and the rest of the nation, focusing on internal factors (interorganizational relationships, program resources, program operations) and the environmental characteristics of the community. The extent to which various planning measures have been adopted for earthquake hazard mitigation was also described. On the basis of survey data used in this description, this chapter identifies internal and external factors of programs that are important in explaining adoption of planning measures in California and all other states. Two basic questions are to be addressed: What is the relative importance of internal factors compared to external factors? To what degree do factors that influence adoption differ between communities in California and those in other states?[1]

A series of regression analyses was used to examine the survey data.[2]

1. As discussed in chapter 7, while programs in communities throughout the country are at different stages of evolution, those in California are far ahead of the rest of the nation (Scholl 1986). Given this difference in development, separate analyses of two groups of survey communities allow us to examine more carefully factors associated with local response to the seismic threat than would examination of pooled data of communities in all states.

2. Due to a large number of independent variables, a data reduction strategy was necessary. This involved two steps. The first step was to enter independent variables into four regression equations for each of the two survey groups of communities. Four equations were required because there were too many variables for a single regression equation. Each equation contained all of the variables of each of the four categories of independent variables (see Appendix A). That is, all variables describing community external environment were entered into one equation, all variables describing program resources were entered into another, and so on.

The dependent variable is the number of earthquake mitigation measures used by the community.[3] The independent variables in the regression analyses were grouped into the four categories of factors that influence community response: the internal factors—interorganizational relations, program resources, and program operations—and external environment factors. (Measures of both dependent and independent variables are presented in detail in Appendix B.) Regression coefficients were standardized to allow variables within each survey group to be compared for the relative magnitude of influence on community adoption of planning measures. Unstandardized coefficients allow variables between the survey groups to be compared (see Pedhazur 1982, 247–49).

FACTORS RELATED TO ADOPTION OF PLANNING MEASURES

The independent variables performed well in explaining variations in community adoption of planning measures (table 8-1).[4] The regression equations predicting the number of planning measures adopted for both survey groups of communities were statistically significant as indicated by F values. Furthermore, the equations explained 31.2 percent of the

---

The second step of the analysis involved entering all variables that meaningfully contributed to explaining variations in community response into a regression equation. Those variables were included whose t values were statistically significant at the .1 level. This procedure controls across categories for the influence of all factors with moderately strong relationships to community response.

3. Because our primary objective was to determine why some communities are doing more to mitigate earthquake hazards than others, the dependent variable consisted only of the number of locally adopted planning measures that were specifically enacted to mitigate earthquake hazards (as indicated by the survey questionnaire) and that are not required for adoption by state mandates. Of the twenty-one measures listed in table 7-2, five (building codes, zoning ordinances, subdivision ordinances, comprehensive plans, and capital improvement programs) can be used to some extent for earthquake mitigation but are typically enacted for nonhazard reasons. To identify which of the measures are required for adoption in California, we referred to a report by the California Seismic Safety Commission (1986). Similarly, we referred to the directory of state building codes (NCSBCS 1988) to identify those states besides California that have mandated local adoption of seismic building codes. None of these states require local adoption of other types of measures.

4. The dependent variable, the number of adopted planning measures, has been used in numerous studies (see Burby and French 1981, 1985; Godschalk et al. 1989; Hansen and Hirsch 1983). Indeed, its acceptance as a measure is one important reason we chose to examine it. However, as discussed in chapter 7 (n. 2), our study seems to have uncovered some flaws in the measure. Problems are obvious, but no clear substitute exists. Our use of the measure should enable clear comparisons between our study and others. Further, it would seem that the same measurement problems should be present in California and other states. Therefore, while we should be cautious about statements concerning the degree of acceptance, conclusions about relative differences among states and relations between independent and dependent variables are less problematic.

Table 8.1 Factors Related to Local Adoption of Planning Measures for Earthquake Mitigation

Factors by Category	Standardized Beta Weights (Unstandardized)	
	California	All Other States
External environment		
Past experience	—	.07 (.07)
Number of seismic related hazards	.21 (.27)**	.22 (.19)**
Interorganizational relations		
Extent of contact with organizations	.06 (.13)	—
Responsiveness of other organizations to local program needs	.20 (.22)*	.38 (.34)***
Program operations		
Presence of an advocate	—	.20 (.68)**
Integration of seismic program formulation with conventional comprehensive planning	—	.29 (.84)***
Linkage of seismic issues to other local issues	.29 (.32)**	.18 (.94)**
Program resources		
Staff hours allocated to seismic safety	—	.12 (.18)
Adequacy of maps that delineate seismic hazards	—	.06 (.07)
R^2 for equation	.312	.407
F ratio	8.735***	7.376***

* $p < .1$.
** $p < .05$.
*** $p < .01$.

variance in response behavior for California and 40.7 percent for all other states, these percentages are quite good for this type of research. In contrast, Godschalk *et al.* (1989), for example, were able to explain only 21.3 percent of the variation in adoption of planning measures for hurricane mitigation in their national study.

Interorganizational Relations. Two factors focus on the relationship between local planning programs and their political environment. The first is the frequency of contact between local program staff and federal, state, and local organizations. We expect that interorganizational contact in a policy-making arena has a positive impact on community response to earthquake hazards. Findings, however, do not support this expectation. As indicated in table 8-1, interorganizational contact has an insignificant impact on local adoption of earthquake mitigation measures.

In contrast, the second factor, perceived responsiveness of federal, state, and other local organizations to local mitigation efforts, has a much more important impact on local response for both groups. This finding supports the Drabek et al. (1983) interpretation of interorganizational relations. That is, frequency of contact suggests nothing about the content or perceived usefulness of contact. For example, highly technical reports from higher levels of government may not foster local understanding of the nature of seismic risk.

Program Resources. Program resources are the resources available for initiation and adoption of local earthquake mitigation programs. The forms of support discussed here include amount of planning staff time devoted to earthquake hazards and adequacy of maps that delineate earthquake hazards.

Staff time was expected to have a positive impact on local response. More time allows staff to devote greater attention to activities required for initiating and adopting seismic mitigation measures. The results for staff time, however, were not consistent with our expectation. Table 8-1 indicates that this factor has an insignificant effect on local adoption in communities from both California and other states.[5]

Our expectation concerning the perceived adequacy of maps that delineate seismic hazards was also not supported. We anticipated that adequate maps would enhance the capacity of public officials to understand the causes of earthquake risk and to clarify the impact of various mitigation policies. Mushkatel and Nigg (1987b), for example, found that the presence of seismic zonation maps contributed to raising public officials' awareness of risk and drew attention to the need for action. Our finding, however, probably reflects that while accurate maps raise awareness of risk, awareness is not necessarily translated into significant action.

Program Operation. The procedural aspects of a planning program are program operation. Factors discussed here include the role of seismic safety advocates and linkage of earthquake hazards to comprehensive planning programs and other local concerns.

The presence of advocates of earthquake hazard mitigation was expected to have a positive effect on local adoption of mitigation measures. The results only partially supported this expectation. While this factor significantly influenced adoption of mitigation measures in communities outside California, it had little impact on communities in California. This difference can probably be attributed to the fact that advocates tend to play a strong role in localities where mitigation planning is a new or

5. An important limitation of the staff hours variable should be noted. The survey did not differentiate between staff time devoted to formulation and enactment of seismic mitigation measures and implementation of such measures. Consequently, staff time may not be an accurate indicator of local adoption.

emergent function (Lambright 1984). In contrast, communities with more established programs are more likely to adopt additional mitigation measures with relatively less change in the status quo. Consequently, compared to communities in other states advocates in California communities may not have been as important at the time the survey data were collected.

A key determinant of adoption of mitigation measures is integration of natural hazard issues, which are traditionally of low political salience, with well-established and politically acceptable ways of doing things. It was expected, therefore, that seismic issues would progress on local agendas when they were integrated with conventional local planning activities. This expectation was only partially supported. Integration had no significant influence in California, but it played an important role in communities of other states.

This difference may be due to California's requirement that communities develop and incorporate several mitigation measures into their comprehensive plans. Requiring integration may deemphasize local involvement and commitment. While preparation of the state-mandated seismic safety element stimulated seismic policy activity and involvement in the Palo Alto case study (see chapter 4), previous research based on thirteen California case communities does not support this finding. Wyner and Mann (1986) found that although California communities integrated seismic safety elements into their comprehensive plans, local officials rated these elements as low in importance in fostering additional community mitigation action. Other states, however, have no such requirements. If communities in these states, like Salt Lake County and Charleston (see chapters 3 and 5), integrated seismic program activities with conventional comprehensive planning activities, the integration effort probably originated at the local level. Planners, therefore, were likely to perceive such efforts as important.

It was expected that linkage of seismic safety issues to one or more other local issues, such as environmental protection, economic development, or recreation, would have a positive impact on adoption of mitigation measures. As one of a group of issues, or in some cases as a tool to be used for very different goals (e.g., stopping new development for purposes of environmental protection or encouraging renovation and reinforcement of buildings in declining downtowns), the earthquake issue can be raised on political agendas. Table 8-1 shows that our hypothesis is supported for communities in California and in other states.

External Environment. As discussed, external environment refers to the conditions in which a local earthquake mitigation program must operate. Of the original ten external factors considered in the survey data (see Appendix A), only the number of earthquake-related hazards was found to be significant. This finding was consistent with our expectations. That is, the greater the number of hazards present in the community, the more likely it is that a greater variety of mitigation measures will be required. Communities that are exposed to only ground shaking, for example, might require a seismic building code ordinance, but communities exposed to ground shaking, landslides, and faults might require both building code and land use controls.[6]

As indicated in table 8-1, disaster experience reached the second regression equation but was not significant. This finding does not uphold previous research, which generally maintains that disaster experience has a strong positive impact on adoption of mitigation measures (cf. Godschalk et al. 1989; Drabek et al. 1983; Wyner and Mann 1986). This suggests that while a disastrous event may provide a window of opportunity for adoption of mitigation measures, the window can close quickly during the immediate disaster aftermath with no ensuing adoption of mitigation measures. The Palo Alto and Salt Lake County case data and other research findings (Alesch and Petak 1986; Burby and French 1985) reinforce this interpretation. Alesch and Petak (1986), for example, argue that Los Angeles did not adopt a structural retrofit ordinance after a series of major earthquake events over a fifty-year period because local officials did not have a readily available solution that was both technically feasible and politically acceptable to various interest groups. Thus, at least for these data, past experience has little influence on local adoption activities.

CONCLUSIONS

Two general questions were addressed in this chapter: (1) What is the importance of internal factors compared to external environment characteristics? and (2) To what degree do factors that influence adoption differ between communities in California and those of all other states?

The first question concerned the relative effects of internal factors, or activities that planners and other decision makers can use to advance planning programs, and community environment characteristics. Overall survey findings indicated that internal factors had an important influence on local efforts to adopt planning measures for earthquake mitigation. In contrast, community environment characteristics played a less important explanatory role. Thus, efforts to advance local earthquake mitigation activities through enhancement of planning process actions have a relatively substantial potential for success.

6. Seismic zone classification (see fig. 1-5) was originally considered an independent variable. However, the variable was not used in the regression analysis due to lack of variation. Of the 82 communities surveyed in California, 81 are in seismic zone 4, and 2 of the 120 communities in other states are in seismic zone 4.

This finding is significant, particularly in regard to several studies in planning and organizational decision making. These studies contend that environments dictate organizational actions and that planners and decision makers can do little to affect organizational responses. That is, decision makers are rigidly constrained by their contexts (Aldrich 1979; McKelvey 1982). This research indicates that, at least for the survey data presented here, this was not the case. Decision makers can have a strong positive influence on responses.

The second question addressed differences in causes of community adoption of planning measures between California communities and those in other states. There were two main differences. First, the presence of advocates was a more important cause of adoption in communities outside California. This difference is likely due to the fact that advocates have a stronger influence in communities outside California, where mitigation efforts are new and emergent. Second, integration of seismic program formulation activities with more conventional comprehensive planning activities was more important among communities outside California. Because communities outside California are not required by the state to undertake seismic mitigation activities, efforts to integrate seismic mitigation with conventional planning probably originated at the local level. Thus respondents are likely to consider such efforts as more important than state-mandated initiatives.

9 • CONCLUSIONS AND RECOMMENDATIONS

Worldwide, earthquakes represent a tremendous threat to life and property. Recent earthquake events in the Soviet Union, the United States, and elsewhere illustrate vividly the potential for devastation posed by these phenomena. At the same time, however, action can be taken to reduce the vulnerability of both people and property to future seismic events. Using data from local case studies and from mail and telephone surveys, this book has presented a documentation and evaluation of many of the more promising and successful efforts aimed at hazard mitigation. In particular, we have examined the extent to which different seismic mitigation tools and techniques are being used by localities around the United States, and we have evaluated in considerable detail the seismic mitigation policy in three specific locales: Salt Lake County, Palo Alto, and Charleston. This chapter summarizes the principal study findings, with special emphasis on evaluating the conceptual framework introduced in chapter 2, and presents recommendations for establishing and improving local earthquake mitigation programs.

CONCLUSIONS

The Status of Local Seismic Mitigation Practice

A host of tools, techniques, and programs, including disaster preparedness and recovery actions, could be adopted by local governments and could greatly decrease the potential losses from a major earthquake. The focus of this book, however, has been on the techniques of development management or land use management. It is clear that the vulnerability of people and property to earthquakes can be substantially reduced *before* a disastrous seismic event occurs. Building codes and seismic construction standards have proven effective in California and elsewhere. Localities can adopt seismic retrofit ordinances aimed at reducing the vulnerability of unreinforced masonry and other high-risk structures. Local comprehensive plans and land use controls can direct development and public facilities away from high-risk locations, such as high-slope regions subject to landsliding, areas of high liquefaction potential, and surface fault-rupture zones. Localities can adopt information dissemination provisions that seek to inform developers and housing consumers about the nature and extent of seismic risks. Land use and development incentives, such as Palo Alto's density bonus system, can encourage more seismically sound buildings and patterns of development. Ultimately, the most effective mitigation strategy is *avoidance* of the hazard in the first place.

For many localities in earthquake-prone areas there are, however, few vacant and undeveloped areas. The best opportunity for substantial mitigation and land use change in these areas may be the one presented by the need for recovery after an actual earthquake. Recognizing that earthquakes will occur in the future, some localities are developing in advance of the disaster recovery or reconstruction plans that will guide postdisaster relocation and redevelopment. The efforts of Los Angeles, for example, in developing such a reconstruction capability are encouraging.

This study has provided a national assessment of the extent to which local governments in high-risk regions have adopted seismic mitigation programs. Our results show a mixed picture. California localities have adopted and implemented a wide variety of mitigation measures, from zoning and development control to facility-siting and information dissemination strategies. Localities in other states, however, have been considerably less ready to adopt seismically oriented development and land use management tools and techniques. While mitigation activity is on the rise in other seismically vulnerable states, our findings suggest that there is room for considerable progress in the vulnerable states of the East and Midwest and also elsewhere. Even in California, many localities consider seismic risks in only the most rudimentary manner, and substantial opportunities exist for better integrating earthquake mitigation into development and land use decision making. The feasibility of such local programs will depend on a variety of political and other factors; our study has provided substantial insight into the political dynamics of seismic mitigation policy making.

The Nature of Seismic Mitigation Politics

Local adoption of seismic mitigation policy is difficult politically because it often has the effect of placing additional economic or regulatory burdens on particular interest groups, such as building owners and land developers, and because the *benefits*, in the form of reductions in loss of life and property are *uncertain* and occur in the *future*. From the point of view of a local elected official, *seismic safety*, if it is to be appreciated at all by the electorate, will be appreciated by *future* constituents, perhaps many years after the official has left office. Moreover, while the costs associated with mitigation programs are generally discrete and manifest, the benefits are more diffuse and do not attach to particular people. It is much more difficult for constituents to *see public safety* than the more visible and tangible results of, for example, construction of a new road or a new library.

Because earthquakes are low-probability catastrophic events, mitigation is likely to be eclipsed in importance, for both public officials and the general public, by more immediate and pressing public concerns. It is generally much easier to elicit a sense of concern from public officials and citizens for issues such as crime, air and water pollution, solid waste disposal, and traffic congestion. These are issues that affect the public on an almost daily basis.

Adaptive Mitigation: Responding to Stakeholder Interests

While adoption and effective implementation of seismic mitigation are politically difficult, our research illustrates clearly that it is possible to formulate acceptable and technically effective mitigation measures in the face of political obstacles. Case study findings suggest that adoption of such measures can be promoted by identifying different stakeholder values and searching for mitigation measures, and packages of measures, that are responsive to these values. Innovation, adaptation, and creative compromise can overcome major objections of stakeholders (Alesch and Petak 1986).

This type of adaptation was strongly evident in two of the communities studied and suggests the importance of *customizing* mitigation measures to take account of different stakeholder and interest group views in the community (see table 9-1). Palo Alto changed from a largely regulatory approach to one based on incentives and information dissemination. Salt Lake County changed from a strategy of optional seismic area review to one that includes both regulatory and informational measures.

For mitigation measures to prevail in the local political arena requires the involvement of important stakeholders in the community. This occurred, for instance, in the Palo Alto case through a citizens' committee

Table 9.1 Mitigation Strategies—Initial and Adapted

Type of Measure	Salt Lake County, Utah		Palo Alto, Calif.		Charleston, S.C.	
	Initial	*Adapted*	*Initial*	*Adapted*	*Initial*	*Adapted*
Incentive	—	—	—	Development density bonus	—	—
Informational	—	Geological reports on seismic vulnerability of existing structures; real estate disclosure for new developments	Engineering report on seismic vulnerability of six classes of buildings	Engineering report on seismic vulnerability of three classes of buildings	—	Public awareness technology transfer programs
Regulatory	Optional application of land use controls	Mandated application of land use controls	Strong building requirements	—	—	Seismic building requirements for new development

Note: — indicates measure not present.

on seismic safety composed of building owners, architects, and representatives of the business and development communities, among other major stakeholders.[1] Through this committee mechanism stakeholder views and values were identified and clarified and compromise positions were developed. The mitigation proposals generated by this committee held political credibility for having incorporated these different stakeholder positions. Our case studies indicate that inflexible attempts by seismic proponents to push initiations without such a process of stakeholder consultation are not likely to prevail. Indeed, this is precisely what happened in the Palo Alto case before the appointment of the citizens' committee.

The local case studies identified a variety of different stakeholders, often with quite different attitudes and perspectives on seismic hazards and the need for seismic mitigation. These different perspectives involved both factual and value disagreements. Factual disagreements existed over the magnitude and seriousness of the seismic threat, and the likely efficacy and economic effects of different mitigation programs under consideration. Basic value disagreements included, among others: whether the risk from earthquakes was sufficiently great to justify major expenses to reduce or mitigate it (some local stakeholders argued that social resources would be better spent making highways safer or discouraging the use of cigarettes); the extent of actual risk reduction believed to be warranted (e.g., preventing building collapse versus preventing significant building damage); whether decisions about seismic risks were legitimately in the public domain or should be left to private individuals and businesses; and who should pay most of the costs associated with seismic hazard reduction (e.g., building owners versus the general public). While factual disagreements can be overcome to some extent through dialogue and information dissemination, many value disagreements cannot. The mitigation case studies examined in the book reflect *creative compromises between these different community perspectives*. Thus, in these communities the development of acceptable mitigation programs occurred through an *interactive learning process* in which major stakeholders were involved in the formulation of, and ultimate compromise on, specific mitigation proposals. The cases

1. It could be argued that caution should be exercised in applying the Palo Alto experience to other localities because the provisions of the retrofit strategy were "watered down" (i.e., changed from mandatory type to incentive and informational types) to achieve political feasibility for successful adoption and implementation. Indeed, while there are numerous examples of such watering down that have led to ineffective mitigation efforts (see, for example, Wyner and Mann 1986), the Palo Alto experience (see chapter 4) does not adhere to this argument. On the contrary, in communities like Palo Alto, powerful private interest groups offer strong political opposition to retrofit, the Palo Alto approach perhaps should be considered the most effective available strategy. As discussed in chapter 4, the ordinance has been effective; almost all owners of targeted hazardous buildings have either undertaken retrofit or are in the process of doing so.

further suggest that the future is not *planned* so much as it needs to be negotiated, processed, and politicked to achieve effective mitigation (Kartez and Lindell 1987).

Factors Influencing the Mitigation Planning Process

A primary objective of the study was to identify and determine the relative importance of different social, economic, and other factors that might influence the local seismic mitigation process. As suggested earlier in figure 2-1, a variety of factors might influence the adoption and implementation of seismic policy. We have found it useful to distinguish between external and internal factors. *External* factors are essentially outside the local planning process and largely beyond the direct control of planners or local officials (earthquakes and other focusing events, social and economic conditions, and political culture). *Internal* factors represent process activities that can be manipulated locally (stakeholder interaction, role of advocates, linkage to other local issues, allocation of resources) and can be modified and reinforced at the federal and state levels. As indicated in table 9-2, we found that both external and internal factors exercised substantial influence on local mitigation policy making. To determine the level of influence of each of these factors, an intercoder reliability procedure was used.[2]

Problem Recognition, Windows of Opportunity, Political Culture, and Socioeconomic Conditions. Among the external factors often attributed importance in hazard mitigation policy making are recognition of an earthquake problem, opening of windows of opportunity (i.e., usually from an earthquake event), local political culture, and local socioeconomic conditions. We found in our study that these factors were important influences but not necessarily the *most* important or determining factors.

The case studies indicated that the chance of gaining adoption of significant local mitigation increases with an increased local understanding and recognition of the potential effects of an earthquake. All stakeholders,

2. The degree of influence of each factor (listed in table 9-2) in mitigation planning was derived from qualitative interview and documentary data (see chapter 1 for a discussion of case study data collection methods). A rating for each factor was determined according to the following procedure. Using coded interview and documentary data, each of the two authors independently rated each of the factors on a four-point scale: high, moderate, low, and not present and no effect. When we agreed on the rating, we used that consensual judgment. When there were disagreements, we resolved the differences by creating a midpoint value. For example, if a factor was rated as high by one researcher and moderate by the other, we then assigned the factor a moderate–high rating. Of the sixty ratings (twenty per case community), there were thirteen disagreements. In no instances, however, did the differences in ratings exceed a value of 1. That is, we did not have an instance in which one factor was rated, for example, high by one researcher and low or not present by the other.

Table 9.2 Factors Affecting Earthquake Mitigation Planning Process—Initial and Current

Factors	Salt Lake County, Utah		Palo Alto, Calif.		Charleston, S.C.	
	Initial	*Current*	*Initial*	*Current*	*Initial*	*Current*
External						
Degree of public regarding political culture	Low	Low	High	High	Low	Low–moderate
Presence of window of opportunity	—	Moderate	—	Moderate	Low	Low–moderate
Stakeholder problem recognition						
• Public officials	Low	Moderate	Low–moderate	Moderate–high	Low	Moderate
• Citizens	Low	Low–moderate	Low	Low–moderate	Low	Low–moderate
• Real estate interests	Low	Low	Low	Moderate	Low	Low
Support from socioeconomic conditions	Moderate	Low	High	High	Low–moderate	Low–moderate
Internal						
Availability of resources	Low	High	Low	High	Low	Low–moderate
Interorganizational coordination and communication	Low	Moderate	Low	High	Low	Moderate
Linkage to established planning activities	Moderate	Moderate–high	Moderate–high	Moderate–high	Low	Low
Presence of advocate	High	High	High	High	High	High

Note: — indicates factor is not present and has no effect.

even those who may be economically affected by mitigation measures, are more likely to support such measures when they are better educated about the potential hazard. In the case communities, increased recognition of a hazard problem was the result of several factors. Sometimes stakeholders' attention was influenced by certain *systematic indicators* of risk. Such indicators might be studies that produced detailed maps of earthquake hazards and identified structurally inadequate buildings. These types of studies often enhanced the capacity of public officials to better understand the causes of seismic risk and clarify the impact of mitigation policy. A second reason for increased recognition of the earthquake threat was the occurrence of a focusing event (e.g., earthquakes or related disaster events) that resulted in elevating the importance and priority local officials and stakeholders gave to the seismic threat. Such events were influential in both Salt Lake County (the Borah Peak earthquake) and Palo Alto (the Coalinga earthquake). While these events did not cause damage locally, they contributed to a sense of the importance of earthquake mitigation and enhanced long-term local salience of the seismic issue to local stakeholders.

While a major geological event can heighten long-term awareness and problem recognition, it can also suddenly open a window of opportunity and cause the seismic hazard to be immediately placed at or near the top of the agenda for action. Once the window opens, however, it does not stay open long. Moreover, local officials must be ready to take advantage of the temporary sense of urgency. Case studies revealed, however, that while public officials gave considerable attention to alternative mitigation proposals, the window quickly closed and adoption of mitigation measures did not occur. The reason for not adopting such measures was the absence of an acceptable mitigation solution that was readily available at the time of the crisis. In Salt Lake County accurate maps depicting seismic hazards were not available, making seismic area impact reviews technically impractical. In Charleston and Palo Alto the key reason for failure of adoption was the absence of a politically acceptable strategy.

Our study agrees with previous studies in attributing importance to the local political culture and socioeconomic conditions (Godschalk et al. 1989; Wyner and Mann 1986). While again not necessarily the most important or determining factors, these factors can make adoption and effective implementation of mitigation measures easier or more difficult, depending upon their dimensions. Clearly, the progressive political culture of Palo Alto made the formulation and adoption of a unique mitigation program there easier. The conservative political culture of South Carolina, with its predisposition against government regulation of land and property, clearly makes adoption of seismic mitigation there more difficult. Socioeconomic conditions have similar contextual effects. The strength of

Palo Alto's building and development industry (and the especially strong market for downtown space) made the adoption of its program more politically acceptable. There were few fears that such new mitigation requirements would negatively affect the city's booming commercial sector. Interestingly, in Salt Lake County the dramatic downturn in the regional economy seems to have enhanced the political feasibility of its program by reducing the political opposition of the development community (many of the larger developers had apparently left the region).

Advocates, Coordination and Communication, Resources, and Policy Linkage. While external factors are important in setting the policy context and may serve either to facilitate or to obstruct the adoption of local mitigation, they are not determinative. Our case study analyses suggest that *internal* factors are often more important. We found that especially important in explaining local mitigation were the presence of credible advocates, coordination and communication among key participants, availability of resources, and linkage to other issues. Even where external supports, such as a progressive political culture or a strong local economy, are missing, internal factors may compensate. Moreover, our conclusions suggest that even with supportive external factors, advancement of local seismic mitigation is difficult without the presence of these internal factors. Survey findings discussed in chapter 8 reinforce these impressions. Survey results showed that internal factors had a strong positive influence, with external factors playing a less important explanatory role.

These findings indicate, then, that public officials and others interested in promoting seismic mitigation can have a strong positive influence on local response to seismic hazards. They have significant theoretical and practical implications. Theoretically, they provide empirical support for a *contingent* approach to the planning process generally (Bryson 1983 and Christensen 1985) and hazards reduction specifically (Kartez 1984). That is, the context within which planning occurs influences the choice of measures to achieve desirable outcomes. Practically, those interested in advancing hazards mitigation planning must account for the context of planning in tailoring appropriate strategies to increase the likelihood of successful mitigation responses.

A second theoretical implication is that public organizational actions are not rigidly constrained by their contexts. While several studies in planning and organizational decision making contend that environments dictate organizational actions (Aldrich 1979 and McKelvey 1982), findings reported in this study indicate that this was not the case. The practical implication is that planners and other public officials can have a strong influence on local response to hazards.

Furthermore, the findings suggest certain recommendations about formulating and advancing seismic mitigation policy. These are presented below, beginning with recommendations for local jurisdictions and then recommendations for higher jurisdictional levels, including state and federal policy for enhancing local capacity to promote mitigation.

RECOMMENDATIONS

Local Actions for Advancing Mitigation

Promote mitigation strategies appropriate to local seismic risks. The design of mitigation strategies should be adapted to the particular seismic hazard conditions that exist in the community and to the opportunities that may exist for public intervention to reduce these risks. For instance, seismic faulting in California is different from faulting in Utah, suggesting the need for a different type of mitigation tool. While a uniform fault setback requirement works in California, the variable nature of faulting in Utah makes such a measure inappropriate. In the case of South Carolina, there is no surface faulting, making fault zone setback requirements inappropriate. As a further example, some localities have high-slope lands subject to landsliding and mass movement during earthquakes, suggesting in turn the need for particular measures (e.g., slope-density matrix), while other localities may not have such hazards. In some communities seismic hazard areas may already be heavily built up (such as in the Los Angeles case), making reconstruction and relocation planning, as well as seismic retrofit, more appropriate mitigation strategies than they are in communities that have large expanses of undeveloped land. Each locality has a somewhat unique set of hazard circumstances requiring a different mitigation strategy.

Integrate seismic consideration into local planning and land use management; link seismic hazard issues with other well-established issues. The feasibility and acceptability of seismic mitigation is enhanced considerably if it is *linked* to other well-established local issues. In particular, this study suggests the potential effectiveness of incorporating consideration of seismic risks into local land use and development management. Most local governments are already undertaking some degree of land use planning or management, and incorporation of seismic hazards usually does not involve creation of a new separate policy initiation, but incremental adjustments to an established program. This type of linkage might occur in numerous ways. For instance, the acquisition of hazard-zone open space may not be politically or economically feasible when seismic mitigation objectives are considered alone, but it becomes feasible when other local issues, such as the need for recreational facilities like parks, are considered as well. Land use controls that reduce development density in hazardous areas may be difficult to justify solely on seismic risk reduction grounds, but, again, they may be feasible when other local issues (e.g., preserving visual quality astride a fault precipice) are addressed as well.

This study provided a number of examples of how seismic mitigation has been incorporated into local land use and development management. In Salt Lake County, seismic mitigation issues were integrated into the conventional and well-established subdivision and zoning permit review process. In Palo Alto, seismic mitigation was a major component of the city's general plan, and incentives for mitigation were incorporated into local growth and development controls.

Involve major stakeholders in the development of mitigation strategies and search for creative solutions responsive to these different interests. Successful advancement of mitigation strategies locally requires sensitivity to local stakeholder values and preferences and the ability to develop compromises that balance a range of stakeholder concerns. For instance, the initial stringent regulatory approach to building retrofit in Palo Alto was rejected due to strong opposition from real estate interests. Only after much negotiation and compromise was an acceptable incentive and informational approach developed that addressed the concerns of building owners and occupants without causing a fatal erosion of local support. Our research suggests that even in the face of tremendous political opposition, creative solutions can be found that respond to the concerns and reservations of various stakeholders in the community.

The political acceptability of local seismic mitigation depends on the direct involvement of all major community stakeholders. Such a process, like that undertaken in Palo Alto through its citizens' Seismic Hazard Committee, not only facilitates the discovery of acceptable compromises but adds substantially to the political credibility of the resulting proposals. In the case of Palo Alto, its seismic ordinance was politically acceptable in large part because it reflected the recommendations of a committee representing major community stakeholders.

Build communication and relationship networks. Effective hazard reduction policy is most likely to be enacted where communication among people and organizations is frequent and sustained. Such communication nurtures good relationships. Communication and relationship networks are delicate bridges over which ideas can travel, information can be exchanged, perspectives can be shared, and values can be clarified. There is more opportunity for bargaining and compromise, and the chances of adoption of an acceptable policy increase.

Sometimes relationships must be built from scratch. Uncertain ones must be strengthened. A key requirement of this strategy is assuring that information is communicated in a form that is understandable by those without a technical background. Simply put, when information is too technical for the audience, it can't be used.

Effective communication and relationship-building activities can take a variety of forms, from workshops that bring together producers of information (scientist, engineers, and legal specialists) with users of information (policy makers, developers, and the general public) to regular reporting of research findings during local planning staff meetings and through the media. The efforts of Salt Lake County planning staff to establish cooperative relationships with community councils appear to be a step in the right direction in this regard. Another positive step was the creation of the Palo Alto citizens' Seismic Hazard Committee. Committee members, including city building inspection staff and developers, became informed about the technicalities of retrofit, exchanged views on various alternative solutions, and negotiated an acceptable mitigation strategy.

Cultivate and support advocates. This recommendation assumes that some people within a given planning and policy arena wish to be involved in activities that give them an opportunity to share their views, arguments, knowledge, and values with others. They in turn persuade others to participate and to support a given policy issue.

A variety of activities can put this strategy to use. One would be to identify those people who have a strong commitment to earthquake hazard reduction and who are members of organizations whose participation and support are desired. These people need to be supplied with up-to-date information on relevant policy issues and encouraged to tell what they know to people they typically associate with. Another activity would be to convene mitigation advocates occasionally. When people with similar points of view are brought together, their positions and attendant arguments are reinforced. Finally, advocates should be given opportunities for public exposure whenever possible. They should be invited to give presentations at conferences and workshops and encouraged to convey their message to the general public through the mass media and public hearings.

Promote involvement in information-seeking activities. This recommendation would both expand the current information base for public policy decision making regarding seismic safety and encourage active involvement in information-seeking efforts of the principal users (local government officials) and interest groups (developers and building owners) affected by public decisions. It would involve ongoing assessment of, among other things, alternative land use planning measures in high-risk zones and new alternative building technologies that minimize occupant risk (e.g., structural reinforcement techniques). Such an assessment would also entail review of expected losses and attendant costs and benefits (loss reduction) of each alternative.

Because technical data derived from this assessment process are helpful and necessary, the principal users and interest group representatives must be able to understand and use this data in voicing their concerns regarding public policy decisions. Hence, a key requirement to the success of this recommendation is active participation of affected groups in information seeking. Activities that give people and their organizations an opportunity to seek information lead to greater political support for mitigation policy making and greatly increase the chances for political compromise and acceptance of innovations. Through participation such groups also become more knowledgeable about the potential consequences of seismic risks and the impacts of alternative mitigation plans and policies. Ultimately, adopted plans and policies are more responsive to the specific concerns of these groups. A successful example of active involvement in information-seeking activities by a wide range of interest groups is the citizens' Seismic Hazard Committee of Palo Alto.

Be prepared to take advantage of disastrous events. The occurrence of an earthquake, close by or in another part of the world, often seems to focus the attention of elected officials, community stakeholders, and the general public on a seismic threat. The occurrence of such an event can help to create a more supportive political climate for local seismic mitigation. Local proponents of mitigation should be prepared to take advantage of such events and to use the knowledge and imagery gained from them to promote seismic mitigation locally.

The Coalinga earthquake occurred during the period in which the Palo Alto citizens' Seismic Committee was meeting, and advocates there presented photographic slides of the damages and otherwise sought to impress upon local stakeholders and decision makers that similar events could happen in their own community. In Salt Lake County, one local seismic advocate who visited the Soviet Union after the Armenian earthquake has been effective in arguing that similar damage levels could occur in Utah (again with the aid of photographs), further heightening a sense of local concern. Such dramatic events capture the attention of the public and may help to elevate, for a time, seismic mitigation on the local public agenda.

While a major earthquake event may increase awareness and the sense of importance given to seismic safety locally, these efforts tend to dissipate over time. Local advocates should prepare to take advantage of the more favorable political climate that may exist after such events. If advocates have an acceptable mitigation solution ready, they should push for its adoption. On the other hand, if a particular local initiative is not feasible, the occurrence of a major earthquake or other disaster even may provide an opportunity to resuscitate an initiative that is feasible.

Select and combine recommendations. These recommendations are complimentary and overlapping. They can be used independently or in combination, depending upon the extent of involvement desired, the amount of time and resources permitted, and the difficulty in achieving consensus among alternative solutions. Building communication and relationship networks is likely to make the other recommendations more effective. Joint inquiry and information gathering is likely to increase the possibility that mitigation measures will be responsive to stakeholder concerns, and that those involved will become more effective at advocating hazard reduction issues. Cultivating and supporting advocates may make it easier to link hazard reduction issues to other well-established issues and to take advantage of disastrous events. Linking hazard issues to other issues can enhance efforts to develop acceptable mitigation strategies. Used together, the recommendations have a greater potential than any single one has for producing support and participation in formulating effective mitigation strategies.

Funding to implement these recommendations is crucial. While federal and state funding should not be overlooked, funds could be derived from the beneficiaries of mitigation programs. As discussed in chapter 6, earthquake-prone localities can establish, for example, special hazard assessment districts or impact fees to fund mitigation. Local funds could also be obtained through the imposition of impact fees on developers and subdivisions. Impact fees are fees that local governments charge new developments for a variety of costs associated with their development, including sewer and water facilities, drainage, public libraries, and parks and open space. A portion of the impact fees could be used to fund a variety of seismic mitigation activities.

The Federal Government's Role in Supporting Local Mitigation

While the primary focus of this study has been on *local* mitigation efforts, it is clear to us that higher levels of government have significant roles in promoting seismic safety. Federal policy makers could undertake some combination of three general types of action to stimulate local seismic mitigation programs: (1) substantially increase existing mobilization efforts that induce local attention to earthquakes; (2) place greater emphasis on the role of nongovernmental interests in promoting existing limited regulatory effort; and (3) shift to a stronger set of mandates that might be part of a general regulatory program (May 1991). The first type of action was exemplified in this study by the U.S. Geological Survey's effort to mobilize local support in Utah through provision of credible information about seismic risks. Products of this effort in Salt Lake County included detailed maps of seismic hazards, ongoing development of an automated geographic information system for risk analysis, and the funding of a county geologist to provide technical assistance in translating hazard information. The positive outcome of the mobilization approach was demonstrated by the adoption of the seismic area review ordinance in Salt Lake County.

Caution, however, should be exercised in considering the efficacy of this approach. As suggested by the study conclusions discussed previously, credible information may not be a sufficient basis for mobilizing local response. Other factors, particularly those that reinforce organizational intention and capacity, are crucial. Furthermore, as indicated in chapter 7, only 20 percent of California communities, where very good maps of seismic hazards are available, reported inadequate maps as a somewhat serious or very serious barrier to local mitigation efforts. The most serious obstacles reported were lack of local political support and lack of public interest in seismic safety. May (1991, 17) notes that the real problem with federal mobilization efforts in Utah and other regions "is as much one of 'needing users' of information as it is of understanding 'user needs.' " May further cautions that the federal resources required for the mobilization approach would have to be substantially greater than the $600 million spent over the past decade under the National Earthquake Hazards Reduction Program.

The second type of action the federal government can undertake in stimulating local response entails substantially increasing emphasis on the nongovernmental interests (e.g., insurers, reinsurers, lending institutions, and professional associations) that undertake limited regulatory activities. These interests have often been active in seismic regulation outside the governmental arena. For example, a lending institution required that a major hotel in Charleston be designed to account for seismic forces before granting a loan to complete the structure. Another example in South Carolina is the role that nongovernmental building code–writing authorities played in integrating seismic design standards in model codes. Such model codes are used by states and localities when they adopt a building code. Thus, strengthening the roles of nongovernmental interests in seismic mitigation policy making would provide more opportunities both to induce localities to undertake mitigation practices and to forge public and private partnerships in mitigating seismic risks.

A noteworthy weakness, however, in the limited regulatory approach regarding code-writing authorities is the difficulties in state and local government seismic code adoption and enforcement. As evidenced in South Carolina, there can be significant resistance to adoption of building code standards at both the state and local levels. Also, there were insufficient technical capabilities, particularly in small localities, to enforce seismic code provisions within local building and inspection departments.

A third action the federal government could take involves shifting to a general regulatory approach that would entail a much greater federal presence in promoting local seismic land use and building regulation than is currently the case. To date the federal government has had no experience with this approach in the seismic mitigation field. A precedent exists, however, with the establishment of the National Flood Insurance Program (NFIP) by the U.S. Congress in 1968. Under this program residents in flood-prone localities are eligible for federally subsidized flood insurance. To qualify for participation localities must adopt and enforce a set of minimal land use and building flood safety standards. It is instructive to note that this program began with positive inducements to encourage voluntary local government participation. However, only 10 percent of all eligible localities entered into the program during the program's initial five years of existence. In 1973 Congress enacted a strong set of sanctions for failure to participate.[3]

Simply adopting the NFIP approach to create a national earthquake insurance program, however, would be a mistake. Seismic characteristics are sufficiently different from those of floods that separate land use and building design regulations would be needed for earthquake insurance. Because scientists know less about earthquake hazard zones and considerable expense is required to gain site-specific knowledge, earthquake maps would not be as precise as floodplain maps. The federal government would also need to hire seismic experts capable of coordinating a program involving the complex physical processes of earthquakes.

Stronger State Role

While federal support of local seismic mitigation efforts is crucial, states have the necessary legal power and access to sufficient resources to play an important role in promoting safer development practices as well. As a first step in considering seismic safety, states should form some sort of interagency council or task force. As evidenced by the Utah Seismic Safety Advisory Council, the lead state organization would facilitate interaction among multiple interests and help produce consensus on how seismic safety might be advanced. Members might include representatives of various affected interests, including federal, state, and local agencies, developers, insurance companies, lending institutions, and professional engineering and scientific organizations.

Key tasks of a lead organization would involve assessment of the magnitude of seismic risks to people and property within the state and

3. For a detailed discussion of the evolution of the National Flood Insurance Program and the use of positive inducements and sanctions, see Burby and French (1985, ch. 1).

establishment of earthquake safety performance standards against which local plans and programs can be assessed. Such safety standards would specify acceptable limits on earthquake zone development intensities, seismic construction specifications, and minimal local mitigation plan and program elements. At a minimum, the standards should require that earthquake-prone localities adopt a building code with seismic design standards. As suggested by survey findings in chapter 7, many localities outside of California have yet to adopt building codes. Moreover, mandated state standards serve to work in favor of local political supporters, as demonstrated by Palo Alto's initiation of a seismic retrofit program in response to a state mandate for local planning. Supportive local individuals and groups were able to point to state requirements as a rationale for undertaking a mitigation program and for linking it to well-established comprehensive planning activities.

Activities a lead organization could perform in formulating standards would vary but might include convening meetings, setting agendas, and identifying the roles of state and local governments, as well as of nongovernmental organizations. As mentioned, nongovernmental interests active in seismic mitigation should be actively involved. These interests should play a strong role in assisting the lead state organization in designing statewide mitigation standards.

Another important activity would be to offer technical assistance and prepare guidelines for local governments charged with carrying out state policy. This assistance can include provisions of funds to localities to undertake mitigation planning and to acquire seismically hazardous lands. It could also involve preparation of model hazard mitigation ordinances and plans for use by localities. In addition, whenever possible states should maximize the amount of staff time spent in contact with locals. Personal contact reduces distrust of outside experts, provides for opportunities to educate and involve key leaders in mitigation, and permits state staff to better understand local problems and adjust their recommendations to better fit local needs.

USING THE INTERNATIONAL AND UNITED STATES DECADE AS A CATALYST FOR CHANGE

As discussed in chapter 1, plans for the 1990 International and United States Decade for Natural Disaster Reduction are taking shape. Various governmental bodies and nongovernmental organizations are increasingly becoming committed to translating the primary goal for the decade—to reduce the loss of life, injury, and property damage due to the ever-growing risk posed by natural hazards—into action. Further, the decade offers those in the hazards field a unique opportunity to assess the gap between existing and desired mitigation efforts and to assess where they would like to be in ten years. Indeed, numerous domestic and international organizations have begun a process to define what they intend to accomplish by the end of the decade and to develop actions that can be taken to reduce risks from hazards (see Toki 1990; Vessey 1990).

Earthquake mitigation policy is likely to be advanced if those involved in formulating it take advantage of the momentum generated by the decade initiatives. A recent report produced by a group of hazards specialists attending a U.S. Decade workshop provides national policy recommendations that specify how the decade could be used as a catalyst in stimulating hazards reduction efforts. These recommendations include, for example:

1. An assessment of progress to date in hazard reduction, including a roster of existing programs, impact trends, and research progress since the last major assessment in the early 1970s and identification of gaps in both knowledge and practice

2. A national, high-visibility conference on the decade, as well as a plan to "market" the decade's purposes and goals

3. Designation of local or regional "demonstration projects" that can be brought under, or newly created as part of, the decade

4. Creation of a consortium of institutions with expertise in hazard reduction to provide advice and assistance with such efforts as the creation of links between research and practice and the monitoring of its progress (Natural Hazards Research and Applications Center 1989, 26).

This study demonstrated how local governments can advance mitigation by linking seismic issues in the hazards policy arena to issues in other arenas. Similarly, linking seismic issues to decade activities could make the seismic problem more attractive to policy makers. The key to making this strategy work is that local officials should not view seismic concerns and the decade as separate initiatives. Rather, the decade can be a focal point for achieving the common goal of risk reduction.

AVERTING EARTHQUAKE DISASTER: A FINAL COMMENT

As the moderate intensity Loma Prieta earthquake (7.1 on the Richter scale) of 17 October 1989 demonstrated only too well in the San Francisco area, it does not take a "big one" like the great 1906 earthquake (8.2 on the Richter scale) to deal a devastating blow. Preliminary media reports indicate that damage from the 1989 earthquake was more than $10 billion, yet fatalities were remarkably low—only sixty-two. A recurrence of the "big one" is likely, however. The question is "not if, but when, for the 'big one,'" according to a notable geological expert.[4] One insurance industry projection estimated that a great earthquake could cause more than $50 billion in damages and result in thousands of casualties (Friedman 1984). The message from the 1989 earthquake and from future projections, therefore, is unmistakable: be prepared.

While there are no ways to prevent an earthquake or reduce its magnitude, there are ways to protect people and property from the most damaging effects. The most effective strategy is to require that all development be directed out of the most hazardous areas, where seismic forces are most destructive. This strategy would also require that building codes with stringent seismic safety standards be adopted and enforced in all moderate- and high-risk areas. As outlined in this chapter, achieving this strategy requires major changes and efforts by federal, state, and local governments, even though the visible outcomes appear only at the local level. These changes are applicable to all earthquake-prone areas, including not only those of California and the West generally, but also those of the Midwest and along the eastern seaboard.

4. Quote from Dallas Peck, Director of the U.S. Geological Survey, *Time*, 30 October 1989, 44.

APPENDIX A

Interorganizational Relations, Program Support, Program Operations, and External Factors Related to Local Adoption of Planning Measures

Factors by Category	Standardized Beta Weights (Unstandardized)	
	California	All Other States
1. Interorganizational relations		
Extent of contact with organizations	.34 (.38)***	.16 (.11)
Responsiveness of other organizations to local program needs	.23 (.25)*	.37 (.35)***
R^2 for equation 1	.258	.248
F-ratio of Equation 1	13.706***	19.292***
2. Program resources		
Staff hours	.10 (−.32)	.23 (.72)**
Planning budget	.26 (1.16)	.10 (.38)
Budget change	.10 (.48)	.10 (.24)
Lack of higher level financial support	−.11 (−.21)	−.21 (−.28)
Inadequate expertise	.10 (.20)	.02 (.02)
Adequacy of maps	.11 (.22)	.24 (.31)**
R^2 for equation 2	.087	.160
F-ratio for equation 2	1.110	2.830***
3. Program operations		
Presence of an advocate	−.08 (.44)	.29 (.97)***
Integration of seismic program	.01 (.06)	.20 (1.04)**
Linkage of seismic issues to other local issues	.38 (.80)***	.25 (.37)**
Media campaign	.09 (.55)	−.07 (−.22)
R^2 for equation 3	.157	.263
F-ratio for equation 3	3.349**	9.827***
4. External environment		
Home value	−.06 (.00)	.02 (.00)
Population size	−.09 (.00)	−.04 (.00)
Conservative attitude	.17 (.39)	−.15 (−.22)
Legal restraint	.06 (.13)	−.07 (−.11)
Lack of public interest	−.06 (−.13)	−.13 (−.20)
Opposition by real estate	−.03 (−.06)	.23 (.32)
Lack of support by local elected officials	.12 (.21)	.16 (.22)
Past experience	−.09 (−.12)	.19 (.20)*
Perceived risk	.08 (.13)	−.14 (−.24)
Number of hazards	.34 (.44)***	.25 (.22)**
R^2 for equation 4	.183	.202
F-ratio for equation 4	1.496	2.024**

* $p < .1$ ** $p < .05$ *** $p < .01$

APPENDIX B

Variables and Measurements from the Survey Questionnaire

Variable	Measurement
DEPENDENT	
Innovative mitigation measures	Respondents were asked to indicate whether each of 21 local land use and development mitigation measures was adopted by their community. Responses were coded 0 = no and 1 = yes and summed. Only those measures that specifically addressed seismic hazards and were not adopted in response to state legislative mandates were used.
INDEPENDENT	
Program operations	
Advocates influencing planning decisions	Respondents were asked if any individuals or groups advocated concern for earthquake hazards in their jurisdictions. Responses were coded 0 = no and 1 = yes.
Hazards integrated into comprehensive plan	Respondents were asked if earthquake mitigation program formulation activities were integrated into comprehensive planning activities of their jurisdiction. Responses were coded 0 = no and 1 = yes.
Number of concerns linked to earthquake hazards	Respondents were asked to indicate which concerns were linked to earthquake hazards in their jurisdiction from a list of seven concerns. Responses were coded 0 = no and 1 = yes and summed.
Media attention	Respondents were asked if there is a media campaign in their communities to make the public more aware of earthquake hazards in their jurisdiction. Responses were coded 0 = no and 1 = yes.

Appendix B *continued*

Variable	Measurement
Program Support	
Staff hours	Respondents were asked approximately how many hours per week were devoted to earthquake problems by their staffs. Responses were coded 1 = less than 1 person-hour, 2 = 1 to 7 person-hours, 3 = 8 to 39 person-hours 4 = 40 person-hours or more.
Percentage of planning department budget	Respondents were asked approximately what percentage of the department's annual operating budget is allocated to earthquake problems. Responses were coded 1 = less than 1%, 2 = 1 to 5%, 3 = 6 to 20%, 4 = greater than 20%.
Change in budget	Respondents were asked to compare the budget percentage allocated to earthquake problems now to the budget percentage 5 years ago. Responses were coded 1 = much less, 2 = less, 3 = about the same, 4 = greater, 5 = much greater.
Lack of state or federal financial support; inadequate staff expertise; inadequate maps delineating earthquake hazards	Respondents were asked to rate on a 5 pt. Likert scale the seriousness of each of these obstacles in reducing earthquake activities in their jurisdictions. Responses were coded 1 = very serious to 5 = not serious.
Interorganizational Relations	
Number of interorganizational contacts	Respondents were asked to indicate the average number of times they were contacted (face to face or by telephone, meeting, letter, report, etc.) in the last year for 8 federal, state, and local agencies and groups. Responses were coded 0 = no contact and 1 = 1 or more contacts and summed.
Organizational responsiveness	Respondents were asked to rate on a 5 pt. Likert scale (1 = not responsive to 5 = very responsive) the responsiveness of 8 federal, state, and local agencies and groups to needs and problems related to earthquake hazards in their jurisdictions. Responses of 1, 2, and 3 on the scale were coded as 0 = not responsive, nd 4 and 5 were coded 1 = responsive. The coded responses were then summed.
Community Context	
Median home value	Census data was recorded to identify the median home value for each respondent's jurisdiction in 1980.
Population size	Census data was recorded to identify the population size of each respondent's jurisdiction for 1980; 10,000 was the lower limit.
Past experience	Respondents were asked to indicate when the effects of an earthquake were last experienced in their jurisdictions. Responses were coded 0 = more than 20 years ago and 1 = 20 years ago or less.

Appendix B *continued*

Variable	Measurement
Number of seismic-related hazards	Respondents were asked to indicate which of 9 seismic-related hazards are in their jurisdictions. Responses were coded 0 = no and 1 = yes.
Perceived risk	Respondents were asked to rate on two separate 5-pt. Likert scales: (1) the chances that a major earthquake will occur in your jurisdiction over the next 30 years; (2) the ability of structures in your jurisdiction to withstand a major earthquake. Responses were coded 1 = very low chance to 5 = very high chance and 1 = very low ability to 5 = very high ability, respectively, and added to form new variables. (Cronbach's alpha = .654.)
Conservative attitude toward government control of private property; legal restraints in state law for planning and managing development; lack of public interest about earthquakes; opposition of real estate or development interests; lack of support by local elected officials	Respondents were asked to rate on a 5 pt. Likert scale the seriousness of each of these obstacles in reducing earthquake activities in their jurisdictions. Responses were coded 1 = very serious to 5 = not serious.

ACRONYMS

BAREPP	Bay Area Earthquake Preparedness Program
CAMA	Coastal Area Management Act
CIP	Capital Improvements Program
COMBS	Citizens and Organizations for Minimum Building Standards
EEC	Earthquake Education Center
EPRI	Electric Power Research Institute
FAR	Floor Area Ratio
FEMA	Federal Emergency Management Agency
MMI	Modified Mercalli Intensity
NBS	National Bureau of Building Standards
NEHRP	National Earthquake Hazards Reduction Program
NFIP	National Flood Insurance Program
NRC	Nuclear Regulatory Commission
NSF	National Science Foundation
PDR	Purchase of Development Rights
PUD	Planned Unit Development
SCEPP	Southern California Earthquake Preparedness Program
SCSSC	South Carolina Seismic Safety Consortium
SMSA	Standard Metropolitan Statistical Area
TDR	Transfer of Development Rights
TIDC	Technology Transfer and Development Council

UACC	United Association of Community Councils
UBC	Uniform Building Code
UGMS	Utah Geological Mineral Survey
URM	Unreinforced Masonry
USGS	United States Geological Survey

REFERENCES

Abney, F. and L. Hill. 1966. Natural Disasters as a Political Variable: The Effect of a Hurricane on an Urban Election. *American Political Science Review* 60, no. 4.

Ackoff, R. L. 1970. *A Concept of Corporate Planning*. New York: John Wiley.

————. 1981. *Corporate Strategy*. New York: McGraw-Hill.

Aldrich, H. E. 1979. *Organizations and Environment*. Englewood Cliffs, N.J.: Prentice Hall.

Alesch, D. and W. Petak. 1986. *The Politics and Economics of Earthquake Hazard Mitigation*. Institute of Behavioral Science Monograph No. 43. Boulder: University of Colorado.

Algermissen, S. T. 1969. *Studies in Seismicity and Earthquake Damage Statistics*. Appendix B. Washington, D.C.: U.S. Department of Commerce.

Alterman, R. (ed.). 1988. *Private Supply of Public Services: Evaluation of Real Estate Exactions, Linkage and Alternative Land Policies*. New York: New York University Press.

Alterman, R. and M. Hill. 1978. Implementation of Urban Land Use Plans. *Journal of the American Institute of Planners* 44, no. 4.

Ansoff, H. I. 1985. *Implanting Strategic Management*. Englewood Cliffs, N.J.: Prentice-Hall International.

Arnold, C. 1988. The Process of Introducing New or Improved Seismic Design Provisions in the Western United States. In W. Hays and P. Gori (eds.), *A Review of Earthquake Research Applications in the National Earthquake Hazards Reduction Program, 1977–1987*. Reston, Va.: U.S. Geological Survey.

Association of Engineering Geologists—Utah Section. 1986. *Guidelines for Preparing Engineering Geologic Reports in Utah*. Salt Lake City: Utah Geological and Mineral Survey.

Bagwell, Joyce B. (ed.). 1986. *Workshop on Lessons from California and Utah*. Proceedings of a workshop held at Baptist College at Charleston, S.C. November 15–16, 1982.

————. 1988. Application of the National Earthquake Hazards Reduction Program through an Earthquake Education Center at Charleston, South Carolina. In W. Hays and P. Gori (eds.), *A Review of Earthquake Research Applications in the National Earthquake Hazards Reduction Program, 1977–1987*. Reston, Va.: U.S. Geological Survey.

Baker, E. and J. McPhee. 1975. *Land Use Regulations in Hazardous Areas: A Research Assessment*. Boulder: Institute of Behavioral Science, University of Colorado.

Banfield, E. and J. Wilson. 1963. *City Politics*. New York: Vintage Books.

Barnes, Jerold H. 1988. Utilization of Hazard Maps in Salt Lake County. In W. Hays and P. Gori (eds.), *A Review of Earthquake Research Applications in the National Earthquake Hazards Reduction Program, 1977–1987*. Reston, Va.: U.S. Geological Survey.

Barrows, H. H. 1923. Geography as Human Ecology. *Annals of the Association of American Geographers* 13.

Beatley, T. and D. Godschalk. 1985. Hazard Reduction through Development Management in Hurricane Prone Localities: State of the Art. *Carolina Planning* 11, no. 1.

Beatley, T., David J. Brower, and Lou Ann Brower. 1988. *Managing Growth: Small Communities and Rural Areas*. Augusta, Maine: Office of State Planning.

Beatley, T. and P. Berke. 1990. Seismic Safety through Public Incentives: The Palo Alto Seismic Hazard Identification Program. *Earthquake Spectra* 6, no. 1: 57–81.

Beavers, James E. 1988. Perspectives on Seismic Risk Maps and the Building Code Process in the Eastern United States. In W. Hays and P. Gori (eds.), *A Review of Earthquake Research Applications in the National Earthquake Hazards Reduction Program, 1977–1978*. Reston, Va.: U.S. Geological Survey.

Belmont, California. 1988. An Ordinance of the City of Belmont Amending City Code Section 7-12 by Adding Subsection (d), Geologic Hazards in the San Juan Hills Area. May 25.

Berke, P. 1989. Hurricane Vertical Shelter Policy: The Experiences of Florida and Texas. *Journal of Coastal Management* 17, no. 3.

Berke, P., T. Beatley, and S. Wilhite. 1989. Influences on Local Adoption of Planning Measures and Earthquake Hazard Mitigation. *International Journal of Mass Emergencies and Disasters.* 7, no. 1.

Bollinger, G. A. 1972. Historical and recent Seismic Activity in South Carolina. *Bulletin of the Seismological Society of America* 62; 851–64.

———. 1973. Seismicity of the United States. *Bulletin of the Seismological Society of America* 63, no. 5: 1785–1808.

Bosselman, Fred, John Banta, and David Callies. 1976. *The Takings Issue*. Washington, D.C.: Council on Environmental Quality.

Brower, David J., William Collins, and Timothy Beatley. 1984. *Hurricane Hazard Mitigation and Post-Storm Reconstruction Plan for Nags Head, North Carolina*. Chapel Hill, N.C.: Coastal Resources Collaborative.

Brower, David J., Timothy Beatley, and David J. L. Blatt. 1987. *Reducing Hurricane and Coastal Storm Hazards through Growth Management: A Guidebook for North Carolina Coastal Localities*. Chapel Hill: Center for Urban and Regional Studies, University of North Carolina.

Bryson, J. 1983. Representing and Testing Procedural Planning Methods. In I.

Davis (ed.), *Evaluating Urban Planning Efforts*. Aldershot, U.K.: Gower Publishing Co.

Bryson, J. and K. Boal. 1983. Strategic Management in a Metropolitan Area. *Proceedings of the Academy of Management 43*.

Bryson, J. and W. D. Roering. 1987. Applying Private-Sector Strategic Planning in the Public Sector. *Journal of the American Planning Association 53*, no. 1.

Burby, R. and S. French. 1981. Coping with Floods: The Land Use Management Paradox. *Journal of the American Planning Association 47*, no. 3.

————. 1985. *Flood Plain Land Use Management: A National Assessment*. Boulder, Colo.: Westview Press.

Burton, I. and R. Kates. 1964. The Perception of Natural Hazards in Resource Management. *Natural Resources Journal 3*.

Burton, I., R. Kates, and G. White. 1978. *The Environment as Hazard*. New York: Oxford University Press.

California Code of Statutes, 1986. Disaster Recovery Act, sec. 8874.5. Sacramento, Calif.

California Seismic Safety Commission. 1986. *A Review of the Seismic Safety Element Requirement in California*. Sacramento, Calif.

————. 1987. *Guidebook to Identify and Mitigate Seismic Hazards in Buildings*. Sacramento, Calif.

————. 1988. *California at Risk: Steps to Evaluate Safety for Local Government*. Sacramento, Calif.

Campbell, D. 1975. "Degrees of Freedom" and the Case Study. *Comparative Political Studies 8*.

Chapin, F. Stuart and Edward J. Kaiser. 1979. *Urban Land Use Planning*. Urbana: University of Illinois Press.

Christensen, Gary. 1987. *Suggested Approach to Geologic Hazards Ordinances in Utah*. Circular 79. Salt Lake City: Utah Geological and Mineral Survey.

Christensen, K. 1985. Coping with Uncertainty in Planning. *Journal of the American Planning Association 47*, no. 3.

Cibrowski, A. 1981. *Urban Design and Physical Planning as Tools to Make Cities Safer in Earthquake-Prone Areas*. Warsaw: Institute of Urban Design and Physical Development, Warsaw Technical University.

Clary, B. 1985. The Evolution and Structure of Natural Hazard Policies. *Public Administration Review 45*.

Cochran, H. C. 1975. *Natural Hazards and Their Distributive Effects*. Monograph no. 3. Boulder: Institute of Behavioral Science, University of Colorado.

Cohen, M., J. March and J. Olsen. 1972. A Garbage Can Model of Organizational Choice. *Administrative Science Quarterly 17*.

Coughlin, R. E. et al. 1977. *Saving the Garden: The Preservation of Farmland and other Environmentally Valuable Landscapes*. Philadelphia: Regional Science Research Institute.

Coughlin, R. E. and John Keene (eds.). 1981. *The Protection of Farmland: A Reference Guidebook for State and Local Governments*. Washington, D.C.: Government Printing Office.

Coughlin, R. E. and Thomas Plant. 1978. Less-than-Fee Acquisition for the Preservation of Open Space: Does It Work? *Journal of the American Planning Association* 44, no. 4 (October): 452–62.

Cox, John. 1989. Earthquake Threat Overstated. Letter to the editor. *The Evening Post—The News and Courier* (Charleston, S.C.), May 30.

Davenport, Clifton and Theodore Smith. 1985. Geologic Hazards, Negligence, and Real Estate Sales. *California Geology:* 159–60.

DeGrove, John M. 1984. *Land, Growth and Politics.* Chicago: American Planning Association Press.

Dillman, D. 1978. *Mail and Telephone Surveys: The Total Design Method.* New York: John Wiley.

Dillon, R. 1985. Integration of Hazard Assessment and Reduction in Existing Buildings. In R. Scholl (ed.), *Proceedings of a Workshop on Reducing Seismic Hazards of Existing Buildings.* Washington, D.C.: Federal Emergency Management Agency.

Drabek, T. E. 1986. *Human System Responses to Disaster: An Inventory of Sociological Findings.* New York: Springer-Verlag.

Drabek, T. E., A. Mushkatel, and T. Kilijarrel. 1983. *Earthquake Mitigation Policy: The Experience in Two States.* Boulder: Institute of Behavioral Science, University of Colorado.

Duncan, O. D. 1964. Social Organization and the Ecosystem. In R. Faris (ed.), *Handbook of Modern Sociology.* Chicago: Rand McNally.

Elazar, D. 1966. *American Federalism: A View from the States.* New York: Crowell.

Ender, R., J. Kim, L. Selkregg, and S. Johnson. 1988. The Design and Implementation of Disaster Mitigation Policy. In L. Comfort (ed.), *Managing Disaster.* Durham, N.C.: Duke University Press.

Faupel, C. and C. Bailey. 1989. Movers and Shakers and PCB Shakers: Hazardous Waste and Community Power in a Rural Community. Paper presented at the Mid-South Sociological Association meeting. Baton Rouge, La.

Federal Emergency Management Agency. 1989. *Estimating Losses from Future Earthquakes.* Washington, D.C.: FEMA.

Findlay, Prentiss. 1989. Armenian Quake Is a Warning. *News and Courier,* May 30.

Fischoff, B., S. Lichtenstein, P. Slovic, R. Keeny, and S. Derby. 1981. *Acceptable Risk.* Cambridge: Cambridge University Press.

Friedman, D. 1984. Natural Hazard Risk Assessment for an Insurance Program. In *The Geneva Papers on Risk and Insurance.* Geneva: International Association for the Study of Insurance Economics.

Glendale, California. 1975. *Seismic Safety Element.* Adopted July 29 by the Planning Division.

Godschalk, D. 1984. *Impact of the Coastal Barrier Resources Act: A Pilot Study.* Washington, D.C.: Office of Ocean and Coastal Resources Management, U.S. Department of Commerce.

Godschalk, D. and D. Brower. 1979. *Constitutional Issues of Growth Management.* Chicago: American Planning Association Press.

———. 1985. Mitigation Strategies and Integrated Emergency Management. *Public Administration Review* 45.

Godschalk, D., D. Brower, and T. Beatley. 1989. *Catastrophic Coastal Storms: Hazard Mitigation and Development Management.* Durham, N.C.: Duke University Press.

Haas, H. J. Robert Kates, and Martyn Bowden (eds.). 1977. *Reconstruction following Disaster*. Cambridge, Mass.: MIT Press.

Haas, H. J. and D. S. Mileti. 1976. Socioeconomic Impact of Earthquake Prediction on Government, Business and Community. *California Geology* 30, no. 37.

Halen, David. 1989. For Alaskan Survivors of 1964 Quake, Tiny Tremors Evoke Tragic Memories. *Washington Post*, March 27.

Hansen, L. and T. Hirsh. 1983. *Effectiveness Study of Wisconsin's Floodplain Management Program*. Madison, Wisc.: Wisconsin Department of Natural Resources.

Harlan, Maurice R. and Charles Lindbergh. 1988. *An Earthquake Vulnerability Analysis of the Charleston, South Carolina, Area*. Charleston, S.C.: Department of Civil Engineering, The Citadel.

Hays, W. 1980. *Procedures for Estimating Earthquake Ground Motions*, Professional paper no. 1114. Reston, Va.: U.S. Geological Survey.

Herman, F., J. Russell, and R. Sharpe. 1988. *Review of Palo Alto's Seismic Hazards Identification Program*. Sacramento: California Seismic Safety Commission.

Kaiser, E. and R. Burby. 1987. Emerging State Roles in Urban Stormwater Management. *American Water Resources Bulletin* 23, no. 3.

Kartez, J. 1984. Crisis Response Planning: Toward a Contingent Analysis. *Journal of the American Planning Association* 50, No. 1.

Kartez, J. and M. Lindell. 1987. Planning for Uncertainty: The Case of Local Disaster Planning. *Journal of the American Planning Association* 53, no. 4.

Kates, R. 1978. *Risk Assessment of Environmental Hazard*. New York: John Wiley.

Keating, W. Dennis. 1986. Linking Downtown Development to Broader Community Goals. *Journal of the American Planning Association* 52, no. 2: 133–41.

Keene, John et al. 1976. *Untaxing Open Space*. Washington, D.C.: Council on Environmental Quality.

King County, Washington. 1988. Sensitive Area Rules. Adopted 1988.

Kingdon, J. 1984. *Agendas, Alternatives, and Public Policies*. Boston: Little, Brown and Company.

Kockleman, William J. 1985. Some Techniques for Reducing Mudflow and Mudflow Hazards. In John Kusler (ed.), *Post Disaster Response and Mitigation of Future Losses*. Washington, D.C.: American Bar Association.

Kuehn, Robert R. 1984. The Coastal Barrier Resources Act and the Expenditures Limitation Approach to Natural Resources Conservation: Wave of the Future or Island unto Itself? *Ecology Law Quarterly* 11: 583–670.

Kunreuther, H. and J. Linnerooth. 1984. *Risk Analysis and Decision Processes*. New York: Springer-Verlag.

Lambright, H. 1984. *Role of States in Earthquake and Natural Hazards Innovation at the Local Level of Decision Making*. A Report to the National Science Foundation. Syracuse, N.Y.: Syracuse Research Corporation.

Lindbergh, Charles. 1986. *Earthquake Hazards, Risk, and Mitigation in South Carolina and the Southeastern United States*. Charleston: South Carolina Seismic Safety Consortium.

———. 1988. Southeastern United States. In W. Hays and P. Gori (eds.), *A Review of Earthquake Research Applications in the National Earthquake Reduction Program, 1977–1987*. Reston, Va.: U.S. Geological Survey.

———. 1989. *The Armenian Earthquake of 1988—The Event and its Implications for*

Charleston, South Carolina, and Other Cities in the Eastern United States: An Eastern Engineer's Perspective. Charleston, S.C.: Department of Civil Engineering, The Citadel.

———. undated. The Establishment of Uniform Minimum Building Standards in South Carolina. Charleston, S.C.: Citizens and Organizations for Minimum Building Standards.

Los Angeles, California, 1986. Ordinance no. 5-67. General Grading Requirements. Adopted November.

———. 1987. Recovery and Reconstruction Planning: Existing Policies and Future Directions. Recovery and Reconstruction Subcommittee, April 10.

Lowi, T. 1964. American Business, Public Policy, Case Studies, and Political Theory. *World Politics* 16.

Mader, G. 1980. *Land Use Planning after Earthquakes.* Portola Valley, Calif.: William Spangle and Associates.

Mapleton, Utah. 1985. Ordinance no. 85-2: Critical Environmental Zone Ordinance. Adopted June 2.

March, J. G. and H. Simon. 1958. *Organizations.* New York: John Wiley.

May, P. 1991. Addressing Public Risks: Federal Earthquake Policy Design. *Journal of Policy Analysis and Management* 10, no. 2.

May, P. and P. Bolton. 1986. Reassessing Earthquake Hazard Reduction Measures. *Journal of the American Planning Association* 52, no. 4.

May, P. and W. Williams. 1986. *Disaster Policy Implementation. Managing Programs under Shared Governance.* New York: Plenum Press.

McKelvey, W. 1982. *Organizational Systematics.* Berkeley: University of California Press.

McNamara, J. 1978. Determining Sample Size in Decision-oriented Research Studies. *Planning and Changing: A Journal for School Administrators* 9, no. 7.

Meek, Clark D. 1988. Four Years after the Borah Peak Idaho Earthquake—What Mitigation Activities Have Occurred? In W. Hays and P. Gori (eds.), *A Review of Earthquake Research Applications in the National Earthquake Hazards Reduction Program, 1977–1987.* Reston, Va.: U.S. Geological Survey.

Merriam, Dwight, David J. Brower, and Philip D. Tegeler (eds.). 1985. *Inclusionary Housing Moves Downtown.* Chicago: American Planning Association Press.

Mileti, D. 1980. Human Adjustment to the Risk of Environmental Extremes. *Sociology and Social Research* 64.

Mintzberg, H. and J. A. Waters. 1985. The Mind of the Strategist(s). In S. Srivastva (ed.), *Executive Mind: New Insights on Managerial Thought and Action.* San Francisco: Jossey-Bass.

Mittler, E. 1988. Agenda-Setting in Nonstructural Hazard Mitigation Policy. In L. Comfort. (ed.), *Managing Disaster.* Durham, N.C.: Duke University Press.

Murphy, F. C. 1958. *Regulating Flood Plain Development.* Research Paper no. 56. Chicago: Department of Geography, University of Chicago.

Mushkatel, A. and J. M. Nigg. 1987a. Opinion Congruence and the Formulation of Seismic Safety Policies. *Policy Studies Review* 4, no. 6.

———. 1987b. The Effect of Objective Risk on Key Actor Support for Seismic Mitigation Policy. *Environmental Management* 11, no. 1.

Mushkatel, A. and L. Weschler. 1985. Emergency Management and the Intergovernmental System. *Public Administration Review* 45, special issue.

National Conferences of States and Building Codes and Standards (NCSBCS). 1988. *Directory of State Building Codes and Regulations*, 4th ed. Herndon, Va.

National Research Council. 1984. *The Utah Landslides, Debris Flows, and Floods of May and June 1983*. Washington, D.C.: National Academy Press.

———. 1987. *Confronting Natural Disasters: An International Decade for Natural Hazard Reduction*. Washington, D.C.: National Academy Press.

Natural Hazards Research and Applications Center. 1989. *Report of the Colorado Works on Hazard Mitigation in the 1990s: Toward the U.S. Decade for Natural Disaster Reduction*. Boulder: University of Colorado.

Nelson, Arthur C. (ed.). 1988. *Development Impact Fees: Policy, Pationale, Practice, Theory, and Issues*. Chicago: American Planners Association Press.

Nelson, Craig. 1987. *Surface Fault Rupture and Liquefaction Hazard Areas*. Salt Lake City: County Planning Division

———. 1988. *Rockfall Hazards, Salt Lake County, Utah*. Salt Lake City: Salt Lake County Planning Division.

North Carolina Administrative Code. 1974. Coastal Area Management Act. Raleigh, N.C.

Nugent, Michael. 1976. Water and Sewer Extension Policies as a Technique for Guiding Development. *Carolina Planning* 1 (Winter): 4–11.

Nutt, P. C. 1984. Types of Organizational Decision Processes. *Administrative Science Quarterly*, 29.

Oaks, Sherry. 1987. Historical Earthquakes in Salt Lake City, Utah: Event and Institutional Response. Ph.D. Dissertation, Department of Geography, University of Colorado, Boulder.

Olson, R. A., R. S. Olson, and D. Messinger. 1988. *Standing Rubble*. Sacramento, Calif.: VSP Associates.

Olson, R. S. and D. Nilson. 1982. Public Policy Analysis of Hazards Research: Natural Compliments. *Social Science Journal* 19.

Onslow County, North Carolina. 1984. *Hurricane Storm Mitigation and Post-Disaster Reconstruction Plans*. Wilmington, N.C.: Henry Von Oesen and Associates.

Palm, R. 1981. *Real Estate Agents and Special Studies Zones Disclosure: The Response of California Homebuyers to Earthquake Hazards Information*. Boulder: Institute of Behavioral Science, University of Colorado.

———. 1990. *Natural Hazards: An Integrative Framework for Research and Planning*. Baltimore: Johns Hopkins University Press.

Palo Alto, California. 1981. *Palo Alto Comprehensive Plan: 1980–1995*.

———. 1984a. Seismic Hazards Reduction Program. Memorandum. Seismic Hazards Committee.

———. 1984b. *Final Report from the Palo Alto Seismic Hazards Committee*. Seismic Hazards Committee.

———. 1984c. Minutes. Seismic Hazards Committee.

———. 1984d. Minutes. City Council.

———. 1986. *Setting Forth a Seismic Hazard Identification Program*. Ordinance No. 3666.

————. 1987. *CD Commercial Downtown District Regulations.*

————. 1988. *Staff Report on Seismic Hazards Identification Program.*

Pedhazur, E. J. 1982. *Multiple Regression in Behavioral Research: Explanation and Prediction.* New York: Holt, Rinehart, and Winston.

Petak, W. and A. Atkisson. 1982. *Natural Hazards Risk Assessment and Public Policy.* New York: Springer-Verlag.

Phillips, Patrick. 1985. Nantucket's Land Bank: A New Direction in Land Conservation. *Urban Land*, December.

Pizor, Peter J. 1986. Making TDR Work: A Study of Program Implementation. *Journal of the American Planning Association* 52, no. 2.

Reaveley, Laurence D. 1988. The Process of Dealing with Existing Hazardous Buildings in Utah. In W. Hays and P. Gori (eds.), *A Review of Earthquake Research Applications in the National Earthquake Hazards Reduction Program, 1977–1987.* Reston, Va.: U.S. Geological Survey.

Reitherman, R. 1983. *Reducing the Risks of Nonstructural Earthquake Damage: A Practical Guide.* Redwood City, Calif.: Scientific Services.

Robinson, Andrew and Pradeep Talwani. 1983. Building Damage at Charleston, South Carolina, Associated with the 1886 Earthquake. *Bulletin of the Seismological Society of America* 73, no. 2: 633–52.

Rogers, Golden, Halpern and Associates. 1981. *Hurricane Evacuation and Hazard Mitigation Study for Sanibel, Florida.* Philadelphia, Pa.

Rohe, W. and L. Gates. 1985. *Planning with Neighborhoods.* Chapel Hill, N.C.: University of North Carolina Press.

Rossi, P., J. Wright, and E. Weber-Burdin. 1982. *Natural Hazards and Public Choice: The State and Local Politics of Hazard Mitigation.* New York: Academic Press.

Rowe, W. 1977. *Anatomy of Risk.* New York: John Wiley.

Salt Lake City, Utah. 1986. *Planning Goals and Policies.* Salt Lake County Planning Commission.

————. 1988a. Hillside Protection Zone, Chapter 19.72. In *Salt Lake County Zoning Ordinance.* County Planning Division.

————. 1988b. *Millcreek Community Master Plan.* County Planning Division.

————. 1988c. *Wasatch Canyons Preliminary Master Plan: 1989–2009.* Salt Lake County Public Works Department and Planning Division.

————. 1989. Natural Hazards Ordinance. County Planning Division.

Scholl, R. 1986. *Reducing Earthquake Hazards: Lessons Learned from Earthquakes.* El Cerrito, Calif.: Earthquake Engineering Research Institute.

Selkregg, L., R. Ender, S. Johnson, J. Kim, and S. Gorski. 1984. *Earthquake Hazard Mitigation: Planning and Policy Implementation: The Alaska Case.* Anchorage: University of Alaska.

Simon, H. A. 1957. *Administrative Behavior*, 2d ed. New York: Macmillan.

Slovic, P., H. Kunreuther, and G. White. 1974. Decision Processes, Rationality, and Adjustment to Natural Hazards. In G. White (ed.), *Natural Hazards: Local, National, Global.* New York: Oxford.

Sorensen, J. and G. White. 1980. Natural Hazards: A Cross Cultural Perspective. In I. Altman, A. Papaport, and J. Wohwill (eds.), *Human Behavior and the Environment.* New York: Plenum Press.

Spangle and Associates. 1988a. *Geology and Planning: The Portola Valley Experience.* Portola Valley, Calif.
———. 1988b. *Putting Seismic Safety Policies to Work.* Portola Valley, Calif.
Sprinkel, Douglas A. 1988. A Review of the Regional Earthquake Hazards Assessment Program for the Wasatch Front Area, Utah—Will Utah Meet the Challenge? In W. Hays and P. Gori (eds.), *A Review of Earthquake Research Applications in the National Earthquake Hazards Reduction Program, 1977–1987.* Reston, Va.: U.S. Geological Survey.
Stroud, Nancy. 1988. Legal Considerations of Development Impact Fees. In Arthur Nelson (ed.), *Development Impact Fees.* Chicago: American Planning Association Press.
Snyder, Thomas P. and Michael A. Stegman. 1986. *Paying for Growth: Using Development Fees to Finance Infrastructure.* Washington, D.C.: Urban Land Institute.
Talwani, Pradeep. 1986. Current Thoughts on the Cause of the Charleston, South Carolina Earthquakes. *South Carolina Geology* 29 (2): 19–38.
———. 1988. The Intersection Model for Intraplate Earthquakes. *Seismological Research Letters* 59, no. 4: 305–10.
———. 1989. Characteristic Features of Intraplate Earthquakes and the Models Proposed to Explain Them. In S. Gregersen and P. W. Basham (eds.), *Earthquakes and North Atlantic Passive Margins: Neotectonics and Postglacial Rebounds.* New York: Kluver Academic Publishers.
Talwani, Pradeep and Keith Collinsworth. 1988. Recurrence Intervals for Intraplate Earthquakes in Eastern North America from Paleoseismological Data. *Seismological Research Letters* 59, no. 4: 207–11.
Talwani, Pradeep and John Cox. 1985. Paleoseismic Evidence for Recurrence of Earthquakes near Charleston, South Carolina. *Science* 229 (July 29): 379–81.
Taylor, B. 1984. Strategic Planning—Which Style Do You Need? *Long Range Planning* 17, no. 3.
Toki, K. 1990. Japan—The Decade Is Underway. *Natural Hazards Observer* 15, no. 1.
U.S. Census Bureau. 1980a. *General Social and Economic Characteristics.* Washington, D.C.
———. 1980b. *Census of Population.* Washington, D.C.: U.S. Department of Commerce.
Urban and Regional Research. 1982. *Land Management in Tsunami Areas.* Seattle: URR.
Utah Office of Planning and Budget. 1988. *Utah Economic and Demographic Profile.* Salt Lake City.
Van de Ven, A. H. 1980. Problem Solving, Planning, and Innovation. P. II. Speculations for Theory and Practice. *Human Relations* 33, no. 11.
Visvanathan, T. R. 1980. Earthquakes in South Carolina, 1698–1975. Bulletin 40. Columbia: South Carolina Geological Survey.
Washington Terrace, Utah. 1988. Ordinance 18–88: Development Overlay Zones.
Weschler, B. and R. Backoff, 1987. The Dynamics of Strategy in Public Organizations. *Journal of the American Planning Association* 53, no. 1.
Wesson, R. L., E. J. Kelley, K. R. Lajoie, and C. M. Wentworth. 1975. *U.S.*

Geological Survey Professional Paper 941A. Washington, D.C.: U.S. Geological Survey.

West Valley, Utah. 1988. *West Valley City's Earthquake Hazards Reduction Program: Phase II.* Community Development Department.

White, G. 1945. *Human Adjustment to Floods.* Research paper no. 29. Chicago: Department of Geography, University of Chicago.

———. 1974. *Natural Hazards: Local, National, Global.* New York: Oxford.

White, G. et al. 1958. *Changes in Urban Occupancy of Flood Plains in the United States.* Research paper no. 57. Chicago: Department of Geography, University of Chicago.

White, G. and E. Haas. 1975. *Assessment of Research on Natural Hazards.* Cambridge, Mass.: MIT Press.

Wiggins, J. 1979. *Building Losses from Natural Hazards—Yesterday, Today, and Tomorrow.* Redondo Beach, Calif.: J. H. Wiggins Co.

Wind, Y. and V. Mahajan. 1981. Designing Product and Business Portfolios. *Harvard Business Review* 59, no. 1.

Wright, J. and P. Rossi. 1981. *The Politics of Natural Disaster: State and Local Elites.* In J. Wright and P. Rossi (eds.), *Social Science and Natural Hazards.* Cambridge, Mass.: Abt Books.

Wyner, Alan J. and Dean E. Mann. 1986. *Preparing for California's Earthquakes: Local Government and Seismic Safety.* Berkeley: Institute of Governmental Studies, University of California.

Yin, R. 1984. *Case Study Research: Design and Methods.* Beverly Hills: Sage Publications.

Zehentner, K. 1990. Germany and the International Decade for Natural Disaster Reduction, *Natural Hazards Observer* 14, no. 6.

INDEX

ABOUT THE AUTHORS

Timothy Beatley is assistant professor in the Department of Urban and Environmental Planning in the School of Architecture at the University of Virginia. He holds a Ph.D. in city and regional planning from the University of North Carolina at Chapel Hill. His primary teaching and research interests include environmental politics and policy, environmental ethics, coastal management, and the conservation of biodiversity. He has recently completed a study on land use ethics under a grant from the Lincoln Institute of Land Policy.

Philip R. Berke is associate professor in the Department of Urban and Regional Planning at Texas A&M University, where he teaches environmental planning, and associate director of the Hazard Reduction and Recovery Center of the College of Architecture. His research at the center focuses on land use planning and growth management in the context of hazard mitigation, disaster recovery, and natural resource policy. He is currently conducting a study of long-term disaster reconstruction in the Caribbean for the United Nations.

Planning for Earthquakes

Designed by Ann Walston

Composed by WorldComp
in Palatino with Eras Demi display

Printed by Thomson-Shore, Inc.,
on 60-lb. Glatfelter Spring Forge